Renaissance Monarchy

Renaissance Monarchy

The Reigns of Henry VIII, Francis I and Charles V

GLENN RICHARDSON

A member of the Hodder Headline Group
LONDON
Co-published in the United States of America by
Oxford University Press Inc., New York

First published in Great Britain in 2002 by
Arnold, a member of the Hodder Headline Group,
338 Euston Road, London NW1 3BH

http://www.arnoldpublishers.com

Distributed in the United States of America by
Oxford University Press Inc.,
198 Madison Avenue, New York, NY10016
Oxford is a registered trademark of Oxford University Press

British Library Cataloguing in Publication Data
A catalogue record for this book is available from the British Library

Library of Congress Cataloging-in-Publication Data
A catalog record for this book is available from the Library of Congress

ISBN 0 340 731 427 (hb)
0 340 731 435 (pb)

1 2 3 4 5 6 7 8 9 10

Production Editor: Jasmine Brown
Production Controller: Martin Kerans
Cover Design: Terry Griffiths

Typeset in 10/12 Sabon by Charon Tec Pvt. Ltd, Chennai, India
Printed and bound in Great Britain by MPG Books Ltd, Bodmin

What do you think about this book? Or any other Arnold title?
Please send your comments to feedback.arnold@hodder.co.uk

For my parents
Alan and Virginia, Lorraine and Robert

I've snapped and plotted all my life. There's
no other way to be a king, alive, and fifty all at once.

Henry II, *The Lion in Winter*

Arthur: Be quiet! I order you to be quiet!
Woman: Order eh? Who does he think he is?
Arthur: I am your King!
Woman: Well, I didn't vote for you
Arthur: You don't vote for kings
Woman: Well, how did you become king then?

Monty Python and the Holy Grail

Contents

Preface

The title of this book should perhaps be explained. It will not be asserted that 'Renaissance Monarchy' was something self-defining, new, or radically different from medieval monarchy. In fact, quite the opposite is true. Sixteenth century monarchs consciously and continually compared themselves with their ancestors and judged themselves against the record of those who had gone before them. They wanted to demonstrate their power in new and dramatic ways, but saw no role for themselves in changing the essential nature of the monarchy or its place in the societies they governed. So the title is used to describe the reigns of three important European kings who ruled together during the period conventionally described as the High Renaissance.

Nevertheless, 'Renaissance Monarchy' is not merely a title of convenience. While the ambitions and anxieties of Charles V, Henry VIII and Francis I differed little from those of their predecessors, they experienced them in a context of rapid intellectual, technological, religious and social change. The past had never before been so thoroughly re-invented as it was in the fifteenth and sixteenth centuries. The hope that the greatness of the past could be revived in the present was palpable among Europe's intellectual and political elites. In this atmosphere, the accessions of three young monarchs within a few short years of each other generated enormous excitement and a momentum which lasted well into their reigns. Whether it was for the revival of morals and 'good letters' for which Erasmus yearned, or the Christian world empire of which Gattinara dreamed, or just for good times, in anticipation of which the English nobility gleefully rubbed its hands in 1509, these kings were all expected to do great things from the outset.

The book is intended to be a synoptic discussion of its subject and is addressed primarily to students of the early-modern period. It does not purport to be a comprehensive treatment of early-modern government or even of the individual careers of the three kings themselves. Rather, it is intended to complement existing monographs and textbooks by offering a more thematic and specifically comparative account of these kings than is currently available.

It presents some of the more interesting research done in the last decade in the fields of administrative, diplomatic and cultural history. Drawing on that research, the book assesses the aims and achievements of these three monarchs according to criteria which they themselves might have recognised and shows how 'personal monarchy' worked in the sixteenth century.

The Preface of a first book provides a welcome opportunity to acknowledge several people whose help and friendship have been of great importance in my career to date. I warmly thank Bruce Mansfield and Roslyn Pesman for guiding me through my final undergraduate year at the University of Sydney and supporting my ambition to do postgraduate study in Britain. My Ph.D. thesis was completed at the London School of Economics under the supervision of David Starkey and I thank him for his expert guidance, encouragement and kindness to me which has continued ever since.

It was a pleasure when the editors asked me to incorporate some of my doctoral research in a contribution to the present series. I would like to thank Arnold's editor, Christopher Wheeler, for the opportunity to write this book and for his interest, advice and support. I wish to thank Pauline Croft and John Morrill for their enthusiasm for the project, for reading the book, and making helpful suggestions. Thanks also to the publisher's anonymous readers who offered positive and sensible advice on the original proposal.

As will be clear from the notes and bibliography, I owe a great debt of gratitude to the many historians whose work has guided and inspired my own. A number of them have offered advice in the course of helpful discussions. In particular I would like to thank Alasdair Hawkyard, Robert Knecht, Glyn Redworth, Mary Hollingsworth and Roger Mettam who have provided useful references and given me encouragement. David Potter and Dominic Omissi read drafts of several chapters and made useful suggestions. Thanks also to my colleagues and friends at St Mary's College who have shown generous and supportive interest in my work. I am especially grateful to Susan Doran for reading a draft of the whole book and making helpful comments and suggestions, particularly about its structure. I also wish to record my thanks to the students I have taught, both at St Mary's and at the London School of Economics, for some stimulating discussions and for their questions which prompted me to think beyond the confines of my initial research interests.

Finally, I would like to thank my wife, Jane, for her support and for letting me read drafts of the text aloud to her in the bath. Her constant encouragement and understanding have been immensely helpful in completing this book. During the course of its writing, I have had the greatest good fortune to meet my birth-parents for the first time. It is to them and to my adoptive parents that this book is gratefully dedicated.

Glenn Richardson
London
September 2001

Abbreviations

AN	Archives Nationales, Paris
BIHR	Bulletin of the Institute of Historical Research
BL	British Library, London
BN	Bibliothèque Nationale, Paris
Brown	*Four Years at the court of Henry VIII: Selection of Despatches of Sebastian Giustinian*
Carolus	*Carolus: Charles Quint 1500–1558* (2001) Exhibition Catalogue.
CSP.Span	*Calendar of State Papers, Spanish*
CSPV	*Calendar of State Papers, Venetian*
DBF	*Dictionnaire de biographie française*
DNB	*Dictionary of National Biography*
CAF	*Catalogue des Actes de François Ier*
EHR	*English Historical Review*
HALL	*The Union of the two noble and illustre famelies of Lancastre and Yorke* (1809 edn.)
HJ	*Historical Journal*
Lanz	*Correspondenz des Kaisers Karl V*
LP	*Letters and Papers, Foreign and Domestic, of the Reign of Henry VII*
Ordonnances	*Ordonnances des rois de France: règne de François Ier*
PRO	Public Record Office
SCJ	*Sixteenth Century Journal*
SP	State Papers (PRO)
St. P.	*State Papers of the reign of Henry VIII*
Weiss	*Papiers d'Etat du cardinal de Granvelle*

All references to calendared correspondence and to Lanz are to document numbers, not pages, unless otherwise stated.

List of maps and genealogical tables

Note on monetary values and coinage

In the early sixteenth century, the English money of account was the pound sterling divided into 20 shillings, each shilling worth 12 pence. The English gold coin, the crown, was worth 4 shillings.

The main French money of account, the *livre tournois*, was similar. 1 *livre tournois* was worth 20 *sous* and each *sous* was worth 12 *deniers* The main French gold coin was the *ecu d'or au soleil* or 'crown of the sun' worth about 40 *sous* in 1516 and 45 *sous* by 1533. 1 *livre tournois* was valued at about 2 English shillings so there were about 10 *livres tournois* to 1 pound sterling.

The basic unit of Spanish currency was the *maravedí*. The Spanish ducat was the principal money of account. At the start of the sixteenth century 1 Spanish ducat was worth 375 *maravedís* or 11 *reales* and 1 *maravedí*. The ducat was also the main gold coin, modelled on the Venetian ducat in widespread use by the early sixteenth century. In 1537 Charles V introduced another gold coin, the *escudo*, worth 350 *maravedís*. During most of Henry VIII's reign the ducat was worth around 4 shillings 6 pence sterling but by the middle of the sixteenth century, it was worth 6 shillings 8 pence sterling.

Note on spelling of names

The names and titles of the three monarchs and their immediate relatives are given in the accepted English translations. All other names are given in the conventional vernacular spellings.

Introduction

On Saint George's Day 1515 at Richmond Palace, Henry VIII received Sebastiano Giustiniani, the new Venetian ambassador to England, recently arrived from a short stay at the court of the newly-crowned Francis I of France. Resplendent in the robes of the Order of the Garter and surrounded by the peers of England, Henry greeted the new ambassador warmly. After orations of welcome and Mass in the Chapel Royal, the court dined in the Great Hall of the palace. Henry conversed with the ambassador in French, Latin and Italian, impressing him with his intelligence and affability. Giustiniani's secretary, Niccolò Sagudino, wrote home to Venice enthusiastically:

> The like of two such courts and two such kings as those of France and of England, have I fancy, not been witnessed by any ambassadors who have gone out of Venice these past fifty years ... so I am very glad to have come on this mission.[1]

Sagudino clearly thought of Henry VIII and Francis I as exceptional types of monarch because of the powerful image of kingship which each projected. Within a year of the reception, they would be joined by Charles I of Spain who was then elected as Holy Roman Emperor in 1519. Together, they formed a triumvirate of kings whose style of monarchy was determined by the values of sixteenth century noble culture. Each of them believed that a truly great monarch was one who was, in the words of Castiglione's archetypal courtier, Signor Ottaviano, 'strong, wise, full of liberality, munificence, religion and clemency.' The great monarch's qualities should be demonstrated in the strict but equitable administration of justice; in the patronage of noblemen, scholars and artists; in peaceful and generous relations with other princes and, when necessary, in the vigorous conduct of magnificent princely warfare. The practice of these virtues demonstrated a king's favour with God and gained him a good reputation among his fellow princes, in a word his *virtus*. This was expected to secure the reverence and obedience of his subjects.[2]

This book examines the way in which this ideal of kingship was embodied, and developed, by these three kings between 1509 and 1558. It first introduces them, providing basic details of their personalities, ambitions and education at the time of their respective accessions. It then discusses how the three-fold model of kings as warriors, patrons and governors integrated classical philosophy of government with medieval experience of monarchy in northern Europe. The writings of Machiavelli, Erasmus, More and others indicate that there was a lively debate in the early sixteenth century about how monarchs ought to behave, what they could legitimately demand from their subjects and what their subjects expected from them.

In considering the role of monarchs in European history, nineteenth and earlier twentieth century historians detected in this period the first stirrings of what eventually became known as the 'absolutist' or 'divine-right' rulers who, using a standing army and an army of bureaucrats, supposedly overrode the traditional privileges of all other institutions of authority within their realms. These included the nobility, representative assemblies, town councils, trade guilds and the church. It was said that these monarchs succeeded in 'centralizing' government in their own hands and that under the Tudors in England, the Valois and Bourbon in France and the Habsburgs in Spain, the modern 'nation-state' was born amidst the death-throes of the great medieval aristocratic families.

In the middle years of the twentieth century this view of the monarchy was modified but to some extent also re-invented in something called the 'new' monarchy, sometimes also called 'Renaissance monarchy.' Francis, Henry and Charles were all portrayed as intent upon if not destroying, then at least severely reducing, the power of the high nobles who had caused civil disruption and bloodshed in the mid-fifteenth century. With men such as Thomas Cromwell in England or Mercurino Gattinara who worked for Charles V, the royal administration was said to have at last broken free from the medieval tradition of government centred on the monarch's household. The role of the royal court was thereafter to be simply a meeting point for the nobility and the king. Meanwhile the legal and financial administration of the kingdom was established on a more efficient, bureaucratic, basis through an alliance with the emerging 'middle men', lawyers and financial experts, whose expertise served the crown's interests. By these means royal authority was extended as far as possible over the kingdom, given the acknowledged constraints placed upon officials by distance and limited communication technology.[3]

During the last 30 years, these views of early-modern monarchy have themselves undergone further reassessment. Some elements of the 'new monarchy' thesis have been confirmed, others discarded. Numerous studies of the fortunes of individual nobles, of particular families and of particular regions of England, France and Spain, have shown a continuing interdependence between the sovereign and noble subjects well into the eighteenth century. Royal authority was extended in the sixteenth century and increasing numbers of the lower nobles and gentry did indeed swell the ranks of royal administrators, but these studies have also shown that monarchs still needed the co-operation of the aristocrats and independent corporate bodies to enforce their rule. While undoubtedly authoritarian in disposition, they had frequently to bargain with their nobles and the various representative institutions of their realms over issues as diverse as levels of taxation, changes to the structure of the church and the operation of royal or seigneurial justice.

Personality has also been restored to a central place in explaining monarchs' dealings with their subjects and their fellow rulers. Their decisions sprang more from personal ambition and dynastic pride than from abstract notions of statecraft, such as 'centralisation' or creating 'spheres of influence' internationally. Sixteenth century kings were not free simply to impose laws on their people or to tax them as they felt inclined. The governance of their states was hierarchical and authoritarian but also fragile in nature. Its structures both facilitated and restricted the executive power of the sovereign in ways that helped to safeguard his predominant position among the political elite.

Relations between the monarch and that elite were mediated most directly through the royal court. This institution has been the subject of intense study over the last few decades. Historians in England and France and those studying the Habsburg rulers, have established that far from being an elaborate side show or glittering prison for nobles, the court was the central institution in the patronage system which the monarchy used to run the kingdom. Although formally distinct, the political world of the court and the administrative world of the royal council's remit were more closely related than has sometimes been supposed. A place in the royal household became vital to the political and social success of upwardly mobile young men, and many women, because the more important court offices gave individuals access to the sovereign and thus the possibility of influencing his decisions. If 'the personal is the political' is a widely accepted idea in the twenty-first century, it was much more so in the sixteenth.[4]

Nowhere is this adage more applicable than in relationships between monarchs, in which the court could also play an important role. The royal activity which consumed more of the emotional and material resources of these three kings than any other was warfare. Henry, Francis and Charles were all driven to acquit themselves well as warriors against each other. None of them in fact enjoyed the unalloyed martial success claimed for them by their propagandists. Rather, they made the most of difficult tactical and logistical situations and usually managed to do sufficient damage or to gain sufficient territory to advance their positions in peace negotiations which followed any sizeable military campaign. Even when they were not actually fighting, rivalry between the kings did not disappear. Making peace was a complex affair in which the hostility between antagonists had to be redirected into less destructive ways of relating. All were kept well informed by ambassadors, spies and merchants resident in the realms of their fellow kings about goings on in their courts and of rumours about their intended courses of action.

In each aspect of Renaissance monarchy with which it deals, the book takes a comparative approach precisely because this it what the three kings themselves did constantly. However, in order to use the available space fully, this comparison focuses mainly on the relevant dominions in Western Europe, the sites of closest interaction between the three kings. Limited reference is made to Charles as overlord of the Spanish Americas. Attention is given to the impact of the Reformation in Germany and Charles's inability, finally, to command the allegiance of his Protestant subjects. However, this study does not analyse in detail the politics of the Holy Roman Empire.

The three-fold analysis of the kings as warriors, patrons and governors, around which the book is structured, is not intended to replace one mechanistic explanation of the meaning of early-modern monarchy with another. Rather, the focus is on showing how these three kings were able to secure the obedience, loyalty and even the affection of their noble and gentry subjects. This approval was their own greatest source of security and strength and it manifested itself in the kind of delighted response expressed by Niccolò Sagudino at Richmond Palace on Saint George's Day in 1515.

1

Monarchs: Personalities and ideals of monarchy

> Nothing brings a prince more prestige than great campaigns and striking demonstrations of his personal abilities.[1]

The Prince, in which Niccolò Machiavelli made this observation, was first published in 1532. During the previous century, in the course of the Italian Renaissance and conflicts in northern Europe, ideals of princely rule had been examined and widely debated. Political philosophers, jurists and princes themselves took renewed interest in medieval and classical models of government. By the time Machiavelli's book was published, Henry VIII, Francis I and Charles V had been kings for at least 15 years. All had been educated in the light of these developments and had contributed to them in words and deeds. They understood from their earliest days as kings what Machiavelli meant. All three had a definite sense of their own talents and what 'great campaigns' they wished to achieve. All understood that prestige, what they called 'honour,' derived from being regarded as three things: a Christian governor, a generous but discerning patron and above all, a successful warrior.

This three-fold ideal of monarchy was itself drawn from three principal and associated sources. The first was the medieval tradition of the monarch as a sacred being charged with protecting the church and upholding justice. The second source of ideals, and undoubtedly the most exciting for the monarchs themselves, was chivalry. The medieval vision of glorious military action in the service of a just cause had enjoyed a new lease of life during the Hundred Years' War and the Italian wars of the late fifteenth century. The third source of ideals lay in the development during the Italian Renaissance of the *studia humanitatis*, the classically inspired curriculum of grammar, rhetoric, poetry, ethics and history which also revived Greek and Roman ideas on government. From these sources, contemporary political commentators developed a model of sixteenth century monarchical government focused on the concept of princely *virtus*.

Moulding themselves to fit this model, Henry, Francis and Charles became, while still young men, a generation of kings unlike any other in European history. All ruled at a time of immense technological, artistic and intellectual innovation and their responses to this innovation profoundly changed the realms which they governed. Charles V united in his own person an empire in Europe and in the Americas unequalled before or since his time. Under Francis I, the kingdom of France was more unified and strong than at any previous time in its history. He rivalled Charles V as no other European king could and was also the single-most important patron of the Renaissance in France. Henry VIII strengthened the authority of the English monarchy, changed the religious life of his kingdom and made England a force to be reckoned with on the European continent. It was to these three rulers that idealists of a later generation looked back nostalgically. They saw them as kings who knew how to be kings; as Renaissance monarchs.

PERSONALITIES AND PATRIMONIES

Henry VIII

Born on 28 June 1491, Henry was the second son of King Henry VII of England. Following his elder brother Arthur's death in 1502, he acceded to the English throne in April 1509. At 17 years of age he was tall, healthy, of athletic build and was considered handsome by contemporaries. He quickly became famous for his strength and physical prowess, losing no opportunity to display these talents to his own courtiers and visiting ambassadors. Their reactions were on the whole favourable and Henry was frequently described as a paragon of princely virtue. On 11 June 1509 he married Katherine of Aragon. It is a fact often forgotten that they were married for 24 years before, as everyone remembers, their marriage was annulled and Katherine found herself merely the first of Henry's six wives.

Henry's mother, Elizabeth of York, had entrusted much of his care as an infant to the women of her household. He spent his early years in the royal nursery at Eltham Palace with his sisters Margaret and Mary. Of his training for kingship we have little direct evidence. Until his brother's death, Henry had been intended for the Church. His education was overseen by his father and his grandmother, Lady Margaret Beaufort, who was a patron of several leading English humanists. Henry was taught by court laureates such as John Skelton, Gilles Duwes and William Horne. He learnt Latin and French, drawing on the books and treatises produced or imported by the scholars of his father's court. Skelton is known to have composed a short work of moral instruction for him in 1501. It is also probable that, as a youth, the king read history, poetry and chivalric romances. He certainly

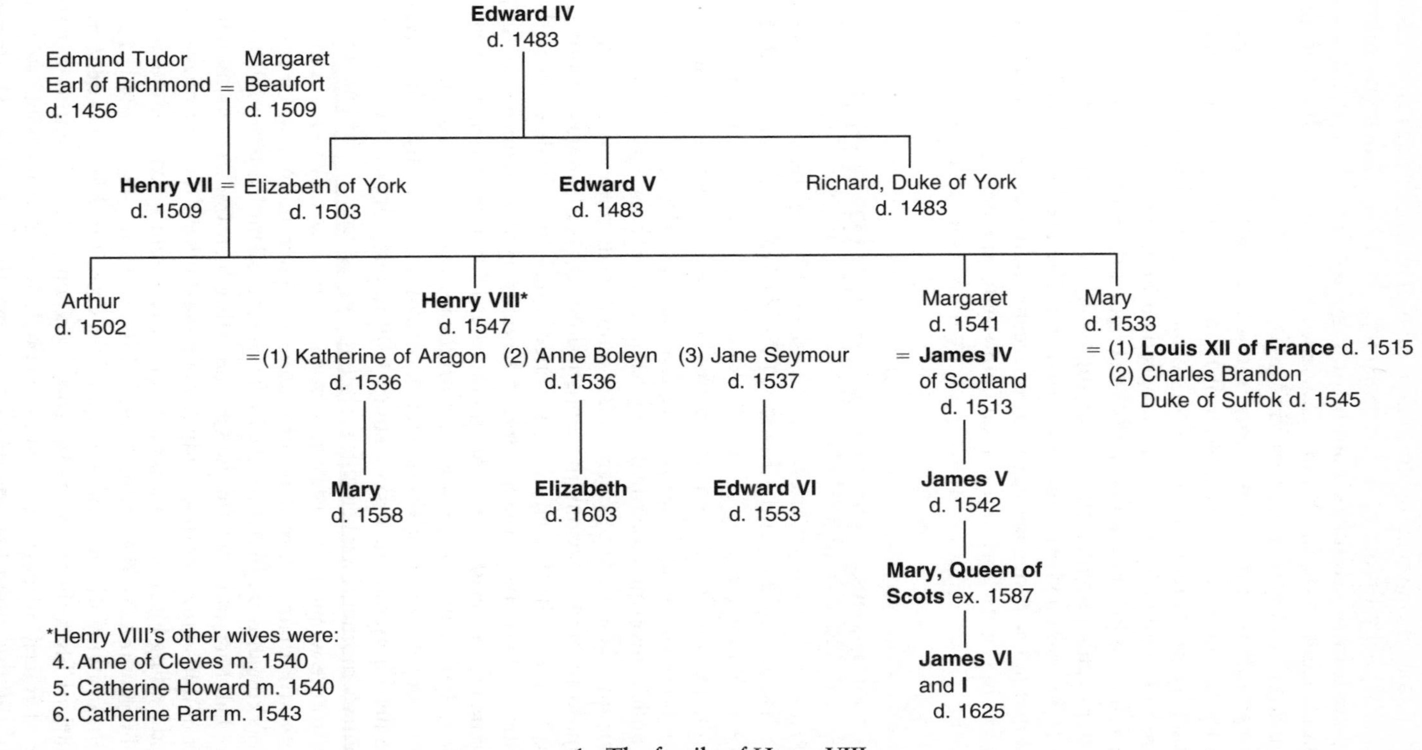

1. The family of Henry VIII

showed great enthusiasm for commissioning or receiving such works as gifts during the earliest years of his reign. Alongside the dynastic emblem of the Tudor rose, Henry took the Beaufort family's emblem, the portcullis, as his personal badge. This symbol of a defensive gate alluded fairly obviously to the personal strength of the new king and of his dynasty.

Henry inherited a kingdom at peace. His father ruled by a mixture of rewards and coercion and he had quietened, if not entirely eliminated, the competitive ambitions among nobles that had provoked the Wars of the Roses. Henry VII's regime employed prudent financial and political patronage to harness noble ambition to the service of the crown. Backed by an effective legal administration, the authority of the monarchy had been re-established and its revenues increased. Although the extent of his fortune is still the subject of debate, the most recent estimates are that at the first Tudor king's death in 1509, his annual income was between £100,000 and £113,000.[2] This wealth was due in no small measure to Henry VII's peaceful, though hardly passive, relations with Europe. From 1492 he received an annual French pension of 745,000 crowns under the Treaty of Etaples. Good trading relations were maintained between England, the Netherlands and France. These facilitated Henry's domestic security and his realm's economic growth. England's engagement with continental Renaissance culture, which had begun during the reign of Edward IV, greatly increased during Henry VII's reign. The values of that culture, particularly its emphasis on magnificent kingship, were articulated in the celebrations that greeted Henry VIII's accession in 1509. These values appealed strongly to the new king and he determined immediately to incarnate them.[3]

Throughout his reign, Henry VIII sought to increase his importance to European princes while simultaneously limiting their potential to threaten his regime. Like his father, he maintained often-difficult alliances with the Habsburg rulers of the Netherlands. His marriage to Katherine of Aragon was intended to secure a parallel alliance with Trastámaran Spain. Dynastic marriages and inheritances were important factors in the structure of early-modern international relations. This was never more apparent than in 1516 when the Habsburg prince, Charles of Burgundy, already overlord of the Netherlands, also became ruler of Aragon and Castile. He thus integrated in his own person England's two main lines of European alliance. Charles was also the maternal nephew of Katherine of Aragon. In the aftermath of Henry's repudiation of her in 1527 and the attendant break with Rome, the Anglo-Habsburg alliance underwent enormous strain. Yet, in the face of France's power, the strategic importance for England of that alliance was strong enough for it to be revived in the 1540s from when it lasted until the final 20 years of the sixteenth century.

Henry always maintained a claim to the crown of France in general and to Angevin patrimony of Normandy, Guyenne, Gascony, and Anjou in western France in particular. These claims were declared visually on the tabards of nine young attendants who rode before the king in his coronation

2. England during the reign of Henry VIII

procession through London in June 1509.[4] By then, the French had regained all the territory once occupied by the English with the exception of Calais which Henry maintained at great expense as a bridghead into France. Henry's armies invaded France three times between 1513 and 1544, in alliance with the Habsburgs. They captured the towns of Thérouanne and Tournai in 1513 and Boulogne in 1544. Thérouanne was destroyed and the other two towns were eventually sold back to the French. Yet for most of his reign, Henry was actually at peace with France. From 1527 his perennial fear of isolation from the Continent was heightened in his campaign for a marriage annulment and the break with Rome. He was also paid a considerable pension by the French king well into the 1530s. In short, it was often worth Henry's while to maintain peaceful, if still tremendously competitive relations, with Louis XII and Francis I.

A constant irritant in these relations was the 'Auld Alliance' between Scotland and France. Henry recognised Scotland's kings and never tried to rule their lands directly but he maintained a residual claim to feudal suzerainty over Scotland. He wanted to prevent the Stuarts pursuing an independent foreign policy and to accord him the respect he felt he was due. James IV and James V asserted their independence from Henry and their international importance by maintaining ties with France and by periodic invasions of northern England, often timed to distract Henry's offensive preparations against their Gallic ally. There were also near constant cross-border raids and lawlessness practised by both sides along the Anglo-Scottish border. On occasions, such as in 1532–34, this raiding led to localised war between the two nations in which the French lent the Scots assistance.

The principality of Wales was progressively united judicially and politically to England between 1529 and 1543 and brought under the sovereignty of the king-in-Parliament. In 1541 English sovereignty over Ireland was declared. The lordship of that country had originally been conferred on Henry II by Pope Adrian I. By declaring himself king, Henry was asserting that his authority over Ireland was now independent of the papacy. This was an obvious and necessary step after the break with Rome and his becoming Supreme Head of the Church in England and in all his dominions.

Francis I

Francis I was born on 12 September 1494 at Cognac in the Loire Valley, the son of Charles of Angoulême and Louise of Savoy. The Angoulême family was a cadet branch of the royal house of Valois. Charles died in 1496 and two years later, his cousin, Louis of Orléans, succeeded to the French crown as Louis XII. The new king had no son and so Francis, his nearest male relative, became heir presumptive. He lived at the French court from 1508. On 18 May 1514 Francis married Claude of France, Louis's eldest daughter by his second wife, Anne of Brittany. This marriage enhanced his status further, making him Duke of Brittany in right of his wife. In January 1514 Anne of Brittany died, leaving Louis two daughters, but no surviving son. After a third marriage, to Mary Tudor in October 1514, Louis XII died, still without a son, on 1 January 1515. Nineteen years to the day after his own father's death, Francis became king of France. He was 20 years old.

Francis's education had been supervised by his mother. From as early as 1504 she had privately, then later more publicly, identified her son with the future of her house and of France. With Louise, Francis learnt Italian and

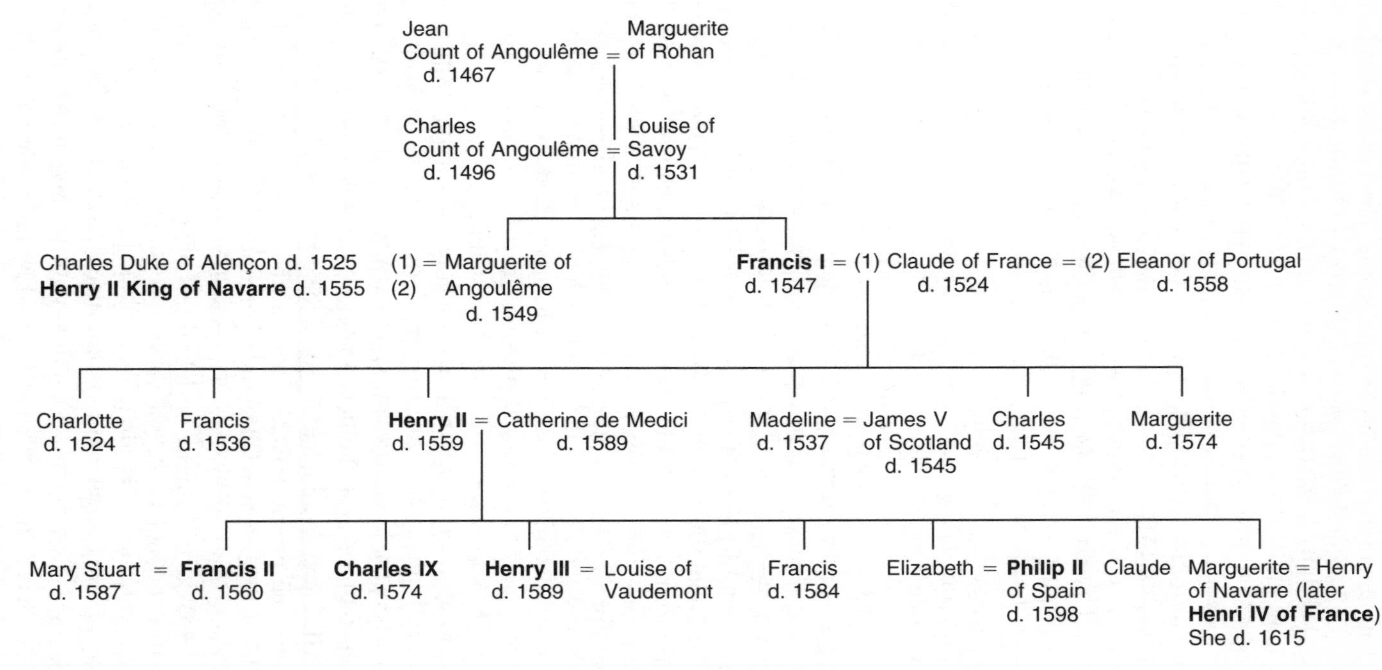

3. The family of Francis I

some Spanish. She was also the patron of a number of French humanists who may have been influential in her son's education. They included François Demoulins, Jean Thenaud and Symphorien Champier. The dominant theme of most of their works was the wisdom of Louise. Some projected a hope that with his mother's advice and guidance, Francis would enjoy security and greatness as king. What Francis made of them at the time we cannot know, but as an adult he was certainly regarded as well read and capable of intelligent discourse. Milanese and Venetian ambassadors took early notice of his rise to prominence and he was favourably mentioned in Castiglione's *The Book of the Courtier* as the consummate French gentleman. In November 1514 while at the French court, the Duke of Norfolk wrote to Cardinal Wolsey of Francis:

> Here is nothing done but the said duke is made privy and doer thereof by the French king's commandment ... My lord I assure you this prince can speak well and wisely.[5]

Like Henry VIII, Francis was of taller than average height and of athletic build. He was a keen huntsman and became a champion jouster, although perhaps not of Henry VIII's exceptional calibre. With his childhood companion, Robert de La Marck, he read exciting chivalric stories and then acted them out in their games and exercises. By such games and by more formal training, Francis acquired the physical skills of horsemanship and combat expected in a young nobleman. Francis's personal device was the salamander amidst flames spitting water from its mouth. It normally appeared with the motto *Nutrisco et extinguo*. According to Ovid, the salamander could live in fire and Francis's device had a double meaning, 'I am nourished by flames and I extinguish them' and 'I nourish good and extinguish evil.' It referred obliquely to the king's passionate nature, his ability to do justice, to sustain his friends and to overcome his enemies.[6]

Like his English counterpart, Francis had grandiose but rather conventional ideas of how to make his mark on the world. One of his first priorities was to secure the Valois succession. His first two children were daughters, Louise and Charlotte. The dauphin Francis was born in 1518. Claude bore Francis seven children altogether before her death in 1524, a few months before her 25th birthday. Only two of the royal children survived into their thirties and Francis was eventually succeeded by his second son, Henry. In 1526 Francis married Eleanor of Habsburg, the sister of Charles V and dowager Queen of Portugal. They had no children together.

Francis inherited a kingdom that was well governed and relatively prosperous. Since the end of Hundred Years' War, an absence of serious famine or conflict and fewer outbreaks of major illness had allowed the population to increase, especially in rural areas. This continued well into Francis's reign. The realm's two principal cities, Paris and Lyon, grew rapidly and both were important centres for printing – the technological revolution of the age. The kingdom's domestic and international trade had also recovered from the slump of the previous century. Grain and wine production in Bordeaux and the north-east of France were again reaching profitable levels although later in his reign there were difficulties in supplying the increasing population with enough food.

In 1515 France was at peace but not free of foreign entanglements. The duchy of Burgundy had been incorporated within the realm by Louis XI in 1477 but the border with the Burgundian Netherlands remained ill-defined and the subject of conflict with the Habsburgs. While the king of France

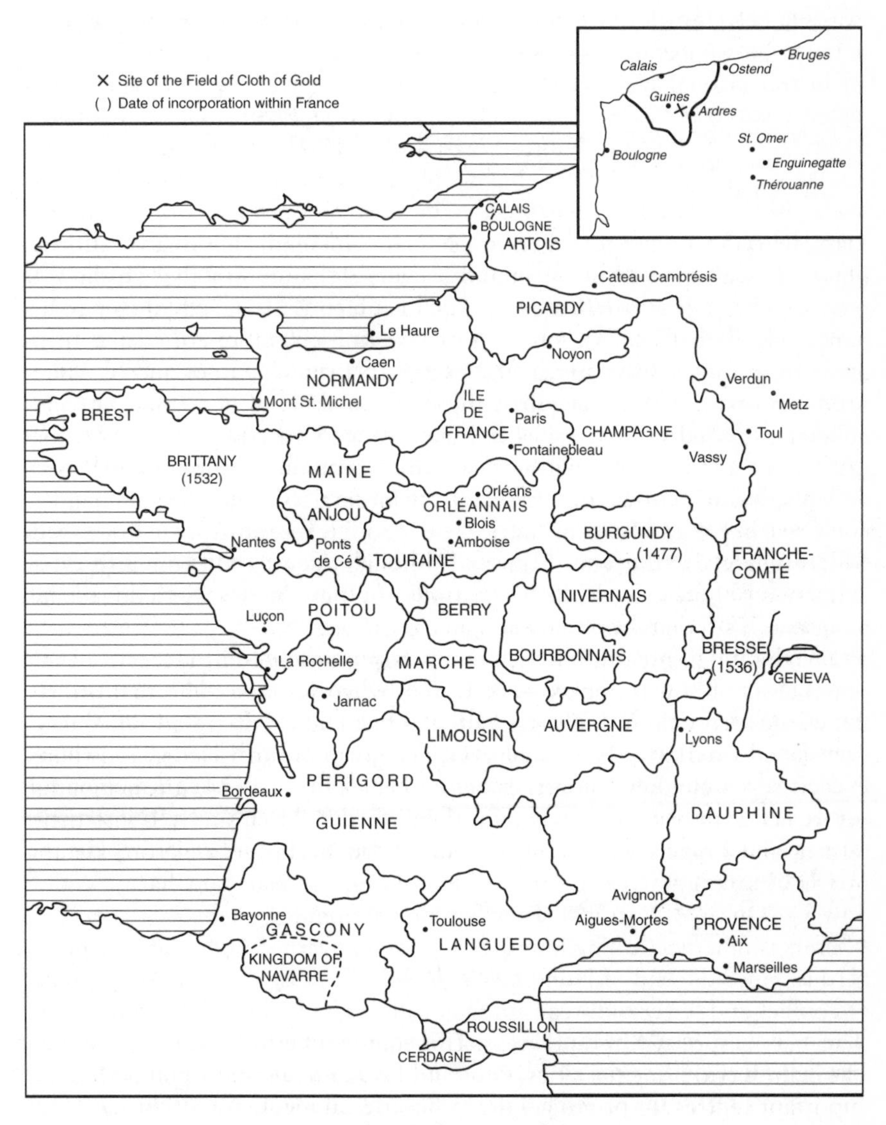

4. France during the reign of Francis I

retained nominal rights over Flanders and Artois, these counties were under Habsburg control. There were other foreign enclaves in the realm. The English still held Calais. Comtat-Venaissin in the south near Avignon was controlled by the papacy. The nearby principality of Orange belonged to the house of Châlons, loyal servants of the emperor. The administration of the duchy of Brittany had been brought into the French king's hands by the successive marriages of Charles VIII and Louis XII to its heiress Anne. She was the daughter of the last independent duke of Brittany and she in turn passed her rights on to her own daughter Claude who married Francis I. The duchy was then given by Claude to her eldest son, Francis, but it was not formally attached to France until he came of age in 1532.

Blessed with an enlarged and relatively stable kingdom, Francis was determined to enhance it, and his own reputation, further. He maintained a large court, was keen to hunt, to feast and make plans for war, and at first showed only limited and variable interest in the mundane duties of government. Above all he was determined to be a warrior and a patron and his primary dynastic ambition was to be the Duke of Milan. He saw the northern Italian duchy as his by birth-right, in exactly the same way that Henry VIII saw western and northern France. The king claimed the duchy through his great-grandfather, Louis I Duke of Orléans. In 1499, Louis XII, also a member of the Orléans dynasty, had asserted this right and conquered Milan from Ludovico Sforza. He then ruled Milan for a dozen years until an alliance forged by Pope Julius II forced him to relinquish it in 1512. In September 1515 Francis made a spectacular debut in international relations by invading and conquering Milan at the battle of Marignano.

Nevertheless, within four years of this victory, Charles V's territories and allies completely surrounded France. Although this was naturally a cause of anxiety for Francis, his main concern was not that Charles would invade his kingdom, but that he would use his great strategic advantages to hem Francis in and to prevent him from keeping possession of Milan. From 1519 onwards Francis was obliged to seek allies wherever he could find them. He found plenty, including Henry VIII of England, the Republic of Venice, German Protestant princes and even the great Turkish leader Süleyman. Nevertheless, he could never secure enough allies, or enough money, for enough time decisively to overcome the power of the emperor. The struggle over Milan became the one fixed point in the king's foreign policy for the whole of his reign.[7]

Charles V

The man who would become the Holy Roman Emperor Charles V was born in Ghent in Flanders on 24 February 1500. His father was Philip the Fair, the Duke of Burgundy, Archduke of Austria and son of the Holy Roman Emperor Maximilian I of the house of Habsburg. His mother was Juana of

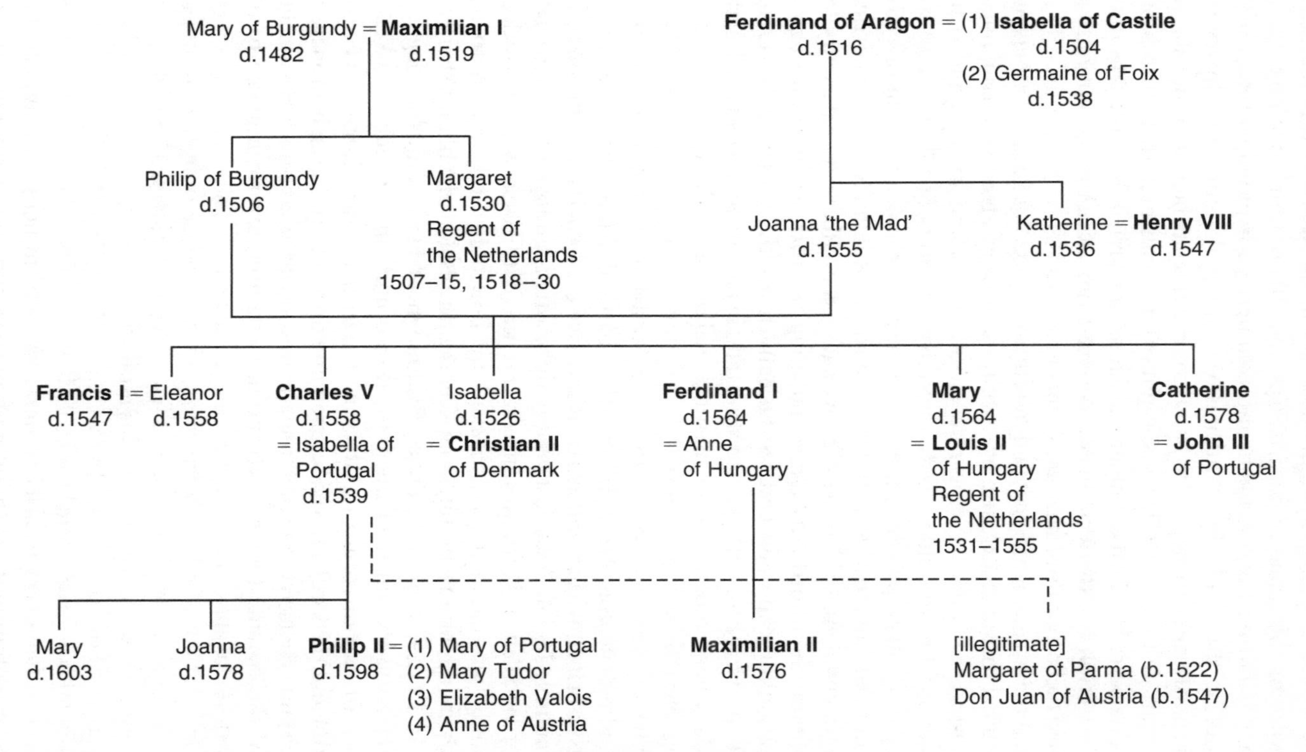

5. The family of Charles V

Castile, the daughter of Ferdinand and Isabella of Spain and the sister of Katherine of Aragon, the wife of Henry VIII. Philip the Fair died in 1506, his wife became insane with grief and so Charles was raised in the care of Philip's sister, Margaret of Austria, dowager Duchess of Savoy.

Charles received a humanist education under his principal tutor Adrian of Utrecht, the future Pope Adrian VI, and under the watchful eyes of two Flemish noblemen Jean le Sauvage, the Chancellor of Burgundy, and Guillaume de Croy, the Lord of Chièvres. They later became Charles's principal advisors. He lived in the Netherlands until his mid-teens, acquiring a deep affection for the aristocratic heritage and the chivalric ideals of the former rulers of the Netherlands, the Valois dukes of Burgundy. He also enjoyed their legendary lifestyle. Fine clothes, good food and exciting entertainments characterised his court as fully as those of Henry VIII or Francis I. Yet Charles was also a deeply religious person and of a rather serious disposition. The moralistic and materialistic aspects of his character were perhaps best accommodated in the aristocratic outlook and traditions of the Order of the Golden Fleece to which he was passionately committed. From 1516 his personal emblem was the twin pillars of Hercules at the end of the world with the motto *Plus Oultre* meaning 'Further Still.' The twin pillars had originally been adjuncts to the emblem of the Order of the Golden Fleece. When joined with 'Further Still' and used personally by Charles, they alluded to his potential as a Christian knight and to the vast extent of his empire and dynastic inheritance.[8]

Charles began assembling this extraordinarily complex inheritance in 1515. It was centred principally on the duchy of Burgundy proper, in eastern France, and most of what is now the Netherlands, Belgium and Luxemburg. In 1477 the last Valois duke of Burgundy, Charles the Bold, had been killed in battle against the French king Louis XI. The duchy of Burgundy was immediately annexed by Louis. In order to prevent the French taking any more territory, Charles the Bold's daughter, Mary, was married to the young Archduke Maximilian of Habsburg. He fought the French to a halt and then ruled a Valois dominion that encompassed the duchies of Luxemburg and Brabant, the counties of Hainaut, Holland, Zeeland and the lordships of Zutphen, Namur and Friesland, held as fiefs of the Empire. He also controlled the counties of Flanders and Artois, held as fiefs of the crown of France. To the east of Burgundy, the Habsburgs now also held Charolais and Franche-Comté centred on the town of Besançon. Maximilian's son, Philip the Fair, had all these titles conferred on him and at his death in 1506 they passed to his own son, Charles. Maximilian acted as regent for Charles until 1515, his authority being exercised by his daughter, Margaret of Austria. In 1515 Charles's majority was declared by the States-General of the Netherlands.

The following year Charles acquired the second major component of his inheritance. In January 1516 his maternal grandfather, Ferdinand of Aragon, died. He had no surviving son from either of his two marriages and so, as his

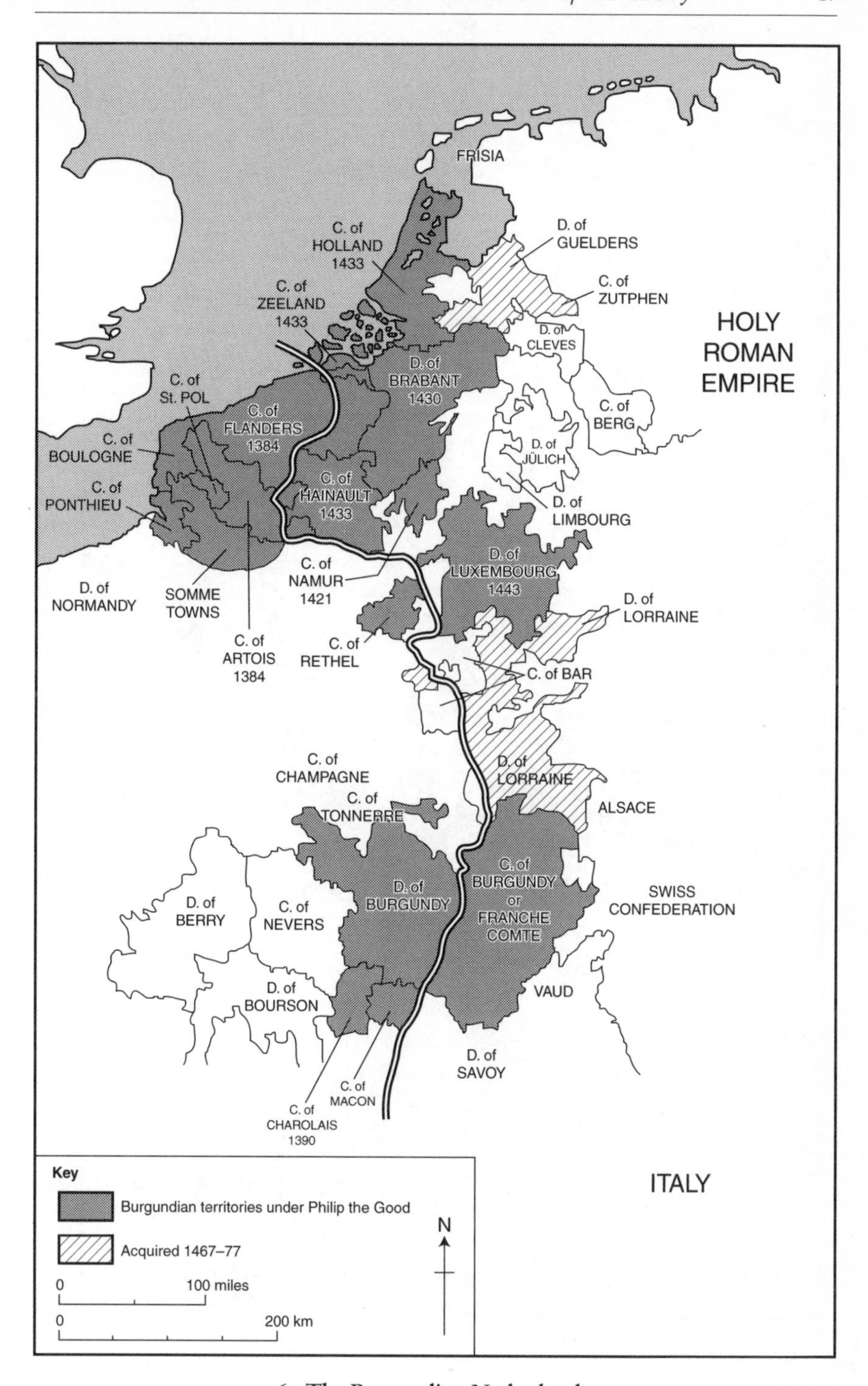

6. The Burgundian Netherlands

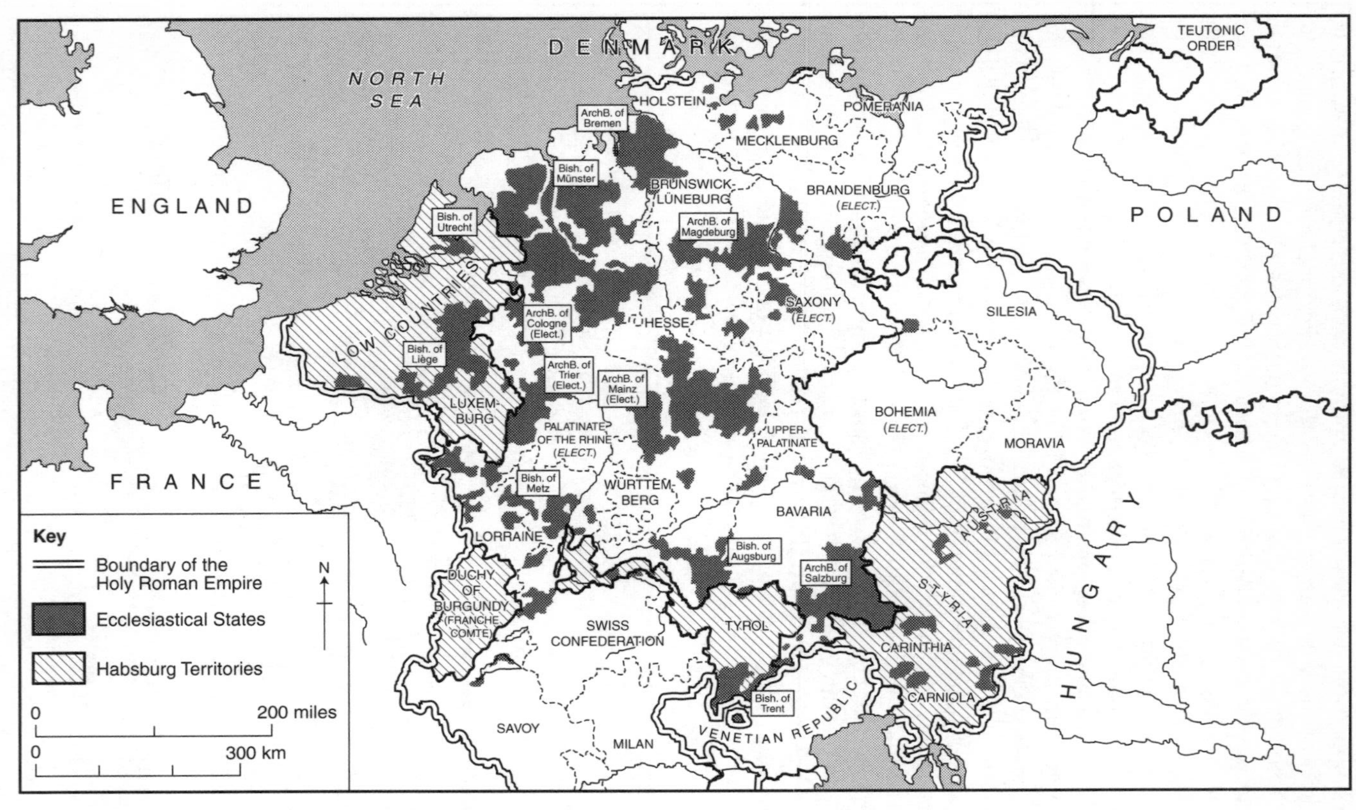

7. The Holy Roman Empire and Habsburg Lands in the early Sixteenth Century

eldest grandson, Charles inherited the kingdom directly. He also became co-ruler of the kingdom of Castile with his unfortunate mother Juana who, due to her insanity, was given no role in its government. After an uncertain start, Castile eventually became Charles's financial power-base and real home. The crown of Aragon also controlled a number of territories in the Mediterranean, the most important of which were Sardinia, Sicily, and the kingdom of Naples. The latter included not just the city of Naples but most of southern Italy. Charles inherited suzerainty of these territories as well.

The third and most prestigious component of his inheritance was the Holy Roman Empire. In January 1519 Emperor Maximilian died, leaving his grandson Charles the Habsburg hereditary lands (*Erblande*). These lands constituted a large block of territory in eastern Europe centred on present day Austria, including the Tyrol. They also included territories on the upper Rhine known as the *Vorlande*, eastern Swabia, the bishoprics of Trent and Brixen and the county of Gorizia together with Friuli and Trieste on the Adriatic. The Habsburgs also ruled in the crown of Bohemia which comprised Bohemia itself (roughly the present Czech Republic); the margravate of Moravia (modern Slovakia); the duchy of Silesia and Lower Lusatia on the border of Poland, which had all been incorporated into the crown by the end of the fourteenth century. The Habsburgs were also related by marriage

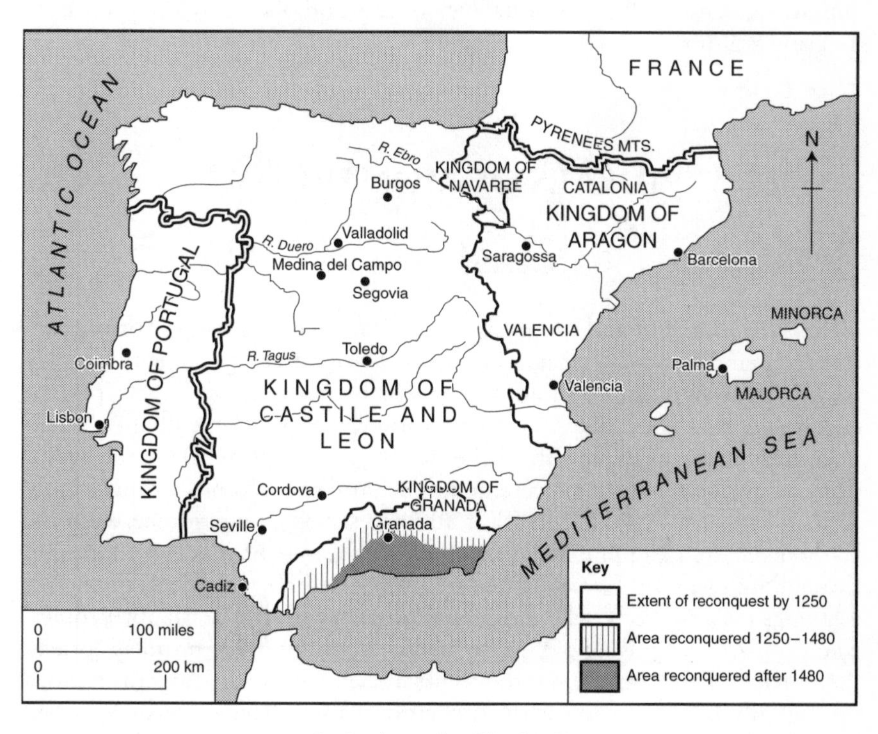

8. Spain under Charles V

to the Jagiellon dynasty which held the elective kingship of Hungary. After the death of the Louis II Jagiellon at the battle of Mohácz in 1526, Charles V's brother, Ferdinand, successively contested the election of Janos Zapolya as king of Hungary. Zapolya was supported by the Turks and Ferdinand was subsequently unable to prevent them conquering all of the kingdom east of the Danube by 1541.[9]

Since 1440 the Habsburgs had also held the elective kingship of the German *Reich* and with it, the title of Holy Roman Emperor. Before his death Maximilian I had secured the promises of a majority of the seven Imperial Electors that Charles would succeed him. After paying enormous sums in bribes, Charles was duly chosen in June 1519 against the strenuous competition of Francis I and the less-serious candidacy of Henry VIII. Charles was crowned as 'German–Roman King' at Aachen in 1520, but he was no more German than he was Spanish and his lack of familiarity with the language, customs and expectations aroused resentment among his subjects there. After some initial and limited success in implementing a more efficient imperial administration in line with his grandfather's policies, Charles chose to concentrate his attention upon his more western dominions. In 1522 under the Treaty of Brussels, Ferdinand received the government of the Habsburg's Austrian patrimony and was made regent for Charles in the German *Reich*. Charles then embarked upon his 30-year long wanderings around Europe in defence of the Catholic church and his own dynastic honour.

IDEALS OF MONARCHY

Sacred kingship

Henry VIII, Francis I and Charles V all considered the Christian faith as central to their identity as monarchs. At all levels of early sixteenth century society there was a profound sense, which monarchs did their best to encourage, that they were sacred persons whose rule was divinely sanctioned. In medieval Europe this belief was expressed primarily in the evolution of elaborate coronation ceremonies. Charlemagne's coronation as Holy Roman Emperor by Pope Leo III in 800 had sealed an alliance between the Catholic Church and Frankish power which became the model for kingship throughout medieval Europe. The ceremony fused Hebrew ideals of anointing kings (as a sign of God's choice and favour) with the Germanic peoples' traditions of recognising a king by acclamation after his promise to lead them well. These remained the central elements of royal coronations throughout Europe in the early sixteenth century. The emperor was still crowned by the Pope, traditionally in Rome, although Charles V was actually crowned in Bologna. The kings of England were crowned in Westminster Abbey, those of France at Rheims Cathedral before the leading members of the lay and ecclesiastical estates of their kingdoms. All swore to protect the Church's privileges and to defend their realms against heresy. They also swore to uphold justice and to treat their subjects equitably.

These monarchs were not simply crowned but consecrated to God, hence the French term for the ceremony, the *sacre*. Dressed in white, quasi-clerical garb modelled on that worn by a deacon, they were anointed on their hands and body with a variety of holy oils which conferred on them a 'sacerdotal' or semi-priestly character. They were then invested with symbols of royal authority. The emperor received a ceremonial sword of state and an orb representing *imperium*. The kings of England and France each received two sceptres. One was the sceptre of authority. The other symbolised justice. In England, it was known as the rod of 'virtue and equity'; in France, it was called the 'hand of justice.' Like the emperor they also received a ring, symbolising their marriage to the Church. Once clothed in purple or blue robes of state, the kings of England and France were enthroned and crowned by the Archbishops of Canterbury and Rheims respectively. They were then presented to the assembled leaders of the nobility and church for formal recognition. After receiving the oaths of fealty, they were then acclaimed as sovereigns. In England the nobles stretched out their hands towards the throne and in France they cried out 'Vive le roi.'[10]

In medieval Spain, the monarchs of Castile and Aragon were so insistent that they owed sovereignty to nobody other than God that they refused prelates any role in their coronations beyond praying for them. They took the symbols of authority, especially the sword of state, for themselves and even placed the crown on their own heads, unassisted. By the sixteenth century coronation services were no longer held. Charles was never crowned as king either of Castile or of the crown of Aragon. The conception behind this lack of formal ceremony was that the kingships of Spain were inherently sacred and needed no liturgical act to manifest this reality. In addition to the crown, the Iberian monarchs' regalia comprised a sceptre representing royal power and justice, together with the sword of state signifying the power of execution. Charles I was also sometimes depicted carrying a baton or staff, signifying command in battle and the protection of his people.

Whereas the kings of England and France were acknowledged by the nobility in the course of the coronation rites, in the Iberian peninsula the king was recognised separately by the Cortes of each kingdom and through the raising of banners or standards bearing the royal arms. This ceremony was performed for the king himself at his first entry to the principal city of the realm. It was also done at the time of his accession in towns and villages across the realm where a local high dignitary, such as the town governor, represented the king. He was presented with the king's banner which was then blessed by the highest ecclesiastic present before being placed on the most prominent public building in the locality. This ceremony signified a residual notion of the new king's election and the realm's giving itself to him in a voluntary, contractual, relationship. Simultaneously it declared the king's authority and protective power. In each of his realms, the king was also required to take an oath to protect the liberties and privileges of his subjects. After his accession in 1516 the Cortes of Castile insisted that Charles come to Spain to take this oath before he was formally recognised as king and not to expect it to obey his orders until he had done so. He did finally swear the oath on 5 February 1518 and was formally acclaimed two days later. The Cortes of Aragon was equally insistent on this point. Charles had already been required to give similar undertakings in all the principal regions of his Dutch and Flemish dominions during 1515.[11]

In the profoundly religious cultures of early sixteenth century Europe, elaborate coronation or recognition ceremonies and related symbols were compelling. They reaffirmed powerful myths, often of rather recent origin, which identified the continued existence of the realm and God's favour upon it with the supposed virtues of kingship. By the sixteenth century in France and England these attributes of monarchy were mixed with, and sustained by, powerful royal 'foundation' myths that were virtually religions in themselves.

In France the foundation myth, developed particularly since the fourteenth century, centred on the conversion to Christianity of the Frankish king Clovis. It was said that at Clovis's baptism the Holy Spirit had appeared in the shape of a dove and presented a phial or ampoule which contained self-replenishing holy oil. With it, Clovis and all subsequent French kings were anointed. This was a symbol of God's favour and Clovis was also said to have received 'the king's touch', the power to heal scrofula. According to the myth, Clovis then united, and in a sense created, the Christian kingdom of France. He rid the French lands of pagans and heretics, fighting under a banner called the *oriflamme* and carrying the symbol of the *fleur-de-lis* or lily on his shield. Both were emblems of divinely ordained military power, protection and approval and the *fleur-de-lis* became the ubiquitous symbol of French monarchy and of France itself.

Colette Beaune has shown that the emergence of a recognisable French consciousness was firmly linked to this royal foundation myth. The strong regional differences in language, customs, trade and social arrangements in late-medieval France meant that if people identified themselves as French at all, they meant primarily that they owed allegiance to the same monarch. The essentially spiritual nature of the monarchy was encapsulated in the royal title *Francorum Rex Christianissimus*, 'the Most Christian King of the French' (literally of the Franks) or *roi très chrestien*. The formula, first used in 1239 and current from the fourteenth century, indivisibly conflated kingship, Christianity and the French people. It signified that the French king received his dominion not from the pope, as it was alleged that the emperor did, but from God directly. The king was therefore 'emperor in his own kingdom' and had ultimate authority over the Church in France.[12]

The English monarchy did not have such a clear foundation myth as its French counterpart. Nevertheless, royal historiographers of the fourteenth and fifteenth centuries drew upon Arthurian legends and those of the ancient Britons to ascribe ancient origins to the English crown. English kings, too, claimed the power to heal scrofula. They also blessed and distributed 'cramp rings' which were believed to have miraculous power to heal muscular disorders and epilepsy. It was not until the reign of Edward II that a myth of English 'holy oil' was developed. The story was that the Virgin Mary had once appeared to Thomas à Becket while he was in exile in France and, consistent with previous heavenly practice, had given him a phial of oil, also self-replenishing. She had told him that the fifth king of England to reign after Henry II, who was of course Edward II, would be a great leader. He and all his heirs would unite their people and conquer their enemies after being anointed with the oil at their coronations. This myth was used to bolster the prestige of Edward's unpopular regime and the usurping Henry IV made even greater use of it in the early fifteenth century to give his monarchy apparent supernatural backing.[13]

Henry IV made such a fuss about the holy oil precisely because, by the fifteenth century, royal blood was increasingly seen as the only essential pre-requisite for the valid exercise of royal authority. In usual circumstances in France, England and the Iberian peninsular, monarchs were made by the death of their predecessors, not by coronation. In the hereditary monarchies the sovereign was still presented to the nobility, a residual intimation of election, but by the sixteenth century it was accepted that the ceremony only declared and sanctified publicly what was already fact.

Apart from the coronation itself, elaborate ceremonial was also important across Europe in declaring the legitimacy of monarchy. The most spectacular of these public ceremonies were the first visits which monarchs made to cities and towns in their kingdoms. On these occasions they customarily confirmed the charters granted to the municipality by their predecessors. The tradition of the royal *entrée* was strongest in France but was also followed in the Netherlands, the Empire and England. In Spain at least until the reign of Philip II, royal entries were colourful and lively but comparatively simple affairs. The leading officials of the town or city government, its guilds and churches would come out to greet the sovereign and escort him or her into the city. Entertainments such as jousts and street theatre would follow on the main public space of the town. When Charles first entered Valladolid on 23 November 1517 his cavalcade itself provided plenty of colour and spectacle, the king was dressed in shining armour and bedecked with jewels, but it passed through only a couple of arches dressed with painted silk.

Elsewhere, the business of royal entries was more complex and involved considerable expense for the town. Their main features were the *tableaux vivants* or 'pageants,' street dramas placed strategically along the processional route to welcome the monarch. Descriptions of them were publicised and kept as records or distributed to advertise the town's wealth and prestige. The pageants usually centred on elements of the royal mythology and praised the personal qualities of the king while simultaneously asserting the importance of the municipality itself. When, for example, Francis I entered Lyon in July 1515, one of the pageants presented to him showed a figure representing the king sat atop a tall, tree-like, *fleur-de-lis* around the foot of which curled a salamander, the king's family emblem. The tree grew in a walled enclosure, signifying France, the key to which was held by a woman representing the city of Lyon. The city was one of the richest commercial centres in the kingdom. It was already giving of its wealth to help fund Francis's imminent campaign for the duchy of Milan.[14]

Like these grand public occasions, the complex ceremonies and etiquette which framed the daily life of monarchs reinforced their sacerdotal status. They declared the sovereign's position at the top of the social and political hierarchy and ranked everybody else by reference to it. The details of ceremonial practice varied considerably across time and location but ritual was a vital feature of monarchy in the early-modern period. The English court had some of the most precise rituals of hierarchy in Europe, many adapted from church practice. Like a priest in the Catholic Mass, the monarch ate off gold and silver plates and drank from covered chalice-like cups. He or she was attended by bare headed servants, of noble or gentry status, who knelt as they served the meal. In France there was less formality over meals but an elaborate ceremony was made of the king's rising in the morning, his going to daily divine service and his retiring at night. These ceremonies of *lever* and *coucher*, like dozens of others practised across the courts of Europe, ensured that the monarchs spent at least some significant part of their day formally acting out the royal role in the midst of their subjects. Ceremonies reminded everyone just who the sovereign was and what was expected of him or her.

Princely virtus

The Holy Roman Emperor and the monarchs of England, France and Iberia were believed to be invested with sacred authority as leaders and law givers. Royal blood and the mysteries of coronation conferred upon them real power for which they were accountable ultimately only to God. Nevertheless, they all operated within constitutional frameworks of greater or lesser precision that had been developed over preceding centuries. These were designed to safeguard the realm from purely arbitrary rule and to ensure that the monarch took account of the interests of other powerful sections of society, specifically, the nobility and gentry, the Church and the mercantile elite. The sovereign's personality and qualities of leadership were crucial in gaining the respect and co-operation of these groups and so ruling the kingdom well.

Ideal princely qualities had of course been discussed since pre-Classical times. Many of these discussions had been rediscovered during the Italian Renaissance and were integrated with those conducted by early Christian and medieval scholars. Cicero and Seneca were drawn upon heavily as were Aristotle and Plato. In particular Plato's conception of the 'philosopher-ruler' was revived and emphasised by early sixteenth century commentators working for princely and royal patrons. According to most, the capacity to do justice was the first and greatest of ideal royal qualities. This meant not only wise arbitration in legal or political disputes but also fair treatment of subjects in all things. Next came prudence, or wisdom, associated with intelligence and a clear understanding of one's position in any situation. It was demonstrated in the ability to take advice so as to ensure a good outcome for the prince and the realm. Temperance meant restraint and balance, in personal matters as well as those of policy; a sense of what was appropriate in every situation, of moderation and sobriety. Fortitude encompassed active bravery in action together with moral strength and patience in adversity. Clemency was construed as a semi-divine forgiveness which had a wondrously unexpected quality. When properly exercised, it reinforced rather than undermined the full force of the law. It was closely related to the final virtue of magnificence or expansive generosity.

These 'virtues' were all important because possessing them, or, more precisely, being regarded as possessing them, brought monarchs 'honour' or prestige, summed up in the Latin word *virtus*; in Italian *virtù*, in French *vertu*. The importance of *virtus* was often discussed by political commentators. However, there was no ultimate consensus as to which of its constituent qualities were essential and which were merely desirable. Machiavelli, for example, saw no necessary connection between Christian morality or 'being virtuous' and *virtus* in an ideal ruler. More typical were scholars such as Marsilio Ficino (1433–99) and Giovanni Pico della Mirandola (1463–94) who sought to reconcile, as far as possible, Plato's ideas with Christian theology. For them the ideal prince was one who was, by birth and education, possessed of the classical virtues integrated within a firm Christian faith. This line of argument was followed in a number of *speculum principis* or 'mirror for princes' books. These usually synthesised neo-Platonic and/or Aristotelian theory with the long northern traditions of monarchy, shaping them with an eye to native experience into manuals of good practice in kingship. Several of the more important of these treatises were dedicated to Charles V, Henry VIII or Francis I.[15]

Erasmus of Rotterdam (1466–1536), the pre-eminent northern humanist of the early sixteenth century, posited the closest possible relationship between Christian sacerdotal kingship and neo-Platonic virtues. He elucidated this theme in *The Education of a Christian Prince*, first published in Basel in 1516 and dedicated to Charles of Spain. A year after its first publication, Erasmus also dedicated a special edition to Henry VIII in hope of attracting his patronage. He argued that a neo-Platonic 'philosopher-king' was one who understood events and people clearly and who acted according to Christian wisdom and truth in any situation, for, he argued, 'being a philosopher is in practice the same thing as being a Christian; only the terminology is different.'[16] Guided by reason, his humanist education and remembering his coronation oath, the prince must uphold the law, preserve peace and place the well-being of his people ahead of his own personal ambitions. He must appoint worthy men to advise him and shun flatterers. Taxes should be kept to a minimum, in part at least as result of avoiding war and eschewing extravagance in his personal style. In other writings Erasmus indicated that princely authority might sometimes have to sanction deeds which were not motivated by the highest ideals of Christian love. God did not require princes to act in as strict accordance with the Gospel as he did priests and popes. Nevertheless, they should strive as far as possible to act according to Christian principles. Such were the essentials of Erasmus's exacting model of religious kingship.[17]

Claude de Seyssel (1450–1520) was the Bishop of Marseilles and Archbishop of Turin, a legal scholar and diplomat who had served Louis XII. In 1515 he wrote *La Monarchie de France*, dedicated to Francis I. Seyssel was more concerned with the rules of effective government than with prescriptions for unalloyed royal worthiness. Nevertheless he still held that the king must live 'in esteem and reputation as a good Christian in order to enjoy the love and complete obedience of the people.' Seyssel naturally assumed genuine Christian belief in the king, but his emphasis on the distinction between the private person and the public actions and reputation of the king is significant. Religion was one of the three *freins* or 'bridles' upon the authority of the French monarchy. Like Erasmus, Seyssel argued that tyranny, though superficially strong, was actually a dangerously insecure form of government. French kings who were truly mindful of their coronation oaths to preserve the Catholic faith would avoid the danger of confusing private whim with public duty. The acceptance of the 'bridle' of religion had held kings in esteem and harmony with their subjects since the time of Clovis. This supposed harmony was encapsulated in the oft-repeated phrase; 'One faith, one law, one king.'

Perhaps surprisingly, Seyssel conceded that a reputation for religious virtue was not so essential for a prince when it came to foreign relations. A prince might, in defence of his realm and without suffering a loss of honour, break his word and deceive both enemies and even unreliable allies if necessary. He should offer mediation of disputes so as to be seen acting according to Christian values but he should never let them distort his judgement about how best to proceed. He should certainly never make peace on terms inconsistent with his own interests and his reputation.[18]

Seyssel's moderate view that a reputation for moral virtue did not constitute the whole of *virtus* has some unexpected parallels with the ideas of Machiavelli (1469–1527). His undeservedly sinister reputation masks the fact that Machiavelli also regarded a reputation for morality as no bad thing in a prince. However, it was not necessary and should never be a primary ambition. The prince must act in ways absolutely contrary to Christian ideals if necessary in order to secure his power and authority. He should know when to break his word and when to show cruelty rather than compassion, especially when dealing with internal dissension. Nevertheless, Machiavelli concluded, ruling by law was ultimately in the prince's interest as it tended to preserve his popularity. Though it was better to be feared than loved, the prince's 'best fortress' was 'to avoid being hated by the people.' The ruler must do things which enhanced a reputation for being an effective and compelling sovereign. This was true *virtus*. Of utmost importance in Machiavelli's view was the prince's capacity to wage war effectively and gloriously.[19]

WARRIORS: WAR AND PEACE IN RENAISSANCE EUROPE

Warfare was endemic in early sixteenth-century Europe. Henry VIII, Francis I and Charles V all invested huge amounts of their money and time in fighting, usually against each other. They considered warfare to be a vital aspect of passing a strong and secure kingdom on to their successors. The nobles also viewed service in war alongside their sovereign as their highest ambition. Central to this mentality was the concept of chivalry that went back to the First Crusade and even to late Antiquity. As the leaders of knights, kings were expected to display the knightly qualities of loyalty, courtesy, hardiness, prowess and *largesse*. In other words they should conduct war as part of the magnificence incumbent upon them as monarchs.

The model of magnificent, chivalric, warfare was exemplified again and again in the heroes of chivalric romances and in treatises on chivalry written from the twelfth century onwards. Among the most famous of them was Ramon Lull's *Libre del ordre de cavayleria* written in the late thirteenth century and published in English by Caxton as the *Book of the Ordre of Chyvalry*. There were three separate French editions of Lull's book published in the early sixteenth century. In England in 1420 John Lydgate had published a translation of Guido della Colonne's chivalric treatise, *The hystorye, sege and destrucyon of Troye* which he dedicated to Henry V. Its dedicatory verses praised Henry V as a king worthy of the ancient heroes. He combined the two supreme royal virtues, success in battle and ruling justly in peace. The book retained its currency right through to the early sixteenth century when Richard Pynson published a new edition on the eve of Henry VIII's first war against France.

The production of these kinds of treatises and panegyrics on warfare reflected and helped to sustain the chivalric milieu into which Henry VIII,

Francis I and Charles V were born. Against the background of dominant noble power in Spain, of the Italian wars, and almost regardless of the constraints upon kings of international politics, great personal valour and a powerful presence on the world stage were still celebrated as the manifest proof of nobility and true kingship. Claude de Seyssel included foreign conquests as a signifier of greatness in his tract, *Les louanges du roy Louis XII*, published in Paris in 1508. In accordance with his ideas set out in *Der Weisskunig*, the emperor Maximilian strove to cast his notoriously ineffective warfare against anyone as heroic. The *Theuerdank*, published in 1517, was a highly fanciful chivalric allegory of the emperor's deeds. It was only one of a proposed series of 12 books glorifying the supposed political and military success of the Habsburg dynasty.

Wars undertaken in defence of Catholic orthodoxy or for the legitimate defence of dynastic claims were generally regarded as glorious. In a deliberate attempt to focus these ideals on themselves and to garner support as military leaders, late-medieval kings had founded orders of chivalry. The most prestigious of these royal orders in the sixteenth century was the Order of the Garter in England, founded by Edward III in 1348. Next was the Order of the Golden Fleece in Burgundy, founded by the Valois dukes. Its ostensible aim was the liberation of Jerusalem and its leadership was enthusiastically taken up by the Habsburg emperors Maximilian and Charles V. The French Order of Saint Michael, founded by Louis XI, came a rather distant, but still honourable, third.

At first sight, there is little evidence to suggest that any of the kings so obsessed with chivalric glory paid much more than lip service to the idea of avoiding war. Historians have often argued that the views of pacifist commentators like Erasmus were dismissed as irrelevant by monarchs. Yet Henry, Francis and Charles all devoted much time and care to defining, asserting and explaining their dynastic claims against each other and all expressed a desire for peace in the right circumstances. Peace-making was never dismissed out of hand by monarchs. If glamorised as an honourable and edifying enterprise between great princes, the ideal of peace could carry conviction. It was seen as the other side of the coin of chivalric warfare and an equally important weapon in international politics.[20]

GOVERNORS: COUNSEL AND ESTATES

It was universally accepted that *virtus* was demonstrated most clearly in magnificent warfare but it also extended to all other aspects of kingship. It should be shown through the maintenance of justice, the first duty of a Christian king and governor. Henry, Francis and Charles were conscious that they needed to take advice on policy and needed assistance to enforce the laws that they promulgated. Such advice was provided in the first instance through royal councils which were chosen by the monarch and usually comprised relatives, particular favourites and the most powerful magnates. Proximity to the ruler brought the opportunity to influence policy and to profit by it. Not surprisingly therefore, the subject of 'counsel' exercised most political commentators. Some favoured Cicero's view, derived from Aristotle, that those born into or raised to the governing echelons of society, should lead an 'active life' in politics. Others, basing themselves on Plato, argued that a capacity to disengage from daily politics in favour of contemplative philosophy was vital in those who governed. There was, nevertheless, a good deal of common ground in this debate as to what made for good government.

In England the view that morally good and well-educated counsellors were the best for the prince was articulated by Stephen Baron, the Provincial of the Observant Franciscans. In 1509 he dedicated *De regimine principum* or 'On the Rule of Princes', to the young Henry VIII. Drawing on verses from the Hebrew bible and Seneca he warned that self-seeking courtiers undermined the well-being of the commonwealth. Royal officials, especially judges, must be chosen for their probity because their acts strengthened or diminished the king's justice for which he was accountable to God. Writing well into Henry's reign, Sir Thomas Elyot (c. 1490–1546) opined in *The Book Named the Governor*, that the 'best' counsellors were, almost by definition, hereditary nobles and the gentry who were the king's servants in the localities. He deplored the king's supposed habit of employing only personal favourites as advisors. Elyot's treatise prescribed a familiar humanist curriculum for aristocratic sons that would enable them to serve the best interests of the prince and the realm in offering well informed, disinterested, counsel.[21]

Machiavelli also warned against small circles of flatterers on robustly common sense grounds. Flattery was natural in humans who wanted something from the ruler. It could be manipulated by the ruler for his own ends but taking it too seriously could deflect him from his real aim which should be to preserve his own power and reputation. Therefore Machiavelli advised him to decide when, from whom, and upon what matters he would be advised. Then the prince must swiftly make his own decision. Drawing on Plato, he laid it down as an 'infallible rule' in keeping power that 'a prince who is not himself wise cannot be well advised.'[22]

This maxim is echoed in Book I of More's *Utopia*. Raphael Hythlodaeus, a neo-Platonist and the main protagonist of the book, argues that his acknowledged intelligence and insight would be rejected in contemporary courts where most advice is self-serving and expedient. In response, the character of 'Morus' enunciates the Ciceronian defence of active involvement in politics. He counters, without finally convincing, that if a counsellor cannot make things good then he must at least make them less bad. The debate between the two remains unresolved but More's view that only the best educated and morally upright should be chosen as counsellors is revealed in Book II where it emerges that the Utopians do have a princely council to settle disputes. The most important decisions however are taken by the Senate, where, because of the highly moral character of the senators, 'the emphasis is on speaking wisely rather than quickly.'[23]

More's reference to the Utopian Senate alludes to the fact that in England, as elsewhere, the monarch was expected to consult yet more widely than the royal council on major decisions, such as demanding the subjects' money for war or when introducing significant changes to the law. By a process of gradual development, the occasional practice of summoning the 'estates' of the realm for counsel, talk, or 'parley' became institutionalised in bodies called *Parliament*, *États*, *Cortes*, and *Reichstag*. By the sixteenth century these assemblies in effect constituted the royal or princely councils at their fullest political and judicial extents. The formal title of the English representative body was in fact 'the king's high court of Parliament'. Although the initiative for summoning and dismissing them remained with the ruler, representative assemblies quickly accustomed themselves to strenuous but careful bargaining with the sovereign. At the heart of such bargaining was the issue of what rights, privileges and obligations the subjects owed the king and what, if anything, he owed his subjects.

Perhaps the clearest statement of the position in England at the close of the fifteenth century was provided by Sir John Fortescue (c. 1394–1476). Chief Justice of the King's Bench under Henry VI and a councillor to Edward IV, he wrote *The Governance of England* in 1471–72. He argued that the English monarch's primary duties were to defend the realm and to do justice. He had broad but finite powers over his subjects and could only rule by laws made with the consent of the Lords and Commons in Parliament. Most importantly, the realm could only be taxed with its consent. This idea of 'mixed monarchy' where estates and king worked together he called *dominium politicum et regale*. In urging the maintenance of this system he drew a false distinction between England and France. He maintained that France was a *dominium regale*, a realm ruled by king alone, with no tradition of effective representation, the majority of whose pathetic people were taxed to penury. In fact *dominium politicum et regale* was the constitutional norm throughout Europe although it often worked in ways unfamiliar to Fortescue. As Professor Koenigsberger has noted: 'In the late-medieval partnership between kings and parliaments throughout Europe, the kings were by far the stronger, although hardly ever the completely dominant partner.'[24]

In *La Monarchie de France*, Claude de Seyssel argued that France too was a 'mixed' or 'constitutional' monarchy. The French monarch had broad powers over his people and did not in any sense share sovereignty. Nevertheless, he freely accepted three restraints upon himself. In addition to religion, discussed above, these were justice and *la police*. Justice was the maintenance of the laws of France that protected the people. The administration of justice, was 'the true pillar of royal authority' and the king could not simply make laws to please himself. It was the judges and the lawyers of the royal courts, known as the Parlements, especially the Parlement of Paris, who represented an aristocratic element in the government of France. They had the right to scrutinise new laws and to remonstrate with the king about them. Although not an elected assembly, the review powers of the French Parlements broadly paralleled those exercised by the English Parliament. *La police* or 'polity' was the most complex of the three restraints comprising as it did three separate elements. The first was the 'fundamental laws' of France which stipulated that the French patrimony could not be alienated without absolute necessity and that females could not succeed to the crown. *La police* also meant not altering in any way those laws, ordinances and customs which had been observed for so long past and which had supposedly kept all levels of French society in harmony. The final element of *la police* was that the French king should follow good counsel especially in matters affecting the commonwealth. In theory at least, the 'bridles' on the French monarch gave the Parlements, the Estates-General of the realm, the provincial Estates and individual noblemen, significant room for argument over the application of royal law.[25]

In 1518 Guillaume Budé (1468–1540), published his *L'institution du prince* which was also dedicated to Francis I. It rehearsed arguments similar to those in Erasmus's 1516 treatise about royal character, the importance of wise counsel, the study of history and doing justice according to the law. Budé endorsed the neo-Platonic ideal of the philosopher-king and saw Francis as having supreme authority unchecked by any restraint other than that imposed by the king's own educated awareness of, and respect for, the ancient laws of France.[26] At first sight this seems a different kind of sovereignty from that formulated by the more Aristotelian Seyssel, and Budé's tract seems to point towards an 'absolutist' theory of kingship. Nevertheless, it is clear that Budé, no less than Seyssel, expected that the king would rule equitably and respect the fundamental laws of France. Budé also maintained strenuously that upholding justice was the vital distinction between legitimate sovereignty and mere tyranny. However, whereas Seyssel allowed royal councillors and the Parlements an active supervisory role in at least the processes of the king's governing if not technically in his sovereignty, Budé allowed no individual or institution such a supervisory role. During the reign of Francis, the broadly 'constitutionalist' view of the French monarchy as advocated by Seyssel was challenged, not least by the king's own legal officials and his propagandists. Yet it largely prevailed until the crisis of the Wars of Religion when accusations of tyranny became the stock-in-trade of warring groups and new arguments were developed about the nature and limits of royal authority.[27]

In Spain theories of mixed or balanced monarchy also competed with those of unfettered royal power. Francesco di Vitoria (1483–1546) was a leading proponent of the ideal of community between the sovereign and the realm, along Seyssel's lines. He articulated what was, at least until the time of the Catholic Kings, a widely held view that the monarchs of Iberia had power delegated to them by God, but on behalf of the people. It had to be exercised for the benefit of the whole community. In the crown of Aragon, there were vigorous institutional safeguards on the ancient privileges of the three kingdoms within it. The Castilian monarch was said to be the highest public official of the realm, but at its service. This view was reiterated by the representatives to the first Cortes Charles summoned, at Valladolid, in 1518. Ferdinand and Isabella tended to clothe their active, interventionist, style of kingship in this rhetoric of service to realm. Charles, too, accepted the traditional and practical restrictions on the power of the Iberian monarchs but insisted on respect for his authority. Especially after the revolt of the *Comuneros* in 1520–21, talk of his owing sovereignty to anyone other than God was restricted to university lawyers. Any public statements to this effect were seen as subversive and tending to anarchy.[28]

PATRONS: 'LARGESSE', PROPAGANDA AND THE ROYAL COURT

The third aspect of successful Renaissance monarchy was patronage. Monarchs always needed the military and financial support of a number of powerful individuals, corporations and interest groups within the realm, each with its own independent traditions of wealth and prestige. Monarchs were also the ultimate authorities and all honours and privileges to which the political and economic elite aspired came finally from them. Therefore, as far as monarchs were concerned, 'patronage' meant, first and foremost, maintaining a mutually beneficial relationship between themselves and the political nation. It also meant employing the services of those who could persuade the political elite to co-operate with the monarchy; that is, technicians, writers, artists and artisans who could present the monarch and his or her regime to that elite in ways that engendered respect and admiration.

Patronage was extolled by classical and medieval writers and in the chivalric concept of *largesse* or extravagant generosity. The feudal system of giving land in exchange for continuing military service to the crown evolved in part from Roman practice and in part from the traditions of the Germanic tribes of late-Antiquity who shared the booty of war out among warriors. Centuries of further political and economic development complicated, but did not obscure, this essential relationship. Sixteenth century European nobles remained acutely conscious of themselves as warriors, as owners of the land and recipients of the privileges which military service entailed. The great magnates in particular expected, as of right, to have from the monarch tokens of esteem and to share directly in the government of the kingdom. They needed influence in order to garner a sufficient share of lands, money and lucrative offices in the church or royal service. This share was then used to enhance their own status and was also re-distributed among their own followers, or clients, further down the social scale. The major noble families, who often had more than a tincture of royal blood themselves, remained a force to be reckoned with.

Late-medieval commentators counselled princes to manage the patronage system carefully. 'Largesse' should be shown with a discerning regard for the character of its recipients. A monarch who indulged only his favourites derogated the honour of the crown. Impolitic generosity caused resentment among those not sharing it and among those whose taxes paid for the king's estate. Royal magnificence should never be confused with dissipation. Seyssel distinguished magnificent display from 'gorgiasetés', unattractive excesses which suggested indifference to the collective wealth of the realm, whose steward the monarch was. In a well-ordered kingdom then, the monarch should ensure that the preponderant share of patronage remained in his or her hands and that it was distributed as evenly as possible, consistent with hierarchical status, to those who served the crown's best interests.

It was exactly to this balance that Fortescue addressed himself in *The Governance of England* which was essentially his prescription to Edward IV for the recovery of the English monarchy after the Wars of the Roses. Fortescue advised that the monarchy needed 're-foundation' on a sound financial basis. Royal lands previously alienated should be reclaimed and used to underpin crown income. The king could then 'live of his own' revenue and resources without recourse to Parliamentary taxation in meeting his 'ordinary' or regular expenditure. This included the costs of the royal household, wages for the great officers of state, for the garrison in Calais and the maintenance of royal palaces and buildings. The king's 'extraordinary' expenses included those for war and the defence of the kingdom, for his ambassadors, for royal judges and the maintenance of law and order. They could be met with help from Parliament because they concerned the king's public role as protector of the realm. With such a re-foundation, Fortescue argued, the king would be the greatest lord of the realm and assured of its support. For, as he also said, 'the people will go with him that best may sustain and reward them.'[29]

Fortescue appreciated that the king had to look the part and the majority of sixteenth century commentators agreed with him. The monarch must have, and be seen to have, sufficient personal wealth so as to maintain an appropriately regal style. He or she should have the biggest, most impressive, buildings decorated in the latest fashion and be well attended by noble and gentry subjects. Royal patronage therefore encompassed architects, painters, musicians, scholars and artisans who did this work for the sovereign and in turn praised him or her for the very generosity upon which they depended. In an elaborately circular process, the work of these artists became propaganda which declared the regime to be worth supporting if the noble elite wished to enjoy a continuing share in the power of a monarch who could command such artistic splendours and in whose company one could lead such an apparently glamorous lifestyle.[30]

The inter-related patronage of nobles, gentry and artists came together most obviously at the royal court, the monarch's household. As monarchs strove to demonstrate their *largesse* to their elite subjects, celebratory banquets and tournaments staged at court became steadily more lavish and spectacular. Pensions and stipends for performing household offices were also available. While modest, these fees and perquisites could still significantly enhance income derived mostly from landed estates. Most important of all was the possibility that proximity to the monarch might secure political influence and with it the chance to profit in more substantial ways from service to the regime.

This helps to account for the extraordinary rise in importance of the royal household in the politics of most western monarchies during the later fifteenth and early sixteenth centuries. Securing a place in the monarch's household became the goal of any seriously ambitious young man. It would enable him to gain prominence within the royal affinity and he might eventually become a substantial patron in his own right. Groups of courtiers gathered around royal favourites and through them attempted to attract and then monopolise the sovereign's bounty. These ever-changing groups, which are known as 'factions', were ubiquitous in early-modern courts. The English and French courts in particular were alive with factional jostling. Baldesare Castiglione (1478–1529) wrote *The Book of the Courtier*, a study in the methods of operating successfully in such a crowded and competitive environment. Written in, and about, the court of the Montefeltro dukes of Urbino, it was first published in Venice in 1528 and widely read in translation throughout Europe from the middle years of the sixteenth century.

CONCLUSION

Henry VIII, Francis I and Charles V all became kings at an extraordinary period of European history. As young men all saw themselves in a similar way. All felt that by birth and the rites of coronation, they had the right to direct the lives of their subjects. They expected the political and financial co-operation of the ecclesiastical establishment and of the papacy in maintaining religion in their kingdoms. They were conscious of their role as governors and took it seriously even if all three often had difficulty settling to the business of administration.

Of their authority as the final arbiters in their own kingdoms and of their right to be obeyed, none had the slightest doubt. All were of a strongly authoritarian disposition from the outset, although each appreciated the need to respect and work with the realm's long-standing institutions and traditions. In Charles V's case, this was to prove both the great strength and weakness of his monarchy. All therefore saw themselves as patrons and expected to use the wealth of the monarchy to maintain the loyal service of deserving subjects. They also expected that their subjects would support them out of their private wealth as need arose, although at the outset, none could have known just how great that need would be. All three were acutely conscious of maintaining the dignity of their royal persons and the importance of visual splendour in conveying the prestige of the crown to domestic and foreign observers alike.

These three kings were absolutely convinced of the importance of political and personal magnificence. They saw this 'virtue' as the key to achieving *virtus* or reputation in the world. Whatever they did, in peace or war, these men were convinced that they must do it superlatively. Whether they always did so is another question entirely. Each was quickly aware of the other two and, whatever the state of their formal relations from time to time, saw them as deadly rivals. They believed that they must defeat or at least neutralise their rivals in the intense personal competition which quickly arose between them to become the incarnation *par excellence* of the royal ideal. It was as warriors that they aimed, first and last, to achieve this goal. Fired by stories of recent victories, or defeats, and educated to some extent at least in the chivalric tradition and the classical histories, they were fiercely determined to assert their greatness on the battlefield.

For all the seducing glamour of revived classical imagery which they adopted and endlessly deployed, Henry, Francis and Charles never forgot the medieval archetype of monarchy. One has only to look at their Great Seals, the ultimate authenticating symbols of their authority, to see the basis of Machiavelli's observation cited at the outset of this discussion. On the obverse, the king was shown crowned, seated in majesty and holding the sceptres of authority and justice. Over his throne was a canopy or 'cloth of estate' usually portrayed in fashionable classical style. On the reverse, the king was depicted in full armour, on horseback, at the gallop with the sword of state upright in his right hand, the very embodiment of knighthood, riding to the defence of his honour and the realm. Around the edges of the seal appeared the king's name and title in Latin.[31] These seals eloquently express the central ideal of monarchy before, after, and most especially during, the Renaissance; the ruler as a magnificent warrior, patron and governor.

2

Warriors: Honour and magnificence in war and peace

> Therefore I cannot but see and feel that time is passing, and I with it, and yet I would not like to go without performing some great action to serve as a monument to my name. What is lost today will not be found tomorrow and I have done nothing so far to cover myself with glory and cannot but blame myself for this long delay. For all these reasons, therefore, and many more, I can see no cause why I should not now do something great. Nor yet do I see cause to put it off any longer, nor to doubt but that with God's grace I shall succeed in it.[1]

These words were written by the emperor Charles V in January 1525 shortly before his 25th birthday. He was conscious of the great inheritance which God had given him, an inheritance then threatened by Francis I who was leading an army against the duchy of Milan, an imperial fief in northern Italy. Alone before his enemy, the emperor felt that his greatest test was at hand. By 'doing something great' Charles meant fighting Francis in a battle in which his armies would be 'either victorious or wholly defeated.' His words, written in this moment of excitement and anxiety, speak for his entire generation of monarchs. Like his grandfathers, Ferdinand of Aragon and the emperor Maximilian, Charles felt an immense personal burden to maintain the standards supposedly set by his glorious ancestors. For him, as for Francis I and Henry VIII, nothing was more intolerable than to be regarded as having failed to equal the deeds of Charlemagne, or Saint-Louis, or Henry V of England.

HONOUR AND THE WARRIOR ETHOS

For Renaissance rulers, war was primarily about asserting personal power and military prowess in a way which secured their fame. Few of the military campaigns fought during the first 50 years of the sixteenth century were, from their inception, motivated by purely strategic or economic concerns. They cannot be explained in the way nineteenth or twentieth-century warfare has been in terms of gaining commercial advantage over rivals, or acquiring 'natural' or 'defensible' frontiers or obtaining 'living room' for a nation's population and so on. The many wars fought on the Italian peninsular between 1494 and 1559 by the kings of France and Aragon and the Holy Roman Emperor were not about incorporating it politically or economically into their respective realms. Rather, these rulers pursued personal claims to rule territories in the peninsula which had come into the patrimony of their kingdoms in a previous generation.

In an age of personal monarchy, 'national interest' and the personal interests and prestige of the sovereign were effectively one and the same. As the emperor Maximilian once put it: 'My honour is the honour of Germany, the honour of Germany is my honour.'[2] Conflicts between monarchs were often referred to as wars of 'magnificence and honour,' reflecting their very personal nature. This international mentality of 'honour' or good reputation operated like a metaphorical stock market where an individual's holdings of the prescribed attributes of *virtus* constituted a share portfolio. Any portfolio's value fluctuated according to the opinion of the 'market' and had at all times to be asserted and jealously guarded. A failure to do so endangered the king and his realm. For, as the Cardinal de Santa Cruz once warned Charles V:

> As soon as a prince loses but one grade of reputation friends will become mistrustful, enemies will be encouraged and in the natural course of events, he will be reduced to the lowest grade.[3]

However, this is only half the story. It was equally clear that monarchs could not be at war the whole time. There were a number of constraints upon the military ambitions of kings. Henry, Francis and Charles were all aware that as Christian rulers, they had to respect, and be seen to respect, Judeo-Christian injunctions against murder and lawless violence. Unnecessary war burdened their subjects financially and potentially threatened their livelihoods. No sensible monarch would readily jeopardise the trade upon which his or her realm's prosperity depended. To disturb international concord without good cause was not simply inept governance, it was a grave sin for which kings were accountable before God. Keeping the peace was as important an aspect of kingship as being a warrior.

The apparent paradox between the duty to practise war and that to keep the peace had, over the course of the middle ages, been resolved by the evolution of the concept of the legitimate or 'just' war and its attendant code of chivalry. Chivalry was primarily a set of ideals, customs and regulations designed to define who in society was entitled to bear arms and to control the expression of their violence and hostility, especially in war. It had evolved over centuries and its component parts and practices were much debated during the sixteenth century but at its heart was a set of agreed rules of warfare. A monarch should declare his 'cause' for war to his enemy, using heralds of varying types who were the messengers and also the 'referees' in international conflict. He should declare his cause to his own people and ensure that it was just. War had to be fought only from necessity and not from hatred. It was theoretically just if undertaken by a recognised sovereign, in defence of the Catholic faith, to recover lost goods or territory, or in defence of his kingdom.[4]

Even if a monarch's cause was just, the successful conduct of war in the sixteenth century required the protagonists to possess sufficient economic and military means to sustain it. Troops had to be recruited, allies found, objectives decided upon and plans put into action which might well miscarry. The weather, the difficulties of moving large armies and the costs of keeping them in the field for long periods often limited severely the potential enemy targets a monarch might launch himself against. No individual monarch was likely to triumph in every campaign he undertook. Losses and disappointments were inevitable. Moreover, in common with every gentleman of arms who ever lived, Henry, Francis and Charles could not guarantee themselves a reputation as a warrior. By definition, repute is something conferred only by others. An individual monarch had simply to do knightly deeds which he hoped proved his valour or *virtus*. A loss in war was not itself disgraceful, provided that the loser had personally distinguished himself in battle. For example, although Francis I was defeated at the Battle of Pavia in 1525 he still fought on until overwhelmed by his enemies. He eventually surrendered to the imperial commander, confident only in his performance as a knight on the day. He summarised his position succinctly in a letter to his mother written shortly after the battle: 'All is lost, save life and honour.'

Despite appearances and the obsession with chivalric glory, war was never made simply from a spirit of reckless bravado. It was entered only after careful consideration of the chances of success, in whatever way that was defined. Peace was a perfectly acceptable alternative to warfare, but, as demonstrated below, it too had to have a chivalric quality about it. It had to enhance, not diminish, the reputation of the kings agreeing to peace with each other. Whether at war or at peace, monarchs had always to answer the demands of the 'magnificence and honour' mentality. This meant doing things which demonstrated their credentials as warriors and leaders. They invested in armies, in new military technologies, in armaments and fortifications. Above all, monarchs constantly acted out their military role through their leadership of the orders of chivalry, by engaging in the paramilitary sports of tournaments and hunting and participating in colourful pageantry. As Blaise de Monluc, one of Francis I's commanders, observed in his memoirs: 'it is nothing to get a good repute if a man do not uphold and improve it.'[5]

Chivalric orders

Since the mid-fourteenth century, European princes had shown a marked interest in the creation of elite societies of knights where the ideals of just and knightly warfare could be clarified and affirmed. These societies were the princely orders of chivalry, the oldest of which was the Order of the Band founded by Alfonso XI of Castile in about 1330. Like the lay confraternities which were their closest antecedents, these orders were distinguished by fraternal exclusivity and by the statutes governing the aims of the order and admission to them. They employed special insignia and liveries and held regular meetings or 'chapters' where members judged each other's behaviour according to the fighting code of the order. Royal leadership gave these orders immense prestige. The prospect of membership could be a strong inducement to powerful nobles to support the royal regime. In turn, the status of such high-born members lent fame to the order and the prince who presided over it. Foreign princes were also included and membership of each other's orders was often used to seal alliances between kings.[6]

The most prestigious princely order in the early sixteenth century was the Order of the Garter. It was founded by the English king Edward III in 1348. Contemporary chronicles made allusions to King Arthur's Round Table as the inspiration for the Garter's foundation and most orders had some similarly fanciful foundation myth. Its patron was Saint George whose obscure but sound crusading credentials were appropriated by Edward to give the war he was then fighting in France the quality of a holy quest carried on by the finest knights of the realm under heaven's protection. The 25 knights of the order and the sovereign met annually on 23 April, its patron's feast day. Henry VIII's desire to assert dynastic right to the French crown during the sixteenth century gave him an intense and lifelong commitment to the Garter. He enlarged and altered the design of the order's collar, which had itself been added by Henry VII, to make it more fashionably grand. In 1534 he commissioned the Black Book of the Garter which is the first surviving register of the order. The men appointed to the order during the first 25 years of his reign were usually genuine soldiers and leading members of the Tudor regime. The future Charles V was made a knight of the Garter in February 1509 and his brother Ferdinand was admitted to its ranks in 1523.[7]

Henry VIII's commitment to the Order of the Garter was more than matched by Charles V's to the Order of the Golden Fleece or the *Toison d'or*. The order was founded by Duke Philip the Good of Burgundy in 1431. The Golden Fleece referred naturally to Jason's famous quest but also more obliquely to the deeds of the Hebrew warrior-leader Gideon. The order's primary aim was a crusade to recapture the Holy Lands. Its patron was Saint Andrew and chapter meetings were held on his feast day, 30 November. Knights wore a gold collar whose design incorporated inter-linked flint stones striking fire on steels. From the collar hung a badge of a golden ram. Charles was made a knight of the order when he was barely 11 months old and his personal device of the two pillars of Hercules was originally an adjunct to the insignia of the Golden Fleece. Its adoption as his own emblem indicates how closely he identified himself with the Burgundian order. Virtually every image of Charles known to us, from a sketch of him as a small boy to the grand portraits of his mature years, shows him wearing its insignia. In 1545 he was painted in his robes as sovereign of the order. Charles increased membership of the Golden Fleece from thirty to fifty knights and the sovereign. Henry VIII had been admitted to the order in 1505, alongside his father who had been a member since 1491. Charles also inherited from Ferdinand of Aragon the leadership of three Spanish crusading orders which were originally independent of the monarchy. In 1523 the masterships of the Castilian crusading orders of Santiago, Calatrava and Alcántara were permanently vested in the crown. Charles used these orders to increase his political patronage in his Iberian kingdoms. Most places in the Golden Fleece were reserved for Charles's relatives, foreign princes, his highest military commanders and local representatives. Their personal loyalty to him as knights of the order was important in maintaining his authority in the lands of his Burgundian inheritance and throughout his vast empire. Consequently, the membership of the Golden Fleece was the most cosmopolitan of all the chivalric orders, having a high proportion of Spaniards, Italians and Portuguese as well as Flemmings.[8]

The French chivalric order during Francis's reign was the Order of Saint Michael, founded in 1469 by Louis XI as a direct, if belated, response to the foundation of the Order of the Garter. The Valois kings adopted the warrior Archangel Michael as their personal protector in the war against the English. He was portrayed in the order's insignia killing a dragon-like Satan, an obvious parallel to the deeds of Saint George. The order had 36 members and Francis was careful to keep to these limits. Its chapter meetings were not held as regularly as for the other two orders and were not marked by such magnificent ceremony, but membership of the order was still prestigious. Charles of Spain became a member in 1516, receiving its insignia at Brussels on 9 November, the same year in which Francis became a *chevalier* of the Golden Fleece. In 1527 Francis I took the significant step of making Henry VIII a member of the Order of Saint Michael. He had suggested an exchange of membership of each other's orders to Henry on at least two previous occasions without success. Henry's election to the French order rather forced his hand and Francis I was soon afterwards elected to the Garter. He thus became the first French king to join the ranks of English chivalry. Francis's election defused some of the Garter's very anti-French ethos and the exchange of orders was rather a public relations coup for the French king.[9]

Tournaments

Like the orders of chivalry, princes and monarchs used tournaments to focus combatants' loyalty upon themselves and as a forum for displaying the knightly expertise of their military elite. The tournament was originally developed in the early medieval period as a training exercise for war. By the high middle ages it had become an integral part of the chivalric ethos and the associated romance of arms. Knights jousted for the honour of their chosen ladies whom they served just as they were meant to serve justice and the Christian faith. They dressed as heroes from the chivalric romances or classical myths and a number of them travelled the tournament 'circuit' becoming renowned competitors, rather like the professionals of modern international sport. Tournaments were occasions for princes and their adherents to display, with marvellous theatricality, their wealth and generosity. The lavishly decorated pavilions and arming tents of the participants, the sumptuous costumes blazoned with badges, mottoes and ciphers, the finest horses decked with brilliant caparisons, the burnished armour of the knights, helms surmounted with crests or plumes, all presented a fantastic and memorable spectacle to observers.

The sheer ostentation of such events enhanced the fame and status of the royal or princely host. He or his consort also distributed the prizes for the various competitions, the peacetime equivalent of distributing booty after battle as a reward to those who had served well on the day. Skills shown on the field were often the making of a young man's career in royal service. In the early 1490s, the Frenchman, Pierre de Terrail, Lord of Bayard, began his career when he demonstrated impressive horsemanship and tournament skills before his patrons, the Duke of Savoy and Louis of Luxemburg. With their support, he went on to join the royal army for successive invasions of Italy under Charles VIII, Louis XII and Francis I. He became known universally as the 'knight without fear or reproach.' It was Bayard who, at the king's insistence, knighted Francis on the field after his victory at Marignano in 1515. He was killed in battle in 1524 and was mourned publicly in France and beyond.[10]

By the early sixteenth century safety improvements such as barriers, known as 'tilts,' reinforcements for armour and new helmets known as 'frog mouth helms' that better protected the face, had reduced the perils of the tournament considerably. The various competitions included jousting against an opponent at the tilt, running at the ring, fighting on horseback or on foot, using 'rebated' or blunted pikes, halberds and swords. The functional relationship between some of these competitions and actual warfare was diminishing but had not been lost entirely. The increased popularity of foot combats in the early years of the century, particularly in Germany and Burgundy, actually reflected changes in real warfare where the infantry increasingly determined the outcome of battles. The emperor Maximilian's book *Die Whiskunig* had a series of woodcut prints illustrating tournament competitions and emphasised foot combat as part of a young knight's training. The tournament remained a very dangerous sport and was intimately connected with war in the minds of participants. It was especially thrilling when the king participated, as Henry, Francis and Charles did regularly.[11]

The undoubted champion of royal jousters was Henry VIII. His mastery of the various competitions derived partly from the fact that, unlike Francis I, Henry spent his first 4 years as king at peace. Tournaments were his only opportunity to display himself as a warrior and in his early years at least, all significant occasions at the Tudor court were marked with tournaments. *The Great Tournament Roll of Westminster* was made to record one tournament held in February 1511 to celebrate the birth of Henry VIII's first and short-lived son by Katherine of Aragon. Its splendid colour illustrations depict the king jousting (and winning) before his wife, dressed as 'Sir Loyal Heart.' He continued to joust well into his mid-thirties. He was listed to participate in a tournament at Greenwich in May 1527 but had to withdraw after injuring his foot playing tennis. Numerous English courtiers, such as Charles Brandon, Duke of Suffolk, Thomas Grey, Marquis of Dorset, Sir Nicholas Carew and Sir Francis Bryan began their political careers with impressive performances in tournaments.[12]

As overlord of the Netherlands and King of Spain, Charles continued the strong tradition of elaborate tournaments or *pas d'armes* begun by the Valois dukes. He attended tournaments as a spectator from the age of nine. When he was 12 his Habsburg grandfather ordered for him from the master-armourer Conrad Seusenhofer, a suit of armour decorated with silver-gilt and etched with emblems of the Order of the Golden Fleece. Whether used purely for ceremony or in actual competition, this armour, now in Vienna, is evidence of Charles's early inculcation in the business of chivalric combat.[13] He appeared in the lists during a series of tournaments held at Valladolid in November 1517 to celebrate his arrival in Castile. On one day he bore a shield with the device *Nondum* – 'not yet'; a humorous gloss on his personal motto of *Plus Oultre*. In March 1522 a Venetian ambassador in Brussels reported that the young emperor excelled all others at a tournament in which Charles and his brother Ferdinand tilted together, dressed as Moors. In June the same year he jousted with, not against, Henry VIII at Greenwich during his visit to England. In July 1524 the young Ferrante Gonzaga, the son of the Marquis of Mantua, was at the Spanish court. His servant and tutor, Pandolfo de Pico della Mirandola reported that a tournament given by Charles 'the emperor ran very well, breaking more lances by himself than all the others put together.' This was exaggeration perhaps but not empty flattery and accords with Venetian reports of the emperor's physical courage and skill in horsemanship.[14]

Tournaments were also popular among the elite in France. Francis I was an able jouster who led teams in the tournament held in 1514 to celebrate the marriage of Mary Tudor to Louis XII and, before injuring his hand, acquitted himself well. At his own accession tournament in February 1515 he delighted spectators with his performance and received favourable mention in reports by English and Venetian ambassadors. He was again the star of a tournament held at Vigevano near Milan in November 1515. At the Field of Cloth of Gold in June 1520 Francis was prominent in jousting and impressed observers with his spectacular costumes and skills. These events notwithstanding, Francis was so soon after his accession engaged upon real warfare, that he does not appear to have been quite as obsessed with tournaments as Charles V or Henry VIII. Nevertheless all major court celebrations from marriages to births of royal princes were marked by impressive tournaments in which the king participated until his middle years.

Hunting

The second great para-military sport was hunting. According to Machiavelli, hunting was the best way for the prince to strengthen his body and steel his nerves in preparation for war. By it he acquired personal knowledge of the geography of his kingdom that might prove essential in its defence. Hunting also provided another opportunity for the prince to impress observers with his courage and skill. There were strong erotic undertones in hunting, still echoed today in Spain in the machismo of bull fighting and the celebrity of matadors. Monarchs hunted on horseback or sometimes on foot with dogs and birds of prey. Deer was the most prestigious quarry; boar was the most dangerous and required real courage to hunt. Unlike today, foxes were not deemed worthy of aristocratic attention.

Francis I travelled and hunted through more of his kingdom more frequently than did either Henry or Charles in their respective realms. He had a large number of hunting lodges and smaller palaces, particularly in the Loire valley. Closer to Paris he hunted frequently in the forests around Fontainebleau and Saint-Germain-en-Laye. The French household accounts of the *vénerie* and the *fauconnerie*, responsible for hunting dogs and birds respectively, show that the king's expenditure on the sport rose steadily over the course of his reign. By 1540 he was spending approximately 58,000 *livres* per year on it, a 71 per cent increase on his earliest years.[15] Francis and Henry often exchanged ideas about hunting techniques and gave each other presents of horses, dogs, hawks and boar piglets. In 1541 Francis even sent Henry some pasties made from deer that he had recently killed. English ambassadors such as Sir William Fitzwilliam and Sir John Wallop considered Francis to be an exceptionally skilled and brave huntsman. During one outing in 1514 before he became king, Francis deeply impressed the visiting Charles Brandon when he single-handedly despatched a rampaging boar which, maddened with fear and pain, had charged directly at him.

This was not the only occasion on which Francis displayed such courage and these episodes illustrate well why contemporaries made such a close connection between hunting and war. This connection was made explicit in François Demoulin's *Commentaires de la guerre gallique*, a three volume work published between 1516 and 1520 which praised Francis as a new Caesar for his conquest of Milan in 1515. Volume II contains two illuminated miniatures in which Francis is depicted while hunting. Francis also received a number of treatises on hunting in which his knowledge was directly or indirectly praised. In another treatise published in 1561 he was posthumously awarded the accolade of, 'the Father of hunters.'[16]

Encouraged by his grandfather Maximilian, Charles V received his first instruction in riding and hunting from Charles de Poupet, Lord of La Chaulx with whom, even as a boy of ten and eleven, Charles often hunted all day. His favourite hunting sites in the Netherlands were the ducal park near Brussels and the forests of Soignes. A decade later Ferrante Gonzaga reported home from Spain how Charles hunted frequently and that his quarry occasionally included bulls. More than twenty years later, the Venetian ambassador reported in 1546 that still Charles's 'chief recreation' was hunting. He usually followed the chase with large numbers of attendants but sometimes hunted with a few friends and 'with an arquebus in his hand.'[17]

Henry VIII enjoyed hunting immensely and usually took his important guests with him on his frequent trips throughout the south-east of England. He and Charles V hunted almost daily together in the summer of 1522 as Henry escorted his nephew by way of Winchester and Bishops Waltham to Southampton. Henry's dedication to hunting easily outran that to formal business. In September 1521 his secretary Richard Pace mischievously told Wolsey that Henry was prevented from answering the cardinal's letter one day by saying his prayers and the next 'by harts and hounds.' Throughout his reign the king's annual 'progress' into the countryside would lay waste to the local wildlife and bring government to a virtual halt. As Edward Hall wrote in 1526 when Henry was in his prime: 'all this summer the king took his pastime in hunting and nothing happened worthy to be written of.' As he grew older and more corpulent, the king hunted closer to London in the parks near Windsor and Greenwich. Stands were built from which he mounted his long-suffering horses more easily or from where he shot at animals driven before him. He now also preferred the sport of hawking which was less demanding on the vast royal physique. At his death, Henry's private apartments contained many items used in this form of hunting.[18]

Pageantry and entertainments

Tournaments and hunting parties were usually followed by banquets which gave monarchs yet more opportunities to show off their physical skills and play the military hero in a romantic setting. Their dynasty and personal virtues were usually celebrated in the decorations for the banquets, the theatrical entertainments and the dancing which followed the eating. Occasionally more specific messages about the king's potential as warrior were delivered to the nobility through entertainments. An example of this phenomenon was the pageant of the 'riche mount' presented to the English court after a banquet at Greenwich palace on Twelfth Night 1513.

An invasion of France was planned for the following summer. A decorated float or 'pageant car' shaped like a hill called the 'riche mount' was wheeled into the banqueting hall. It was decorated with precious stones and flowers made of silk. These were red and white roses, broom flowers, the emblem of the Plantagenet dynasty, and irises or *fleurs-de-lis*, the emblem of France. At its summit sat Henry VIII with five of his knightly friends. Out of the hill came several ladies of the court, wearing French bonnets and adorned in the French fashion. The king and his companions came down from the hill and danced with them before the float was then drawn from the hall. The hill's floral decorations and its punning name referred to the Plantagenet/Lancastrian and, by extension, Tudor patrimony of France. In a light-hearted and romantic way this pageant promised the success to be had in France in the coming war under Henry's leadership.[19]

During the early sixteenth century, these royal regimes became increasingly concerned to present this same message of the monarch as successful warrior to much wider audiences. These included the men of the lower social orders who would actually do the fighting in war and who had to be inspired with the martial talents of their royal commander. Royal entries to cities were ideal occasions for this sort of propaganda. The decorations for such events were primarily the symbols of the royal dynasty or personal emblems of the sovereign such as Tudor roses or Habsburg eagles. For example, in the pageants presented by the aldermen and Mayor of London to welcome Henry and Charles V to the city in June 1522, Charles was greeted as the descendant of Charlemagne, the head of the Order of the Golden Fleece and the defender of Christendom against its infidel enemies. One of the pageants linked the descent of both monarchs from John of Gaunt. Although the emphasis remained on Charles, Henry was also likened to King Arthur. The strongest theme in the series of pageants was that the friendship, equality and joint political and military power of the two rulers together promised great future success.

The rapid development of printing technology during the early sixteenth century meant that this kind of temporary pageantry could be recorded and communicated to still-wider audiences through pamphlets and news-sheets, engravings and woodblock prints. In December 1529 Charles made a formal entry to Bologna where he would be crowned Holy Roman Emperor the following February. The entry was depicted in a series of coloured woodblock prints published by Robert Péril in 1534 showing Charles being greeted as a conquering victor by the city with triumphal arches erected across the main thoroughfare to the central Piazza and the Palazzo Pubblico. These arches and columns bore figures of the greatest Roman emperors, including Augustus, Titus and Trajan. Full use was made of his emblem of the pillars of Hercules and its *Plus Oultre* motto.[20]

Treatises, official orations, and histories of the dynasty were also published by licensed royal printers. Richard Pynson in London and Jean Gourmont in Paris kept up a steady stream of propaganda for their sovereigns. In 1512 Pynson printed a poem entitled *The gardyner's passetaunce touchying the outrage of France*, an allegorical justification of Henry's planned invasion of France. In the poem God appears as a gardener who prefers the sweet smelling rose of England to the proud and malodorous lily of France that he wishes to cut down. The work's jingoistic tone would have appealed to popular prejudice against the French which was particularly strong in the south-east of England were there was also a big market for printed material.[21] In 1523, as his armies once again invaded France, Henry received from John Bouchier, Lord Berners, the former Deputy of Calais, the first volume of a new translation of Froissart's *Chronicle* of the Hundred Years' War which the king had commissioned. The second volume followed 2 years later and became the standard English version until the modern era. A decade later, when Anglo-French relations were rather more peaceful, Wynken de Worde published *The maner of the triumphe of Caleys and Bulleyn*, a flattering account of Henry's meeting with Francis I in October 1532.

In 1556, at the end of Charles V's reign, Maarten van Heemskerck produced the *Divi Caroli Victoriae* which praised the emperor's success as a warrior. The illustrations from the work were engraved under imperial licence by Dirk Coornhert and present Charles V as a Roman emperor in armour at all significant victories of his reign. One of the most dramatic in the series is the first which shows Charles enthroned between the pillars of Hercules, holding a sword in his right hand. Between his feet sits his imperial eagle tethered to whose beak by prisoners' ropes are all Charles's enemies, including Süleyman and Francis I. Equally striking is a woodcut of Charles printed in Antwerp in 1550 as part of a series of equestrian portraits published by Hans Liefrinck the Elder. The emperor is shown in full armour galloping into battle on a magnificently caparisoned war-horse. He carries a huge mace and the collar of the Golden Fleece jangles at his neck. To the left of the page is his emblem of the pillars of Hercules with motto and on the right his coat of arms and imperial crown.[22]

THE CAUSES OF WAR

The ancient royal tradition of leading men in battle was reinvigorated in the early sixteenth century by the accession of three young men who, between them, governed most of Western Europe. They were ambitious, proud and deeply conscious that they were expected to provide the nobility with opportunities to bear arms in battle, its *raison d'etre*. Each of them considered that their causes were just and each convinced themselves that they fought in defence of the Catholic faith and dynastic possessions, the two greatest causes of war in early-sixteenth century Europe.

The most dangerous perceived threat to the Catholic faith in the minds of early-sixteenth century rulers was the advance of the Ottoman Turks who had made alarming incursions into the West in the century after the fall of Constantinople in 1453. It was not Charles, Henry or Francis, but Süleyman I, 'the Magnificent,' who was the greatest warrior of the age. Apart from extensive campaigns in the Middle East, throughout the Mediterranean and in North Africa, Süleyman launched successive invasions of Eastern Europe. The central Balkans and Belgrade fell to him in August 1521. Five years later the Turks destroyed the medieval kingdom of Hungary killing the last Jagiellon king, Louis II, at the Battle of Mohácz. There was panic but no collective response or support from Western Europe. Süleyman returned in 1529 and installed Janos Zapolya as his vassal in Hungary. When Archduke Ferdinand responded by besieging Buda in 1531, Süleyman counter-attacked the following year with a huge army, advancing almost to Vienna itself. Charles V and Ferdinand had some successes against this onslaught in 1532 and 1535 but the long-term consequences of their victories were inconclusive. Henry and Francis continually paid lip-service to the idea of a European crusade but neither of them contributed financially or militarily to their rival's fight against the Ottomans and Francis even signed a number of alliances with Süleyman.[23]

The Ottomans were not of course the only enemies of the Catholic faith in Europe. Just war also encompassed those fought against European heretics and schismatics but here the lines of demarcation between religious and dynastic motives in warfare became so unclear as to be practically meaningless. An important element in creating military conflict in the early sixteenth century was the pope's power to sanction action against schismatic leaders. Successive popes from Alexander VI to Paul III labelled as heretics those princes who opposed them on any grounds at all. 'Holy' leagues were created to punish these princes supposedly for their spiritual obduracy. In fact they were usually designed to enhance not only temporal papal power in Italy and beyond but the grandeur of the popes themselves and their families. For example, in 1511, Julius II excommunicated Louis XII as part of his effort to expel the French from Italy and take back papal lands which his predecessor, the Borgia pope Alexander VI, had alienated to his own family with French help. The pope's declaration of a crusade against France gave Henry VIII the opportunity to attack France in alliance with Aragon and the Holy Roman Emperor that he had been looking for since his accession in 1509.

The increasingly bitter controversies of the Reformation gave popes and princes yet more scope to label opponents heretical, though with perhaps more justice, and created armed ideological camps. The formation in 1531 of the Protestant League of Schmalkalden, presaged armed conflict between the forces of Catholic orthodoxy and those German princes and cities supportive of religious reform. Here too, the French king's action, and occasionally that of Henry VIII, in supporting Lutheran princes helped to confound Charles's attempts to impose orthodoxy on the Germans. When war between the League, in the person of John Frederick of Electoral Saxony, and Charles V finally came in 1547 it was as much about disputed territory held by both sides and arguments about recognition of Charles's sovereignty in Germany as about any attempt to secure religious conformity among the German princes. Charles's capacity to win the peace after defeating the League in 1547 was undermined by the direct intervention of Henry II of France pursuing age-old dynastic quarrels with the emperor.

Dynastic ambition was therefore the most virulent cause of war in sixteenth century Europe. Lineage and ties of blood through marriage produced a myriad of claims and counter claims between nearly all European monarchs. Many of these claims were founded on little more than family connections made generations earlier, or on accidents of birth and death. Yet royal blood was one of the most sacred and compelling entities known to the late medieval mind. It was inconceivable to Francis, Charles or Henry that dynastic claims, inherited or acquired through marriage, should not vigorously be asserted or defended. These claims are best examined separately.

Henry VIII

Henry's primary cause for war against France was his dynastic claim to the French crown. His attack on France in 1513, although couched predominantly in the language of a holy war against the schismatic Louis XII, was dynastic in motivation. He never relinquished the claim but, in circumstances to be explained more fully in the following chapter, he allowed himself to be bought off by the French king, much as his father had done, through a series of immensely profitable peace agreements. They were secured by the payment of a large annual French pension. His ostensible motive for ordering the invasion of France in 1523 was Francis's rupture of the Treaty of London of 1518. In 1544 he again invaded France because Francis had ceased payments of the pension. In Henry's view, this last war was just because Francis had again breached a peace treaty between them.

Henry's wars against Scotland held for him little of the glamour of fighting in France. His causes for war were essentially defensive or retaliatory in nature but there was also a dynastic element to them, particularly in the 1540s. Following the death of James IV at Flodden in 1513, the English king meddled in Scottish aristocratic affairs for a generation. James's widow was Henry's sister Margaret, and Henry expected her son to treat him as suzerain over Scotland. Yet when James V came of age he showed little or no respect for his English uncle. He re-established the alliance with France most effectively, strengthening it in 1538 by his marriage to Mary of Guise. It was Henry's chagrin at being 'injured, condemned and despised' by James V, and the threat of Scottish interference with any potential attack on France, which prompted him to send armies into Scotland on a series of raids in the summer of 1542. The defeat of James's counter-attacking army at Solway Moss in November and the king's death the following month leaving his infant daughter Mary as queen, effectively restored Henry to the position he had occupied in 1513. His further attempts to control the Scots, through a marriage of James V's daughter to his son Edward, backfired and led to a series of vindictive but ineffectual raids on Scotland in 1544 and 1545.[24]

Francis I and Charles V

Rather more complex as a cause of European war was the web of claims and counter-claims between Francis I and Charles V. These claims fell into three broad groups and most had their origins in Charles's inheritance of territories and claims from his Flemish, German and Spanish forbears.

(i) The Netherlands and Burgundy

The first group of claims arose from Charles's power in the Burgundian Netherlands. The Treaty of Senlis in 1493 had confirmed Habsburg possession of Flanders and Artois which bordered on the French province of Picardy. The French king claimed suzerainty over them but this was purely nominal. However he did have actual authority over the town of Thérouanne and the city of Tournai. Charles did homage to Francis in 1515 for Flanders and Artois but wanted to reclaim Tournai and Thérouanne. His other, more significant, claim was to the duchy of Burgundy itself. Francis was supposed to return the duchy to Charles under the terms of the 1526 Treaty of Madrid but repudiated that agreement the following year. In 1529 under the Treaty of Cambrai, it was Charles who relinquished his claim in return for 2 million *écus* from Francis. Francis then relinquished his sovereignty of Flanders and Artois. He also gave up his title to the towns of Tournai, Hesdin, Arras and Lille. However these concessions were repudiated in subsequent wars between Francis and Charles. Towns and territories swapped hands several times during the wars of the 1530s and 1540s and a more secure border was not agreed until the Treaty of Cateau-Cambrésis in 1559.[25]

(ii) Navarre

The second group of competitive claims between Francis I and Charles V centred on the kingdom of Navarre which lay across the Pyrenees and itself formed a corridor connecting the kingdoms of Castile and Aragon. After Isabella of Castile's death in 1504, Ferdinand of Aragon married Germaine

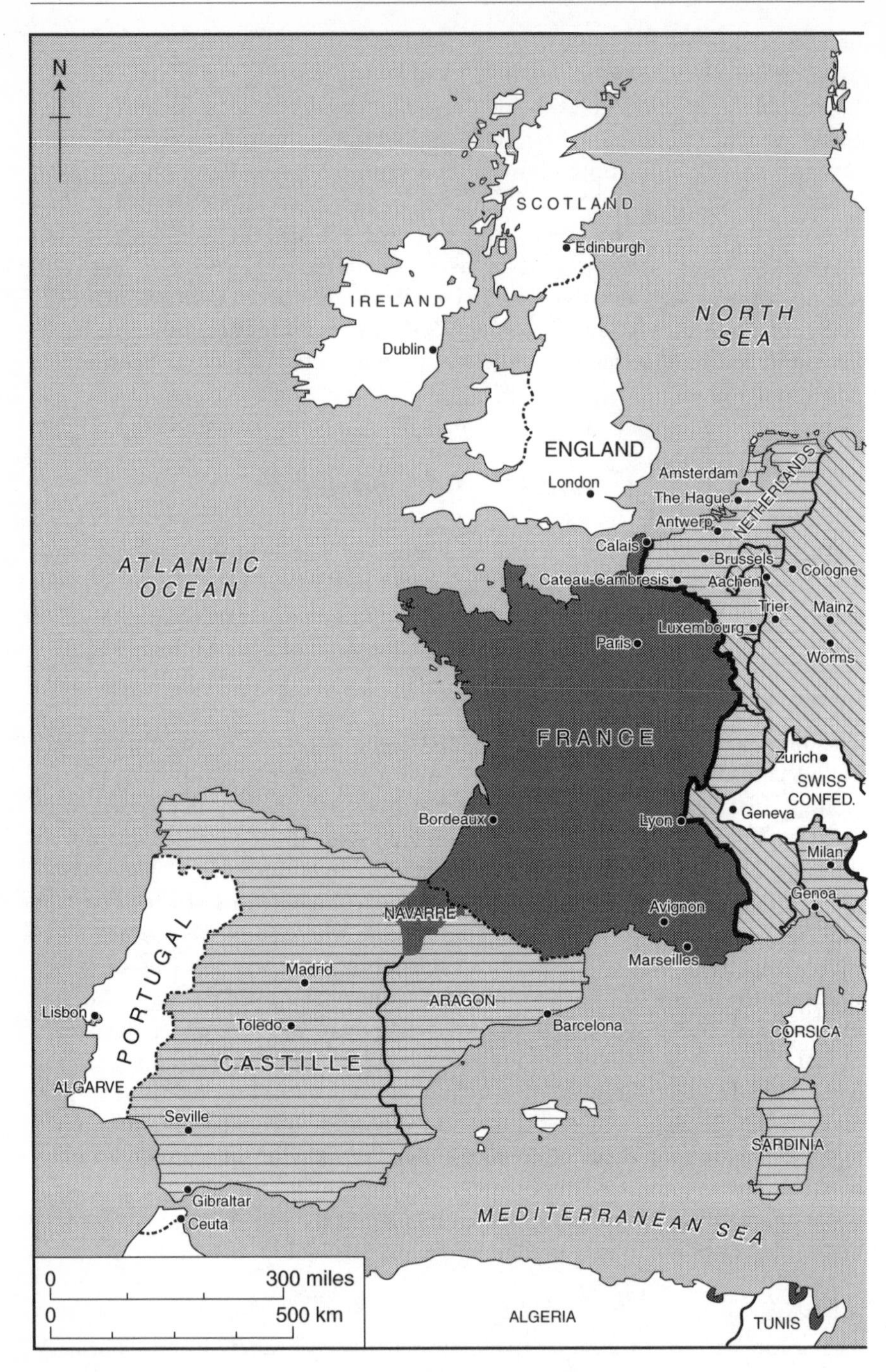

9. Valois and Habsburg possessions

Key
Dominions of Charles V, c.1530
Spanish Habsburg possessions
Austrian Habsburg possessions
Boundary of the Holy Roman Empire
Valois possessions
NORWAY
Oslo
SWEDEN
Stockholm
SWEDEN
Reval
ESTONIA
DOMINION OF THE TEUTONIC ORDER
Riga
DENMARK
Copenhagen
BALTIC SEA
Königsberg
Gdańsk
PRUSSIA
LITHUANIA
Hamburg
HOLY ROMAN EMPIRE
Berlin
Warsaw
Leipzig
POLAND
SILESIA
BOHEMIA
GREEK ORTHODOX
Augsburg
Munich
MORAVIA
Vienna
AUSTRIA
TRANSYLVANIA
MOLDAVIA
Mohacs
HUNGARY
VENETIAN REPUBLIC
TUSCANY
Belgrade
WALLACHIA
BLACK SEA
Florence
PAPAL STATES
Rome
OTTOMAN EMPIRE
ADRIATIC SEA
Naples
NAPLES
AEGEAN SEA
Lepanto
Palermo
SICILY

de Foix and through her laid claim to the kingdom of Navarre. At that time it was ruled by Jean d'Albret, a Gascon nobleman who held it in right of his wife, Catherine, a member of a more senior branch of the house of Foix. In 1512, with the help of Henry VIII, Ferdinand invaded and annexed the kingdom to Castile. Jean d'Albret asked for and received Francis's help on several occasions. In 1521 Jean's son, Henri d'Albret, who married Francis's sister Marguerite, invaded Navarre with the French king's backing but was repulsed. He was forced to renounce his claim to Navarre in 1526 but 12 years later came to an agreement with Charles V partitioning the kingdom.

(iii) Naples

Another group of claims which provoked several wars between Charles and Francis centred on Italy. The oldest concerned the kingdom of Naples. The Valois dynasty claimed the kingdom of Naples after 1481 when Charles III, the last of the Angevin counts of Provence who had also once ruled Naples, died bequeathing his title to the king of France. By 1481 the kingdom was actually under the suzerainty of Ferdinand of Aragon who governed it through a family of client kings. Charles VIII and Louis XII both asserted the Valois claim in the 1490s but by 1505 the French had been forced to withdraw. When Ferdinand died in 1516, Charles of Spain inherited all the Aragonese dependent territories including Naples, Sardinia and Sicily.

The Treaty of Noyon signed in 1516 effectively recognised Francis's sovereignty over Naples by providing that Charles would marry Francis's infant daughter whose dowry it would be. Until they married, Charles was to pay 100,000 crowns annually for it as tribute. However, this agreement proved a dead letter and Francis I sought several times to assert the Valois claim. In 1524 he detached a force from his main army then in northern Italy and sent it to conquer Naples but it was unsuccessful. Four years later he tried again, but after initial successes the French army under Marshal Lautrec was forced to lift its siege of Naples. The French made one more unsuccessful effort to wrest the kingdom from Spain in 1557. Thereafter Naples remained in Spain's possession for over two centuries.

(iv) Milan

If all this were not enough, there was yet another Valois claim in Italy which consumed more military and diplomatic energy in the early part of the century than any other. This was the claim to the duchy of Milan, an imperial fief. In 1387, Louis of Orléans had married Valentina Visconti, the daughter of the Duke of Milan. The marriage agreement provided that the duchy was to go to the Orléans family if the Visconti dynasty died out, which it did with the demise of Filippo Maria Visconti in 1447. However, 3 years before Filippo's death, Francesco Sforza, a successful *condottiere*, had married his daughter Bianca Maria and he was eventually recognised as Duke of Milan. He died in 1466 and was succeeded by his son Lodovico. In 1494, as part of his continual efforts to strengthen his position, Lodovico secured the marriage of his niece, Bianca-Maria Sforza, to the Habsburg Emperor Maximilian. In 1499 Louis XII of France asserted the Orléans claim, conquering Milan from Lodovico Sforza and ruling it until forced by yet another papally organised alliance to relinquish it in 1512. The Sforzas were then restored to power. Pursuing Louis's claim, both in right of his wife Claude, who was Louis's daughter, and as his direct successor, Francis I invaded Italy in 1515 and regained control of Milan. Four years later, Charles of Spain succeeded Maximilian as the emperor. He refused to accept the French claim that, during Louis XII's occupation, Maximilian had renounced the imperial fiefdom of Milan in favour of the French king. His Chancellor, Mercurino Gattinara, urged him to establish his power in Italy and from 1519 the duchy of Milan became the primary bone of contention between himself and Francis I.

Years of war between 1521 and 1525 culminated in Charles V establishing control of the duchy and ruling it through the Sforzas. There followed a decade in which Milan was not actively fought over but during which Francis tried to put military pressure on Charles elsewhere in Italy in the hope of forcing him to relinquish Milan one way or another. French hopes that Charles might concede the duchy in marriage to Francis's youngest son, Charles of Orléans, were at their highest in 1539–40 during a short-lived *entente* with the emperor. Francis was enraged when Charles finally invested his own son, Philip, with the duchy in October 1540. The final war between Francis and Charles was provoked by this decision. It was fought, not in Italy, but in their ancestral homelands in northern France and the Netherlands. Francis died in March 1547 still maintaining his right to the duchy.[26]

HONOUR AND PEACE

The catalogue of claims and counter-claims between the Habsburg, Valois and Tudor dynasties presented above is by no means exhaustive. Deeply conscious as each of these kings was of his God-given duty to protect and uphold his kingdom and all territories and claims inherited from his predecessors, they were not easily discouraged from taking military action against each other. But the sheer complexity of these claims meant that it was rarely, if ever, possible for them to be resolved simply by the outcome of battles. Because of compelling strategic limitations or difficulties, war was not always possible anyway. International relations also functioned through treaties and princely peace agreements.

In the opening decades of the century there was a great deal of talk about peace. Biblical humanist commentators regularly praised it. Erasmus expatiated upon war's horrors in two of his most famous tracts, *Dulce bellum inexpertis*, 'War is sweet to those who know nothing of it' and *Querela pacis* or 'The Complaint of Peace', both published in 1517 by Johanes Froben. For Erasmus, war was sinful in the most profound sense unless undertaken in the last resort to punish or restrain evil-doing. He always remained sceptical that any war could ever be described as wholly just. Thomas More took a similar line in *Utopia* as did the Spanish humanist Juan Luis Vives in his *Concordia et discordia in humano genere*, dedicated to Charles V after the signing of the Treaty of Cambrai in 1529. Biblical humanists argued that building cities and sponsoring learning were the truest proofs of princely virtue. Claude de Seyssel was more in step with contemporary noble expectations. War should not be undertaken from 'disordered passion' but to secure rights which could not be had by peaceful means. Seyssel's panegyric to Louis XII strongly suggests that he regarded dynastic wars as at least justifiable if not always wholly just. Seyssel also warned that a prince should never humiliate himself to have peace, nor seek it too easily.[27]

Henry VIII, Francis I and Charles V all frequently expressed a desire for peace. However, each of them saw international peace not in abstract or theoretical moral terms, but as intimately connected to his sense of personal honour and closely related to his military achievements. Sixteenth century monarchs never made peace for the sake of it. For all three rulers, 'peace' was ideally what happened when all their individual territorial rights, claims and jurisdictions were universally acknowledged and not threatened by anyone. It is hardly surprising therefore that ideal peace was rarely achieved. Nevertheless, when peace was agreed between princes it was invariably publicised in very idealistic language, replete with humanist rhetoric about the joys of Christian harmony. The parties promised permanent concord and their agreements were often termed 'holy', 'eternal' or 'perpetual.' In practice of course, they were usually arrived at when there was more to gain strategically by avoiding conflict. Most treaties failed in their stated aims of securing lasting peace between the signatories. In the face of this apparent contradiction, there is a tendency to assume either that princes wanted, but failed, to make peace for the reasons favoured by the Christian humanists, or that they merely paid lip-service to such ideals with no intention of living up to them. Both explanations have frequently been advanced by historians but they do not really explain why princes made peace when and in the way that they did.[28]

There had always to be a 'cause' for peace just as there were causes for war and both were formulated according to the Christianised fighting ethos of chivalry. To join with other knights in an enterprise of arms enhanced the status of any individual nobleman. To defeat and ransom an honourable opponent was proof of one's own prowess and a great triumph in the career of a Christian knight. In the same way, kings who made peace by joining themselves in alliance with honourable partners or who granted magnanimous peace to a defeated opponent while ensuring justice for themselves, achieved a mark of great distinction. For this chivalric model to work, one thing was essential. Each party to the agreement had to feel that he had made peace with honour. That is, his status as a powerful prince had been at least protected, and ideally increased, by the agreement. Sufficient financial, territorial or other sort of gains had to be made in order to offset the greater or lesser concessions which were usually required to obtain peace. The agreement had also to re-direct any pre-existing hostility and aggression between the signatories. The usual way to do this was to suggest a common enterprise against some third party. Once this position was reached, the agreement could be celebrated by the parties to it and presented to the world in the aspirant language of the Christian humanists with due emphasis on the ideal of Christian love and unity between princes.

PEACE-MAKING

It is therefore important to distinguish 'peace' from 'peace-making'. Ideal peace, in the sense of a complete absence of conflict, was rarely if ever achieved between Europe's principal monarchs during the early sixteenth century. Peace-making was a useful tool in their constant efforts, which went far beyond military conflict, to have others acknowledge their status as great kings. Peace was a blessing of fortune, but peace-making was a serious business.

In 1514 Henry VIII gave a textbook statement of how this peace-making worked in a letter to Cardinal Wolsey. He related an audience he had granted to Louis of Orléans, the Duke of Longueville, who sought peace with Henry on behalf of Louis XII of France following the war of 1513. Henry began his letter to Wolsey by noting, with evident satisfaction, that Longueville feared failing in his mission and was 'as ill afraid as ever he was in his life, lest no good effect should come to pass.' Henry stressed to the duke that he was well able to continue the war which he had begun the previous year, but, 'since your master has sought so gently to us' he was prepared to listen but that Louis would have to pay handsomely for peace. He wanted 100,000 crowns yearly from Louis partly to cover the costs of the war and mostly 'to recompense me for [his] withholding of my inheritance, which, if he be slack in, my subjects would murmur at.' In other words, Henry's 'just' peace involved Louis's tacit acknowledgement of his dynastic claim to, his 'inheritance' of, the crown of France. The reference to his subjects was really to his own sense of prestige which demanded that Anglo-French peace be seen as proof of his victory over Louis XII.[29]

These conditions became the *sine qua non* of every treaty which Henry VIII ever signed with a king of France and are typical of the way in which peace was often made by his fellow European monarchs. Louis of course saw the 100,000 crowns a year he agreed to pay Henry not as 'tribute' for the crown which he wore but as a worthwhile investment which hopefully kept Henry quiet and could be useful in persuading him to join in Louis's new plans for war against his erstwhile ally, Ferdinand of Aragon. Henry was therefore a 'pensioner' of the king of France as Henry VII and several English kings before him had been. From the French point of view, Henry's acceptance of this pension made him in a vague sense one of Louis's servants, and certainly not superior to him. In this way the personal prestige of both princes was safe-guarded and peace between them could be agreed. In the autumn of 1514 Louis XII married Henry's younger sister Mary Tudor, securing a new Anglo-French alliance. This markedly improved Henry's strategic position and was trumpeted by the English as proof of his high international status.

Successful peace-making between Renaissance monarchs, such as that between Louis XII and Henry, was never done simply or quietly. There was too much personal prestige at stake for that. Its most straightforward form was an alliance, usually secured by dynastic marriage between leaders whose interests and ambitions were generally compatible. Alliances provided defensive and offensive support against mutual enemies and fostered economic and cultural interaction between kingdoms. Alliances between Henry VIII and Charles V or between Francis I and the Venetians were of this sort. Such agreements were celebrated as the greatest proof of princely friendship and as the ideal of how relations should be between all Christian leaders. Even so, arranging and maintaining them was a difficult business. Each regime was driven by the hope of making agreements which improved its position relative to all others. It was a rare prince who kept an alliance if the prospect of a more advantageous one elsewhere presented itself. The result was a complicated and ever-changing patchwork of alliances which largely determined the course of international relations throughout Europe, and beyond.

Whether made between erstwhile enemies or between traditional allies, all treaties involved strenuous bargaining in order to satisfy claims and counter-claims between the protagonists or to establish each party's respective contributions to an alliance. Delegations of high-ranking churchmen, lawyers and nobles negotiated on the basis of detailed formal instructions given by the king and his council. They were always acutely conscious of the prestige of their sovereign. They spent a good part of any negotiations defending him against any imputation of fault, or ensuring that he was being dealt with fairly and respectfully by the other prince. As a result, negotiations routinely took many months and not infrequently ended in failure.

Negotiations could also be used to buy time to organise new alliances or to await better fortune on the battlefield. This happened in August and September 1521 at a Franco-Imperial peace conference called at Calais by Cardinal Wolsey. The Imperial chancellor Mercurino Gattinara and the French chancellor, Cardinal Duprat spent 2 months bitterly recriminating over who bore responsibility for the war which Robert de La Marck had begun earlier that year. This gave the Imperialists the opportunity to take the upper hand in the fighting against France and also to sign an alliance with England.[30] Most peace negotiations began in similarly rancorous mood but did eventually make progress. The parties' initial bargaining positions were slowly altered until an agreement was reached which enabled them to have peace with honour.

This emphasis on honour was expressed fully in the inauguration and publication of treaties. Frequently, the delegations that had concluded an agreement would be joined by much larger embassies of courtiers who participated in the formal ceremonies and festivities to celebrate the peace. The highpoint of these formalities was usually a Mass or some similar religious ceremony, at which the monarch signed the treaty and swore on the Bible or holy relics to uphold it, in the presence of his erstwhile opponent's representatives. The treaty documents themselves were often richly decorated with portraits of the princes involved or of classical goddesses of wisdom, love and marriage, together with scenes displaying friendship or peaceful commerce between kingdoms.

Elaborate Latin orations in praise of peace were commonly delivered during these formalities. These speeches expressed universally accepted sentiments and ideals about the desirability of peace and cannot therefore be taken at face value as reliable guides to the parties' attitudes. However, the more sophisticated orations often had subtexts which alluded to the basis upon which a particular peace agreement was made. For example, in September 1532 the Venetian ambassador in England noted that when Henry VIII swore to an alliance treaty with Francis I, Edward Foxe, the royal almoner, made a speech:

> expatiating on the greatness [i.e. the great power and danger] of the Turk and the extreme ill-will he bore Christendom without ever styling him 'Turk' but merely 'the perpetual enemy of our Lord Jesus Christ.'

This ambiguity was also noted by Eustace Chapuys the imperial ambassador. He correctly interpreted it to mean that the real intention of the alliance was not the defeat of Süleyman, but of Charles V.[31]

It was no accident that most peace agreements and alliances were also inaugurated with lavish tournaments, such as the Field of Cloth of Gold in 1520 or that held in 1559 for the Treaty of Cateau-Cambrésis. Tournaments expressed the close connection in the minds of participants between military prowess and peace-making. Competitors in a tournament did not aim to kill each other but aggression, daring display and risk of injury were absolutely vital to a good spectacle. So it was with peace-making. A successful peace treaty was like a tournament in that it 'rebated' or blunted military aggression between princes and set rules for their future relations. It usually did not eliminate princely competition altogether. Instead, a successful peace treaty created room for each of the parties to assert his own status and power against the other in less dangerous activities than outright war between them. One monarch could only maintain a peaceful and generous relationship with another if he possessed sufficient personal and material resources. Henry VIII always strove to play the part of the magnanimous friend, the equal, or better, of Francis I. The king of France responded in kind, not overtly as a warrior but as a great lord and patron.

Nowhere is this sort of extravagant and competitive interaction better illustrated than at the Field of Cloth of Gold, where Henry and Francis first met in June 1520, surrounded by virtually their entire courts. For a month the two kings entertained each other's nobles in the fields between the towns of Guînes and Ardres in northern France with lavish banquets, pageants and para-military combats. Their guests were accommodated in hundreds of acres of tented pavilions, many dressed with velvet and the cloth of gold which has ever since given the encounter its name. The meeting was widely reported and several detailed contemporary descriptions of it survive. Reading these descriptions, historians have puzzled over the aggression displayed by both sides and the elaborate care taken to avoid any open conflict between them. This, together with the fact that Henry met Charles V in England shortly before it and at Gravelines soon afterwards, has led some to dismiss the Field of Cloth of Gold as a wasteful, pointless, junket designed to celebrate a peace in which neither side believed and which was nearly ruined by ill-concealed aggression.[32]

Yet the competitive one-upmanship that characterised the event was in part at least, exactly what the Field of Cloth of Gold was held to allow. The meeting was, first and foremost, a tournament at which the two kings personally affirmed and celebrated their alliance under the Treaty of London. It was on this occasion that they declared to each other personally the grounds on which peace between them could be maintained. That this was so was revealed at their first meeting on the evening of 7 June. Having embraced Francis, Henry is said by a number of sources to have reminded him of the Treaty of London and told him that provided it was 'observed and kept, I never saw a prince with my eyes that might of my heart be more loved.' That is to say, peace between them depended upon Francis keeping his word. Francis's effective reply was to say, when Henry's title of 'King of France' was announced, that in friendship he welcomed Henry even as the king of France he claimed to be, provided that he kept the alliance. In other words, Henry could call himself whatever he liked, the fact remained that he depended upon Francis's co-operation if he were not again to be marginalised in Europe. The message from each side to the other was that peace between them signified strength, not weakness.

This message was driven home during the extended tournament which began 2 days later. On Thursday 14 June Henry jousted in a costume covered with lozenged eglantine flowers. According to Hall, these flowers represented England which was:

> Sweet and pleasant and green if it be kindly and friendly handled, but if it be rudely dealt with it will prick and he will pull up the whole tree by the top, his hands will be hurt.

On 16 June Henry jousted in costumes blazoned with the motto: 'God willing my realm and I . . .', left pointedly unfinished.

In contrast Francis was presented in the jousts and later in the foot combats as the master of the moment and a philosopher-king whose heart and mind were centred on the highest ideals of chivalric monarchy. On each of four days he jousted, Francis's costumes progressively spelled out in words and in symbols of little books and chains the phrase: 'heart fastened in pain endless/when she/delivers me not of bonds.' This motto was discussed among *savants* present and generally interpreted to mean that Francis bore arms in the service of love, learning and justice as befitted a true knight.[33]

The Field of Cloth of Gold was designed to re-package the ideal of princely peace in a new and exciting way. It was invigorated, made heroic, and thus acceptable to the military elites of England and France who participated in it. In meeting each other the two kings were able to indulge what may have been an illusion, but a very important illusion, that each met the other on his own terms. Both sides marshalled immense resources in an attempt to convince the other of the dangers it faced if the agreement between them was broken. The hidden fear of each monarch was that should the other not be persuaded by the glamorously packaged prospect of peace, he would himself be left vulnerable; to attack in Francis's case, to isolation in Henry's.

RENAISSANCE DIPLOMACY

Once peace was agreed, it had to be kept. Misunderstandings about the implementation of a treaty could easily arise or the signatories might wish better to co-ordinate their actions against a third party, necessitating further negotiations. By the late fifteenth century the custom of sending resident ambassadors had been established between the cities and princely states of Italy to improve communications. Ferdinand of Aragon also used resident ambassadors and by the start of the sixteenth century there were resident Spanish agents throughout Italy and beyond. Charles V inherited this network of ambassadors from his grandfather and improved the efficiency of the system considerably so that by the mid 1530s he was probably the best informed sovereign in Europe.

The need to establish and maintain alliances in the face of Charles V's power also prompted the kings of England and France progressively to adopt the practice of appointing resident ambassadors. Initially they were sent to the Papacy and to Venice but then also to Spain and the Netherlands. Like their imperial counterparts, English and French resident ambassadors during the early sixteenth century were drawn from the clergy, the aristocracy and the ranks of the lower nobility or gentry. Clerical ambassadors were usually bishops or deans of cathedral chapters. They had the advantage of speaking Latin, the international language of the sixteenth century, and usually also had significant administrative experience. They could represent the king with all the solemn dignity of high church office but this also tended to make them less engaging figures at the courts in which they resided.

In an age so conscious of personal honour and reputation, rulers commonly found it useful to send a secular ambassador, often a comparatively young man, who could cut a more dashing figure in representing his master. A nobleman or gentleman ambassador might more easily ingratiate himself with the circle of important subjects in his host's court. His own experience as a courtier and a soldier could also be invaluable in making sense of the regime to which he was sent. Provided he had sufficient clerical assistance, such an ambassador could send home the necessary reports and advice while still maintaining a high profile at the court on his master's behalf. It was these considerations which in 1522 prompted Charles V to replace the Spanish bishop Bernadino de Mesa, as resident ambassador in England with Louis de Flandres, Lord of Praet, a younger Burgundian nobleman and soldier.

Many of these ambassadors were the most intimate friends and closest servants of their masters. They had daily contact with their sovereign through the offices that they held at court. In France they were known as *gentilshommes de la chambre du roi*, and in England, following the French model, as *Gentlemen of the King's Privy Chamber.* As their titles imply, these men were entitled to enter the king's private chambers which were forbidden to most courtiers, most of the time. They dressed him, they dined and hunted with him, they entertained and talked to him. Sending these men as ambassadors ostensibly expressed each sovereign's regard for the other. Such intimate servants knew their master better than anyone else so they could stand in for, or literally impersonate, their master in his relations with his 'good brother and friend' as Francis and Henry habitually titled each other. Many of these men served as resident ambassadors, others were also sent as special envoys with specific messages. They were usually treated with exceptional generosity and familiarity by their host, frequently speaking with him in private and hunting with him. By the early 1520s it was customary for men such as Sir Richard Wingfield, Sir William Fitzwilliam or Anne de Montmorency, to be treated by their host as one of his own 'chamber' gentlemen. As Sir Richard Wingfield told Henry in April 1520, Francis had allowed him this privilege and 'could no more familiarly use [i.e. treat] me than he does continually.' This flattered Wingfield and his sovereign, but it also challenged Henry to match the princely 'virtue' shown by Francis in such a gesture.[34]

Treating any ambassador well expressed the trustworthiness and munificence of the prince to whom he was sent. Conversely, ignoring or mistreating an ambassador, especially one of the noble rank, was an insult to his master. It was also true that an indiscreet ambassador might easily insult his host. However, as Charles also discovered with Louis de Flanders, such representatives could sometimes find it hard to maintain the necessary detachment when their master's interests or reputation were impugned. In 1539 Henry VIII's representative in France, Bishop Edmund Bonner, so offended Francis I with his demands that he hand over to Henry a man suspected of plotting against him, that Francis insisted upon the ambassador's recall.[35] Partly in order to overcome some of these problems and partly in an attempt to increase the expertise of ambassadors, a less personalised, more legally codified, kind of representation began to emerge by the middle years of the century. Clerics and soldier-ambassadors were replaced as resident ambassadors by gentleman bureaucrats. These were gentlemen who were university educated, trained in the law and in languages. Formal protocols for receiving such ambassadors were developed across Europe and numerous treatises were published on the talents and duties of the ideal representative. All of this heralded the arrival of creatures whom we today would call diplomats.

Nevertheless, neither the speed with which this trend emerged nor its universality should be exaggerated. As will be demonstrated below, courtier and soldier-ambassadors were used alongside clerical representatives well into the 1550s. There was nothing uniform or codified about how Francis and Henry maintained relations with each other and with the emperor. For these kings, the essential task of the ambassador was always to represent his master effectively and personally at the courts of his fellow rulers.[36]

CONCLUSION

The causes of war between Charles, Francis and Henry were many, and each of them felt the justice of his complaints with passionate intensity. It was in warfare that noblemen proved who they were and it was this powerful group of supporters within their realms that these kings had constantly to reassure with their potential as military leaders. As noblemen themselves and because of their early training, Henry, Francis and Charles were all genuinely fascinated with and committed to the military ethos so cherished by their noble subjects. In these circumstances, the leadership of the military orders, participation in tournaments and hunting and the patronage of writers and poets who celebrated the ideal of princely warfare were all designed to focus the loyalty of the nobility upon themselves. The large sums devoted to these activities, recorded in surviving household accounts, are evidence of how fully these monarchs appreciated the need to be seen doing things that publicised their commitment to the ideals of noble warfare, especially in the absence of actual conflict. The same message was communicated in propaganda to their kingdoms and beyond. Royal entries to towns, the production of widely circulating medals and coins and the publication of literature extolling the virtues of the king as a warrior leader and the legitimacy of his causes were designed to garner support for the royal regime among literate and semi-literate subjects.

At the same time, these Renaissance monarchs knew that they could not always be at war. Maintaining advantageous peace treaties or alliances was also important. Because of the risk of isolation he faced, peace with France became one Henry VIII's major concerns for most of his reign. Guided initially by Wolsey and subsequently by his own grandiose instincts, the king invested considerable time and money in negotiating and then declaring his several alliances with Francis I. This enhanced his political influence and his reputation as a monarch in Europe. While real peace was rarely achieved between Francis and Charles V, each of them regularly asserted his desire for peace with the other, but on his own terms. For both, creating peace had to be, and be seen to be, an active expression of their power, not a passive response to that of the other. When circumstances and their political agendas allowed it, as they did briefly in 1538–40, peace between them could be a way for both to demonstrate royal magnificence and *virtus*.

Whether at peace or in war, these kings strove to associate themselves with, indeed to personify, the chivalric ethos as they understood it. Later in the century the personalities and priorities in international relations began to change. Ideas of personal honour and dynastic ambition were not forgotten by the heirs of Charles V, Henry VIII and Francis I, but they were expressed in different ways. For a time the need to impose religious conformity on their own people became more pressing to monarchs than pursuing dynastic quarrels in each other's territories. The power of the French monarchy collapsed in the Wars of Religion. Philip II sought to use this to his advantage but he too faced religious conflict, fighting strenuously but ineffectively against Calvinist revolt in the Netherlands. Elizabeth I expressed her princely honour in international relations more by defending her Protestant realm from European powers, than by an aggressive assertion of English claims in France.

Elizabeth's attitude to international relations might well have been understood by her father, but for him, as for his great role-model Henry V, the hostility and aggression of his nobles, when properly channelled against a common external enemy could achieve a great deal in the interests of the monarchy and the kingdom. Francis I and Charles V knew that equally well and so in the opening decades of the sixteenth century whenever an opportunity arose to make war in which a satisfactory outcome seemed probable, these kings seized upon it eagerly.

3

Warriors: Warfare and international relations

> ... it behoved him to enter upon his first military experience in so important and difficult a war in order that he might, by a signal start to his martial knowledge, create such a fine opinion about his valour among all men that they would clearly understand that his ambition was not merely to equal but indeed to exceed the glorious deeds of his ancestors.
>
> Polydore Vergil[1]

Thus Henry VIII explained to his council his decision to go to war against France in 1513. Some royal councillors had expressed concern that the king intended to hazard himself in such a major undertaking. They were soon shown their error. Henry insisted that he would personally lead his army in what, he was certain, was a just war against Louis XII. That warfare was the business of kings was axiomatic well before the early sixteenth century. Nevertheless, it is remarkable what an all-consuming business it became for Henry, for Charles V and for Francis I. While owing much to medieval precedents, the campaigns which they actually engaged in proved to be on a scale and of an intensity quite unlike those of preceding centuries. So too did the political machinations which provoked, or dealt with, the consequences of the wars. The military campaigns and diplomatic intrigues in which Francis, Henry and Charles engaged, demanded a greater investment of human, material and financial resources, sustained over a longer period, than any of those of the heroic ancestors who so inspired this generation of kings.

MILITARY ORGANISATION AND TECHNOLOGY

Royal armies of the sixteenth century usually comprised three major elements; the cavalry, the infantry and the artillery. Fortifications and naval forces could also play a vital role in certain circumstances.

The cavalry

The English cavalry under Henry VIII was formed predominantly by the nobles and gentry of his realm. Fighting in its ranks was considered a great honour and was how a nobleman fulfilled his role as warrior and defender of his society. At its core were the king's tenants-in-chief, who owed military service in return for lands held from the king. They were summoned to appear at a certain time and place with a prescribed number of fighting men ready for war. At his accession Henry considered that many young nobleman were 'unexercised in the feat of arms and in the handling and running of spears.' Accordingly, in November 1509 he established a prestigious royal guard called 'the king's spears,' drawn from the ranks of the lower nobility and gentry. It was also intended to be the basis of a permanent cavalry force like those established in France the previous century. Each nobleman swore a personal oath of loyalty to the king. His main weapon was the lance, which, together with armour and horses were supplied for him by the king. The wages of his page and a 'custrel', an attendant armed with a dagger, were also paid for by the royal treasury. Each nobleman was to provide 'two good archers well horsed and harnessed.' In fact the guard proved too costly and was disbanded after 1513. Only in 1539 did the huge profits generated by the sale of monastic lands allow Henry to re-establish it as the 'Gentlemen Pensioners.' The company numbered fifty and its first public appearance was at the reception of Anne of Cleves in January 1540 when it was commanded by Sir Anthony Browne, Henry VIII's Master of the Horse.

The king also invested heavily in the accoutrements of gentlemanly warfare. Between 1511 and 1515 Henry established armouries initially at Southwark and later at Greenwich overseen by two Milanese armourers, Giovanni Angelo de Littis and Filipo de Grampiss. They were followed by German and perhaps Flemish armourers. The establishment at Greenwich was known as the 'Almain Armoury' for this reason although it was later staffed entirely by English craftsmen. The Greenwich armoury produced high quality tournament and field armour for the king himself, his leading nobles and for use as diplomatic gifts. The items which have survived retain their exceptional characteristics and at their production more than held their own with the finest work of continental armouries.[2]

In 1515 Francis I inherited what was undoubtedly the most formidable cavalry force in Europe. In 1439, King Charles VII had established fifteen units called *compagnies d'ordonnance* each of 100 'lances' of heavy cavalry paid for out of the proceeds of a new property tax, the *taille*. A 'lance' initially comprised a fully armed and mounted nobleman, an *homme d'armes*, attended by two or more mounted *archers*, together with a dagger-wielding *coutelier*, a page and servants to look after its horses. For his first campaign in Italy in 1515, Francis was accompanied by some 7000–9000 cavalrymen. In 1534 the formation of the *compagnies* was rationalised. For each *homme d'armes* there was to be one and a half *archers* so that a company of

100 *hommes d'armes* actually comprised 250 combatants. Commanders were drawn from the higher-ranking noble families and chose their men from their local networks of noble clients. These companies assembled regularly for training to ensure their readiness for the king's summons to war. The king also employed the mounted troops of the royal household and could raise additional cavalry by summoning the feudal levy or *ban et arrière-ban*. All those who held land from the king in fief had to supply troops according to their means. Although called periodically in the sixteenth century, the force raised by *ban* could only be kept in the field for short periods and was of limited use in offensive roles.[3]

Charles V also inherited a permanent cavalry in Spain. In the course of the re-conquest of Granada in the 1490s twenty-five companies of 100 mounted men-at-arms comprising heavy and light cavalry had been established by Ferdinand and Isabella. Meanwhile in the Netherlands, the sons of noblemen who had served the Valois dukes of Burgundy, served in the cavalry of the Habsburg emperor Maximilian which was organised along lines broadly similar to the French cavalry. Maximilian had also established an armoury at Innsbruck under the master-armourer Conrad Seusenhofer, which produced high quality armour for the imperial cavalry. Its work was also very influential upon styles of armour throughout Europe.

The infantry

In England, the infantry was raised by traditional methods. Nobles and gentry acting as recruiting agents for the monarchy contracted or 'retained' men for service in war. These 'retinue' forces had formed the armies of Edward III and Henry V in their French campaigns. The Tudors supervised retaining closely in order to avoid falling victim, as their mid-fifteenth century predecessors had done, to the military power of 'overmighty' subjects whose retinues constituted private armies. Only those nobles and gentry who were closest to the regime were temporarily licensed to retain in significant numbers for warfare.

Henry VIII still faced the problem that these retinue forces were insufficient for the ever-increasing scale of warfare during his reign. In the early sixteenth century, victory in battle was determined in part by deploying larger and larger blocks of infantry troops armed with pikes, whose massed weight and numbers overwhelmed opponents, forcing them to break ranks and render themselves vulnerable to further attack by archers, artillery and cavalry. Henry had to recruit more men directly through militia forces raised by commissioners in the counties and larger towns. However, these militia troops were not always of the highest calibre, nor always well equipped. They frequently required further training and even arming at the king's expense. Henry had also to use Burgundian and German mercenaries in all his continental campaigns. This was standard practice across Europe but mercenaries were notoriously expensive and often unreliable troops.

The French infantry under Francis I was initially composed of a volunteer militia force of archers, crossbow-men and pikemen first established by Charles VII called the *francs-archers*. This force was supplemented by a large number of German mercenary soldiers. For his first campaign in 1515 he is estimated to have fielded approximately 30,000 infantry troops. In November 1516 Francis signed an agreement with the Swiss cantons known as the 'Perpetual Peace' of Fribourg. In return for an annual subsidy he obtained their promise not to attack him and the right to hire Swiss mercenaries. These very able troops fought in squares which were excellent in defence against traditional cavalry but which had also proved devastating in attack in several battles of the late fifteenth century.

In 1534 Francis rationalised his infantry forces in an attempt to reduce his dependence upon mercenaries. He replaced the *francs-archers* with seven *légions* each of 6000 men. These *légions* constituted a reserve army paid for by the cities and towns of the major French provinces. They were to be mustered twice yearly and were commanded by provincial noblemen. They fought with halberds, pikes and arquebuses. However, not every province actually set up a *légion* and the *légionnaires* were not as well trained as Francis had originally intended. They were used mainly to garrison border areas and Francis continued to need mercenaries for the bulk of his infantry long after 1534.[4]

Charles V hired German volunteer adventurers, known as 'companions of the country' or *landsknechts*, for his infantry. He also hired Dutch, Italian and Irish mercenaries. In Spain, Ferdinand and Isabella had raised a large, semi-permanent, infantry of 40,000 for the re-conquest of Granada in 1492. Troops were drawn mainly from the league of Castilian urban militias, known as the *Hermandades* and organised by Gonsalvo de Córdoba, one of the heroes of the re-conquest. Charles's Spanish troops continued to be recruited from these sources. In 1534 Charles also decided to rationalise his infantry. Imperial troops were organised into '*tercios*' or thirds, units which combined three types of solider. Theoretically each *tercio* had 3000 men; 1500 pikemen, 1000 swordsmen and 500 arquebusiers grouped in ten to twelve companies. In practice each *tercio* often numbered under 2000 troops.

Like their Swiss and German counterparts, Spanish pikemen formed squares at the centre of which were the swordsmen ready to attack the enemy in hand-to-hand fighting. Smaller firearms began to play an increasing role in mid-sixteenth century battles and the arquebusiers of each *tercio* could also be used separately to give the pikemen protective fire against the enemy, often in conjunction with the artillery. The pike nevertheless remained the predominant weapon of the Spanish infantry forces until the seventeenth century. These *tercios* were based in Sicily, Naples, Milan and Sardinia which were also the main supply bases for Charles V's military campaigns. Body armour and armaments for the infantry were manufactured chiefly in the Basque country.[5]

The artillery

Henry VIII was passionately interested in military equipment but its acquisition had not been a priority under his father. The new king was acutely conscious of how England's military technology and expertise had fallen dangerously behind that of his continental rivals. Henry moved swiftly to redress the balance and the first major expenditure after his coronation was on artillery and small-arms. Between May 1509 and November 1512 he paid nearly £3000 for ordnance from English and Continental gunsmiths. In January 1510 Hans Popenruyter of Mechelen was contracted to produce 48 cannons of different calibres, the biggest 12 of them were each to weigh 4000 lbs and fire shot of 35 lbs. These weapons were delivered over a two-year period and included the famous 'Twelve Apostles' used in Henry's first French campaign. During the 1520s the king's stocks of guns were maintained from the Low Countries and Spain and were substantially increased in the late 1530s when gun foundries were set up in London and in the Weald of Kent under continental gunsmiths. In the early 1540s Henry also established a new foundry in Sussex where successful experiments were carried out in casting safe iron cannon. Weapons so made were put to effective use in the siege of Boulogne in the summer of 1544. At the end of Henry's reign the Tower of London alone housed 400 heavy guns and 6500 handguns.[6]

The French artillery suitable for offensive action at the time of Francis I's accession numbered about 60 weapons. The majority of these were of medium to smaller calibres. Francis invested heavily in the artillery throughout his reign and it was a major factor in virtually all his campaigns. He spent over half a million *livres* on weapons and ammunition between 1521–25, the years of his first war with Charles V. At Pavia he commanded 53 canons of varying calibres. In the last war against the emperor and Henry VIII he spent 1.5 million *livres* on his artillery. Even with such vast sums it was a constant struggle to provide sufficient weapons and enough gunpowder and ammunition for them. One 1544 survey of artillery available in 15 locations along France's northern border put the figure at 279 canons with a further 733 heavy arquebuses equipped with firing stands. The authorities in the north considered they needed roughly twice as many weapons as this against the combined forces of Charles V and Henry VIII.[7]

The production of artillery increased significantly in Spain in the years of the re-conquest of Granada. This was reflected in the fact that at Charles's accession, foundries were located mainly in the south, in Andalusia, at Baza and Malaga. During the late fifteenth century there was great variety in the types of canons produced, most being of medium to heavy calibre. Under Charles, greater efforts were made to standardise the calibres of artillery and increase their mobility in line with developments elsewhere in Europe. The production of munitions for both the artillery and the infantry was concentrated in Andalusia, in Murica and at Egui in Navarre and was closely supervised by the crown.

Fortifications

A corollary to artillery development was the modification of defences, the better to deploy and also withstand the more powerful cannons used in the early sixteenth century. The new designs originated in Italy and spread rapidly throughout Europe. The traditional tall, square medieval keeps or 'donjons' in the centre of castles were replaced by shorter, stronger, keeps designed as firing platforms for cannons. Walls were thickened considerably and given projecting bastions. These bastions, angular or curved in shape were also used to position artillery and in conjunction with small arms could set up a withering cross-fire to repel invaders. Curved edges and faces on walls were designed to deflect the iron balls fired against them. The bastions were accompanied by ditches, detached forts, called 'ravelins,' and earthen or stone slopes which made it more difficult for attacking artillery both to get in range of and then to penetrate the central walls.

Francis I was persuaded of the virtues of new designs in the years after 1525. He heavily fortified Turin in 1536 adopting the bastion system and employed it again at Vitry-le-François and elsewhere along the north-east border of the kingdom in the mid 1540s. These fortifications are estimated to have cost him in excess of 700,000 *livres*. After his conquest of Metz in 1552, the Duke of Guise rapidly improved the existing fortifications of the town. He strengthened the central citadel, building a new inner wall thicker than the old outer one and constructing extensive outworks. These modifications capitalised on the local terrain and provided effective defence against an imperial army that besieged the city the following winter. The same techniques were used in the fortifications built to hem the English in at Boulogne after their conquest of the town in 1544.

Charles V supervised two major programmes of fortification in his empire. The first, begun in the 1530s, centred on the Mediterranean. New, bastioned, fortresses were constructed in Tunis and in Palermo, Syracuse and Messina in Sicily. Naples and Genoa were heavily fortified as were Barcelona and Perpignan in Roussillon near the border with France. The biggest individual project in the Mediterranean region was the extension and fortification of Milan, begun in 1549 under the imperial governor, Ferrante Gonzaga. Charles saw plans and maps of these fortifications and, as at Naples and Barcelona, he inspected the sites personally with the architect. The second programme of fortifications was undertaken in Flanders and the Netherlands. A new citadel was built at Ghent between 1540 and 1544 following a revolt in the city. Charles surveyed the city in March 1540 and personally laid the first stone of the new fortress, designed by the Italian military engineer Donato de Buoni, on May 12 the same year.

The largest single fortification work begun by Charles was the expansion of the city of Antwerp. As the most important trading and financial city in the central Netherlands, its security and prosperity were vital in maintaining his wealth and security. Accordingly, a new area called the Nieuwstad was incorporated within the city and over several decades was established as a residential and commercial district. Work on fortifications began under Donato de Buoni in 1542. The most important fortified gate, the Keiserspoort, was inaugurated by Charles himself in November 1545.[8]

In 1539–40, when a joint Franco-Imperial invasion of England seemed a distinct possibility, Henry VIII oversaw the construction of a chain of defensive castles and blockhouses around the southern coasts of the kingdom from the Wash to Milford Haven. Many, such as Walmer, Deal and Camber survive to this day. Typically quatre-foil or cinque-foil in shape, these buildings adapted features of European fortress design. Their projecting bastions were blunt rather than pointed, with thick, squat, walls pierced by firing ports. They functioned as shore batteries whose powerful guns could attack enemy ships which had to come close inshore if they wished to fire upon coastal settlements or to land troops. These fortifications were stocked with a total of 2250 pieces of ordnance.[9]

The navy

Although he was no great sailor himself, Henry VIII appreciated the importance of naval power for English trade and defence. He made the navy the centre of his military establishment, investing heavily in its expansion and proper maintenance. He built new dockyards at Deptford and Woolwich and retained designers and builders at the forefront of naval technology. The first ships in English history known to have side-firing guns below the main deck level were the *Mary Rose* and the *Peter Pomegranate*, both dating from 1509. Ships were used mainly for coastal defence, to protect merchant vessels from piracy and, less frequently, to attack French ships and coastal settlements during war. Henry had around 90 major ships when the largest maritime battle of his reign was fought against the French in the Solent in 1545. To this figure must be added ancillary ships, row-barges and transports which were usually civilian ships converted to naval use as needed. The inventory of the king's possessions at his death in 1547 lists a total of 53 'ships, galleys, pinnaces and rowbarges.' The largest vessel Henry owned, with a displacement of at least 1000 tons, was his flagship, the *Henry Grâce à Dieu*, known usually as the *Great Harry.*[10]

The sea-borne forces commanded by Francis I were divided into two main fleets whose size and effectiveness fluctuated considerably. The Mediterranean fleet, based chiefly at Marseilles, was equipped with galleys. These long, comparatively shallow draught, vessels of varying sizes were powered by sail and up to 180 oarsmen. They were armed with smaller calibre, deck-mounted, guns. Until the late 1520s, Francis also relied heavily on the fleet of the Genoese admiral and mercenary Andrea Doria. Following a rupture with Doria in 1528 over pay and other matters, Francis was forced to invest more heavily in the navy and thereafter his annual expenditure exceeded 200,000 *livres*. The Atlantic fleet comprised larger vessels able to withstand the rough conditions off the west coast of France and in the English Channel. Like their English counterparts they were armed with powerful canons fired from gun ports in their sides. To a fleet of older vessels of between 80 and 100 tons built for Charles VIII and Louis XII, Francis progressively added larger ships of between 500 and 800 tons. These included several massive vessels such as *La Cordelière* weighing 2500 tons with a complement of 2000 men and *La Grande Maistresse*. Of a similar size was *La Grande Françoise* which was built at Le Havre in 1521–22. In practice, the Atlantic and Mediterranean fleets often operated together as need arose. There were a number of galleys in the fleet of around 400 ships that sailed against England in the summer of 1545. In 1543 Francis's naval strength was temporarily increased by the Turks who used the port of Toulon as a base for ten months, to the general scandal of Christendom.[11]

The one area where Charles V's direct military power was weaker than either Henry VIII's or Francis I's was in naval operations. During his visit to England in 1522, Charles had reviewed the English fleet off Dover. Edward Hall proudly related how the emperor and his large entourage were impressed; they 'much praised the making of the ships, and especially the artillery, they said they never saw ships so armed.' Charles V had no royal navy as such in the Atlantic and had to rely on refitted ships contracted from private individuals. In the Mediterranean he had a small Aragonese fleet but also the fleets maintained in Naples, Sicily and Sardinia. In July 1528, following his defection from Francis I, Andrea Doria placed his fleet at the emperor's command. Thereafter he operated as Charles's admiral of the Mediterranean. In 1530 he attacked pirates on the Algerian coast and two years later captured Patras and Castelnuovo from the Turks. In 1535 Doria's ships were part of the massive fleet of Spanish and Portuguese vessels that Charles led against Tunis. In 1541 Doria again provided ships for Charles's failed expedition against Algiers. Charles also used converted merchant ships to escort the bullion fleets coming from South America to Seville against Corsair, French and English raiders. Such ships as were built on the Iberian peninsular tended to come from the Basque country where Spain's comparatively meagre resources of timber and expertise in ship-building were concentrated. However, it was not until Philip II's reign that the Spanish crown began building warships for its own use in significant numbers.[12]

TACTICS IN WAR AND THE COST OF WARFARE

Warfare in the late fifteenth and early sixteenth centuries was certainly fought on a larger scale and often had more specific objectives than that of a century before. In the fourteenth and fifteenth centuries, raiding from a stronghold and capturing the resources of the locality, or *chevauchée* as the French called it, was the predominant form of warfare. Those attacked shut themselves up in defensible strongholds, usually larger towns and cities, and withstood any ensuing siege until such time as they were relieved or, more usually, the opposing forces retired.[13]

The *chevauchée* never went out of fashion and indeed was practised with renewed vigour in the later wars between Charles V and Francis I. Nevertheless, the deployment of new types of artillery meant that sieges became, for several decades between about 1480 and 1520, comparatively rapid and more successful. It was harder for fortresses and towns to withstand bombardment by more powerful, more manoeuvrable and accurate guns. In addition, the use of large companies of mercenary infantry who were notoriously difficult to keep happy for long periods, meant that an open battle might be both tactically and economically more effective than either initiating or attempting to withstand a siege. On the other hand, deploying big armies on the field was a hazardous business and the chances of a quick victory had to be balanced with those of an equally sudden and devastating defeat.

The wheel came full circle in the course of the 1530s. As a result in part of a number of very bloody disasters for the French during the Italian wars, commanders on all sides became increasingly reluctant to risk pitched battles unless they believed circumstances were extremely favourable. The dominance of infantry pike formations aided by small-arms and field artillery led to very high casualty rates among all ranks of the losing armies. As we have seen, new types of fortifications were developed. Their strength and complexity made them extremely hard to breach and large numbers of attacking troops could be delayed for months in the attempt. As the French military expert Raymond de Beccarie observed of such fortified towns in 1548 'one will loose more than one gains by besieging them.'[14] During these sieges mercenaries might desert for lack of pay, and the besieging army succumb to hunger and disease. The average length of sixteenth century sieges was about two months, similar to pre-fifteenth century warfare. Withstanding sieges again became a superior defensive strategy. As a result, warfare in the 1530s and 1540s was characterised more by stalemates and destruction of the countryside than by decisive open battles.

The relative sophistication of sixteenth century military technology and tactics resulted in massive expenditure among the principal combatants. Total expenditure for Henry VIII's war between 1512 and 1514 has been estimated at around £1 million. The wars of 1542–46 cost him approximately £2.1 million. The total cost of Francis I's first campaign against Milan in September 1515 has been estimated at 7.5 million *livres* or just under £1 million. His longest period of sustained warfare, between 1542 and 1546, is estimated to have cost him 30 million *livres* or approximately £3 million. Charles V's campaigns cost even more. That for Metz alone in

1551 cost him 2.5 million ducats. All three kings drew relentlessly on the wealth of their subjects in taxation and adopted a range of expedients, from expensive loans to devaluing their currencies, in an effort to meet this expenditure. Impressive though these efforts were, their expenditure always out-stripped their income.[15]

THE DYNASTIC WARS OF HENRY VIII

Henry VIII's first major war was undertaken with the ultimate objective of claiming the crown of France. In June 1513 he personally commanded an invasion of northern France by 3000 cavalry and approximately 15,000 infantry troops. He was allied to Ferdinand of Aragon and the emperor Maximilian who supplied a further 4000 *landsknechts*. Louis XII of France was facing attacks on three fronts during that summer and had ordered his field commanders not to give the English open battle as they advanced across Picardy from Calais. Raiding parties harassed the English troops but, much to Henry VIII's frustration, gave him no opportunity to fight in the heroic manner of Edward III or Henry V at Agincourt. However, Henry did conduct two successful sieges in which the firepower he had assembled during the previous five years played a significant tactical and psychological part.

The English deployed an estimated 180 pieces of artillery in these sieges of the town of Thérouanne and the city of Tournai in the summer of 1513. The first fell in August after a failed attempt by some French cavalry to re-victual the town early on 16 August. A French cavalry detachment planned to drop some supplies at what had been until then, an unprotected section of the town's walls. Unknown to the French, the previous night Henry had ordered the middle-ward of the army to move to plug the very gap into which they headed. They were intercepted by rounds of artillery fire and engaged by a force of English cavalry. In a short, sharp, skirmish, the English killed or captured a large number of the French. Henry was disappointed when the encounter was over so soon after it started. He had initially thought that the French cavalry detachment was part of a much larger force coming to raise the siege of the town. Nevertheless, the battle was still an important moment in the campaign because a significant number of French noblemen, including the Lord of Bayard and the Duke of Longueville, were captured. Thérouanne shortly afterwards capitulated. The encounter was thereafter known as the Battle of the Spurs because of the way the French urged their horses to escape. Thérouanne was evacuated and then burned to the ground on Maximilian's orders. From here Henry moved on to the much more important city of Tournai which also surrendered after a siege of only a few weeks in September. Henry made a triumphant entry to the city on 24 September then withdrew to England in October. Henry returned home as the conquering hero but it was actually his wife who had overseen the most significant English military action of that year. Katherine had been left in charge of the kingdom with a handful of councillors. An attack from Scotland was traditional when England was at war with France and James IV did not disappoint. In August he bade Henry defiance and prepared his forces. Thomas Howard, the Earl of Surrey, raised the northern counties in defence and the Scottish royal army crossed the border at the end of the summer. On 9 September 1513 it was comprehensively defeated at the Battle of Flodden. A dozen Scottish earls, a handful of prelates and the king himself were killed. The defeat signalled twenty years of disillusioned and rancorous intrigue among Scottish nobility, which the English did their best to worsen, until James V grew to maturity.[16]

Despite the absence of a major battle during his French campaign, the conquests of Thérouanne and Tournai and the victory at Flodden, got Henry noticed internationally. They lent credibility to his threats of further military action which he used to full advantage in the peace treaty he subsequently signed with Louis XII in 1514. As we have seen, Henry made a dramatic *volte farce*, allying himself to Louis in return for the payment of a sizeably increased French pension. Unfortunately for him, this effort to secure his reputation as a warrior whose future potential had to be taken seriously was overshadowed by the international debut of Francis I in 1515. His conquest of Milan in September that year catapulted him to the forefront of international politics and secured for him an enviable range of allies, including the pope. Charles V's political agenda rarely accommodated Henry's ambitions against France and between 1516 and 1518, the king of England was politically and militarily isolated.

It was Cardinal Wolsey who first saw that if the king's reputation could not be maintained through magnificent warfare in France, then peacemaking with France would have to be made magnificent. Beginning in 1518, Wolsey arranged a series of alliances between Henry VIII and Francis I in which peace between them was made glamorous and portrayed to the rest of the world as proof of Henry's status as a great king. The first of these agreements was the Treaty of London. Taking his cue from Pope Leo X's call for an international crusade against the Turks, Wolsey arranged a 'Universal Peace' between all the major European powers. Warfare, at which Francis I had proved himself alarmingly adept, was to be outlawed. Any prince who transgressed the international agreement would be attacked by all the others. Henry was to oversee the treaty, arbitrating disputes between princes and arranging the punishment of any who hindered peace. The international peace was sealed with an Anglo-French alliance under which Princess Mary, previously betrothed to Charles of Spain, would marry the dauphin of France. The city of Tournai, captured from Louis XII in 1513, would be sold back to Francis for 600,000 crowns and Henry's annual French pension was confirmed and increased substantially. In making these arrangements Wolsey was able to place Henry once again centre-stage in Europe and give him in theory at least, more international influence than he had hitherto achieved.[17]

The Treaty of London was inaugurated with spectacular ceremonies in which Wolsey's flair for theatrical presentation was crucial. Henry rose splendidly to the occasion, as the cardinal knew he would, showing off to the many embassies which came for the signing of the treaty as the very definition of princely generosity and style. The treaty was sworn to at St Paul's cathedral on 3 October 1518. Before an international audience, the royal secretary Richard Pace lauded Henry as the prince of peace, a new Solomon, the apparent embodiment of the hopes of Erasmus and other influential intellectuals. Yet within Pace's speech that Sunday there were also glowing references to Henry's extraordinary physical prowess and personal courage. His skill as a warrior commander was highly praised and Pace alluded frequently and flatteringly to the king's victories in France in 1513. A warning note was thereby sounded that Henry was not abandoning military action merely for the sake of peace. He could make war if he wanted to, but chose to be a peace-maker. Nobody, least of all the French, should underestimate his right and his willingness to wield the sword of just war against those who infringed the agreement.[18]

Pace's speech effectively declared that for Henry VIII, peace with Francis I was acceptable provided that Francis acknowledged his authority by keeping the terms of the Treaty of London. Henry believed that the new international peace had curbed Francis I's Italian ambitions and obligated the French king to him. Francis also considered that he had won by the treaty. He got back the city lost under Louis, purging the disgrace of defeat and re-asserting his power in Flanders. He secured himself against any English invasion, consolidated his hold over the duchy of Milan and obliged Henry to assist him should Charles challenge any of his recent gains. He had also positioned himself well to demand Henry's support in his bid to become the next Holy Roman Emperor. By late 1518 the jockeying to succeed Maximilian had already begun. These were themes articulated in the French celebrations of the treaty, which were held in Paris at Christmas 1518 before an English delegation charged with receiving Francis I's ratification of the agreement.[19] So, for all the humanistic rhetoric associated with it and the diversity of hopes invested in it, the Treaty of London essentially conformed to the 'chivalric' model of peace-making current in the early sixteenth century. Each party felt he had won significant advantages by it.

Henry did not personally lead an army against France for another thirty years but in September 1523 the Duke of Suffolk led an invasion by a comparatively small army of 10,000 English troops and Burgundian mercenaries into Picardy. Henry had declared war on Francis the previous year in alliance with Charles V after Francis covertly organised attacks on Luxemburg and Navarre in 1521, thereby breaking the Treaty of London. As part of a planned tri-partite invasion, the English were to descend upon Paris from the north. Charles V and the Duke of Bourbon,who had rebelled against Francis I, were to close the attack from the south. Initially the English army raided Picardy but made no significant advance towards the French capital. Henry wanted first to consolidate the English presence in the north of France. Cardinal Wolsey urged the king to order his troops to advance to Paris as soon as possible but it was not until late September that Henry was persuaded and the English army made rapid progress. Unfortunately for him, this was also the moment when the strategy to which he had so lately agreed fell apart. Neither Bourbon's nor Charles V's armies made any headway against the French in the south. The English found themselves stranded 50 miles north of the French capital. With winter and its diseases closing in and deserted by his Burgundian mercenaries, Suffolk turned homewards, much to the king's anger. Bourbon was chased out of France in 1524 and by the end of that year Francis I was once again on the offensive.

Henry's next opportunity to conquer France was not long in coming. Following Francis I's defeat at the Battle of Pavia in February 1525 initial plans were made for another joint Anglo-Imperial invasion. Charles V then decided to make a comprehensive peace with Francis. That decision, and Henry's wish to have his marriage to Katherine of Aragon annulled, prompted him to make the second great *volte-farce* of his reign. Under the Treaty of the More signed in 1525 and the Treaty of Westminster of April 1527, Henry once again allied himself to Francis; not this time from any pretensions to indifferent arbitration of international affairs, but in order to assert his independence of Charles. Francis promised to pay Henry two million crowns in annual instalments of 100,000 and to assist in obtaining an annulment of his marriage.

Following the sack of Rome by mutinous imperial troops in May 1527, the Medici pope, Clement VII, was effectively made Charles V's prisoner. It became imperative for Francis and Henry to work even more closely together. In July 1527 Wolsey travelled to France accompanied by a large suite of courtiers and officials with a grand plan to compel Charles to ensure the pope's safety and independence. He was greeted in France as the 'Cardinal Peacemaker.' In August he met Francis I at Amiens and there amplified the Anglo-French alliance. They agreed to Princess Mary's betrothal to Francis's son, Henry of Orléans, and that in any war with Charles, English merchants would have the same trading privileges in France as they traditionally enjoyed in the Netherlands. In November Henry VIII ratified the agreement and as a sign of what was now called a 'perpetual' alliance, the two kings exchanged membership of each other's chivalric orders.

Despite the fact that his own dynastic ambitions did not impinge on Charles's territories and despite the value of strong commercial ties between the Burgundian Netherlands and England, in January 1528 Henry VIII declared war on Charles in alliance with Francis. Although there was never any actual fighting, English merchants found themselves in a trade war. They quickly lost significant business for which the French markets could not compensate. Fear of completely alienating the emperor led the English to a truce with Charles and peace with the Netherlands was eventually restored under the Treaty of Cambrai in 1529.

Although it was a conspicuous failure militarily, the Anglo-French alliance of 1527 was grander, indeed more grandiose, than that of 1518. It instituted almost twenty years of peaceful relations between Henry and Francis. The power of Charles V was so great that neither king could afford to allow the other to isolate him. They had to work together, albeit often in an atmosphere of deep suspicion and recrimination. In September 1532 another important alliance was concluded by which Francis agreed to aid Henry if he was ever attacked by the emperor. In return, Henry gave Francis money to assist him in plans he was then making to stir up trouble for Charles among some of the German protestant princes. In October 1532 the two kings met again, at Calais and Boulgone. Amidst scenes of luxury and theatricality reminiscent of the Field of Cloth of Gold, Francis met Anne Boleyn, lately made Marquess of Pembroke in her own right by Henry. Emboldened by the September agreement and Francis's apparent assurances that he would persuade the pope to annul the English king's marriage, Henry and Anne wed secretly in early 1533.

As queen, Anne Boleyn supported the Anglo-French alliance and her relatives were frequently sent as ambassadors to Francis. However, in the wake of her fall in 1536 and as the English Reformation advanced, Anglo-French relations slowly but steadily deteriorated. The French regime tried to keep Henry on side without endorsing his religious position. A number of trading and maritime disputes arose and Francis's refusal to abandon his support of James V and the pro-French faction in Scotland led to a 'cold war' between England and France during the later 1530s. Most significant of all was Francis's failure to keep up the pension payments due to Henry under the 1527 settlement. These had been regarded by Henry since 1514 as tribute for 'his' crown of France. Because peace with Francis could no longer be taken as proof of Henry's equality with, or superiority to, Francis he returned to the one path which he knew would compel co-operation, an invasion of France.

In 1542, mindful of the Scots' potential to attack England during his projected absence, but perhaps overestimating their present inclination to do so, Henry tried a mixture of diplomacy and intimidation to overawe James V. In September he received Scottish assurances that James would come to England at Christmas to establish better relations but soon afterwards Henry sent troops on destructive raids into the borderlands. Angered by this action, James counter-attacked but was defeated at Solway Moss in November. He died a few weeks later, leaving his infant daughter Mary as the pawn in Henry's subsequent attempts to control Scotland through an 'English' party among Scottish nobles. These culminated in the Treaty of Greenwich signed in July 1543 by which Mary was to marry Henry's young son Edward but the agreement proved a dead letter.

Henry now turned his attention fully to France and despite their troubles of the previous 15 and more years, a new Anglo-Imperial alliance was signed in February 1543. Henry and Charles agreed to invade France together but the specific objectives of the Anglo-Imperial campaign which finally began in June 1544 were, in the end, no clearer than those of 1523. The dukes of Norfolk and Suffolk jointly commanded an army of 42,000 men. They were supposed to join with their imperial counterparts at a suitable place in northern France before sweeping down to the conquest of Paris. Henry was determined that the coastal towns of Boulogne and Montreuil should first be secured, so as to protect his lines of supply and to give his troops an immediate objective. He intended to conduct the siege of Boulogne himself. He also remained sceptical both about Charles's ability to overcome speedily some of the well fortified towns in north-eastern France and about how quickly Paris itself would fall. He seems to have taken one lesson from 1523 and decided that enlarging the English holdings in France came before chasing after any greater glory, however desirable it might still be. Charles argued, rather as Wolsey had done 20 years earlier, that if co-ordinated well and done quickly enough, the march on Paris could be achieved and the war over before an unsecured Boulogne presented much real danger to the English army.

On 14 July 1544 the king arrived at Calais and four days later the siege of Boulogne began. It took considerably longer than those of Thérouanne and Tournai in 1513 but unlike most sieges of the time, it was also successful. Much rejuvenated by his performance as campaigning commander, Henry made his formal entry to the town as conqueror on 18 September 1544. At nearby Montreuil, Norfolk made no headway at all. Meanwhile Charles V had done the unexpected. He had marched as far into France as Soissons, taking Saint-Dizier en route on 17 August. The siege of that town had taken a mere six weeks. Henry was therefore still at Boulogne a month after Charles was ready for the final push against Paris. On the day Henry entered the town, the emperor agreed to the Treaty of Crépy with Francis. Henry was furious. Discharging accusations of treachery at his erstwhile ally, he supervised the further fortification of Boulogne and then returned to England at the end of the month. French forces were now freed to operate fully against the English and reluctantly Henry allowed Norfolk to abandon the siege of Montreuil and prepare for the defence of king's new war trophy.[20]

In May 1545 Francis assembled a force of 30,000 troops and fleet of nearly 400 ships at Le Havre for an attack on England. This was designed to break English lines of supply before the French besieged Boulogne. Francis also hoped to take one of Henry's coastal towns, probably Portsmouth, to avenge the loss of Boulogne and to use as a bargaining counter in negotiations over it. According to an English spy in France, Francis swore, 'to win as much as the Englishmen had on this side of the sea, or else he would give battle.' The French fleet appeared off the Solent in mid-July and Henry moved to Southsea Castle to direct defensive operations. The subsequent battle became an extended duel with Francis I in Le Havre.

The French admiral, Claude d'Annebault, wanted to entice the English fleet into more open waters and out of range of the coastal artillery which Henry had so recently and expensively installed. The English commander-in-chief refused to be drawn into any very close engagements. The closest, off Southsea on 19 July, saw the *Great Harry* in action but also the disastrous loss before Henry's eyes of the *Mary Rose* as she manoeuvred against the tide and wind. When the French attacked the Isle of Wight a few days later Henry secretly shipped over troops from the Hampshire and Wiltshire militias to reinforce the garrison at Carisbroke Castle. The French were driven off the island. They later attacked Seaford in Sussex and Spithead before slipping away on 15 August. Shortly afterwards negotiations for an Anglo-French peace were resumed.[21]

It was a very grudging peace that Henry and Francis finally agreed on 7 June 1546. Under the terms of the Treaty of Ardres Francis would buy the city of Boulogne back from Henry VIII after eight years for two million crowns. For the English these terms were as good as an admission that the city was Henry's. For the French, honour had at least been satisfied insofar as Henry had been made to bargain over his recent conquest. The opportunity to take the city back by force could not be far away. This treaty, like all those between Henry and Francis, was proclaimed as proof of the greatness of both princes, in line with the chivalrous and humanist ideals outlined above. In fact, like two kings, the grand idea of Anglo-French peace had become rather tired and worn out by 1546. Nevertheless, over the previous 20 years the idea of peace and its practical benefits had outweighed the prospective spoils of war. It kept Henry and Francis in a difficult but workable alliance for two decades, a long time indeed in the turbulent politics of the sixteenth century.

THE DYNASTIC WARS FRANCIS I AND CHARLES V

On 1 January 1515 Francis I became king of France and on the same day Charles of Habsburg's personal rule over the Netherlands began. Although their relations started cordially enough, they were, from the outset, locked together by reason of their inheritances in a dynastic struggle in which neither side found much imaginative room to manoeuvre. Unlike Anglo-French relations, Charles and Francis were never able to find some sufficiently grandiose ideal or compelling joint ambition that could make lasting peace between them an exciting or rewarding prospect.

In the spring of 1515 Francis's primary concern was to keep the new overlord of the Netherlands quiet while he pursued his own dynastic ambitions in Milan. He was helped by the fact that at his majority, Charles was still influenced by the francophile nobleman Guillaume de Croy, Lord of Chièvres. He wanted an end to the uncertainty over the Burgundian lands which had poisoned relations with the kings of France for 30 years. With this hope in mind, Chièvres negotiated an immediate alliance with Francis, the Treaty of Paris, signed on 24 March 1515. Charles was promised the hand in marriage of Francis's sister-in-law, Renée of France. The treaty temporarily pacified the dispute over boundaries between the two princes' native lands. It allowed Francis to pursue his Italian ambitions but did not settle the root cause of so much subsequent conflict between them.[22]

Francis I's debut as a warrior-king followed hard upon the heels of this Franco-Burgundian alliance. It was radically different to Henry VIII's in France two years earlier, marked as it was by a major open battle and the conquest, not just of a number of towns, but the whole duchy of Milan. In 1515 Milan was held by Massimiliano Sforza. He had regained control of Milan when the French were forced out by Pope Julius II's Holy League in 1512. Sforza was supported by a coalition of Ferdinand of Aragon, Emperor Maximilian and Pope Leo X. Francis was allied only to Venice. He crossed the Alps in late August 1515 with between 7000 and 9000 heavy cavalry. His infantry consisted of 23,000 landsknechts together with some 10,000 volunteer pikemen, raised mainly in Gascony and the Basque region. Milan was defended by approximately 12,000–15,000 Swiss mercenaries with a small cavalry force of about 200 horse under Cardinal Schinner.

What turned a prospective siege of Milan, thoroughly conventional in itself, into an epic open battle was the decision by the Swiss commanders to attack the French immediately in the hope of stopping an assault on the city and in order to prevent them linking up with their Venetian allies. On the afternoon of 13 September the Swiss infantry marched out of Milan towards the French, stationed just north of the town of Marignano. During the early hours of a moonlit night, three Swiss squares, each of about 7000 men, clashed with Francis's landsknechts. Initially both armies were arranged as series of blocks, one behind the other, designed to engage the enemy in successive waves, or to manoeuvre so as to outflank their opponents. The moonlight later vanished and the two armies broke apart, skirmishing intermittently in the darkness.

At daybreak on 14 September the two armies re-engaged as one long line. The right flank of the French army pushed back the Swiss. At the centre, Francis's infantry fell back but the king counter-attacked at the head of his *gendarmerie* and repulsed the Swiss. On the left flank the Swiss also gained ground and looked likely to prevail but for the timely arrival of Venetian troops. The entire French line then counter-attacked, the Swiss collapsed and Francis was finally victorious. The city of Milan surrendered on 16 September although Sforza held out in the citadel until 4 October. News of Francis's conquest spread rapidly throughout Europe. Within a year of this victory Francis had signed the Peace of Fribourg with the Swiss cantons and acquired the right to hire their mercenaries for his own campaigns. In December Francis signed the Concordat of Bologna with Leo X under which the pope recognised Francis's conquest of Milan.[23]

During the four years after Marignano, Francis tried to keep Charles tied to him. In January 1516 Charles became King of Spain and in August 1516 his alliance with Francis was prolonged under the Treaty of Noyon. This agreement substituted Francis's daughter Louise, for Renée as Charles's future bride and gave her Naples, or more precisely, the French claim to the kingdom, as her dowry. Charles promised to pay Francis an annual sum of 100,000 crowns until they were married, thereby implicitly recognising Francis's claim. In March 1517, Maximilian also became part of this alliance under the Treaty of Cambrai. This, as we have seen, isolated Henry VIII and prompted Wolsey to start working on what became the Treaty of London of 1518. Charles's election as Holy Roman Emperor in June 1519 was a serious blow to Francis's hopes of containing him. His greatest fear was not of a direct invasion of France, but that the new emperor would use his enhanced status and territorial advantages to threaten Milan and prevent Francis pursuing the French claim to Naples.

In order to pre-occupy Charles while he secured his position in the peninsular, Francis attacked him covertly. In March 1521 Robert de La Marck, the Lord of Sedan invaded Luxemburg pursuing a claim to some ancestral lands. Meanwhile, Henri d'Albret, King of Navarre, invaded the kingdom which Ferdinand of Aragon had taken in 1512. Both were supported by the French king. However, the plan back-fired. By the summer these attacks had been repulsed, Francis had been exposed as the true aggressor and suddenly faced invasion himself. He appealed to Henry VIII for assistance under the terms of the Treaty of London and thus was convened the Calais conference, chaired by Cardinal Wolsey at which these disputes were supposed to be resolved. The only thing agreed in the course of the Calais conference was an Anglo-Imperial alliance against France. As the conference dragged on into the autumn, Charles's armies invaded French territory, laying siege to Tournai which Francis had only re-purchased from Henry VIII in 1519. He also ordered his armies to retake Milan. During the autumn Francis fought on two fronts. Unable to move quickly enough in the deteriorating weather in the marshes of Scheldt, he could not save Tournai which capitulated to its imperialist besiegers in early December. Meanwhile events in Italy had taken the worst possible turn. Milan fell to the imperialists on 19 November 1521.

At the start of the next year's fighting season Francis ordered Marshall Lautrec to retake Milan. The French attempt on the city was defeated by the imperial commander Prospero Colonna who then forced them to retreat north to Monza. In April, Lautrec's Swiss mercenaries complained about their wages and demanded to be allowed to turn and face their enemies. Lautrec reluctantly agreed whereupon they attacked Colonna's army encamped around the nearby villa of La Bicocca. A combination of well placed artillery and arquebusiers decimated the ranks of the Swiss pikemen, killing as many as 3000, around 10 per cent of his force. The devastating deployment of firearms and cannon at that battle reinforced the message of Marignano, signalling the decline of the Swiss as the once-invincible fighting force of the previous century. Lautrec's army collapsed in the wake of this defeat and he retreated to France.

Following hard on this defeat in Italy, in September came the English invasion of northern France under the Duke of Suffolk. Mercifully for Paris and for Francis, it petered out in confusion. The planned simultaneous invasion from Spain by Charles V never came and the treasonous Duke of Bourbon, who had raised an army to take central France, was left stranded. He retreated south and besieged Marseilles but was defeated and chased out of France by the end of 1524. Internal order restored, Francis once more attempted to conquer Milan.

In October 1524 he crossed the Alps with an army of 1200–1400 heavy cavalry and between 24,000 and 26,000 infantry. This campaign was to culminate in another epic battle like Marignano, but one with a very different result. The French army actually entered Milan without resistance in October, the imperial garrison withdrawing ahead of it to the smaller towns of Lodi and Pavia. The imperial commanders planned to use these towns as the bases for a counter-attack on Milan. Francis decided to lay siege to Pavia, to force out the imperial troops and thus safeguard his new conquest. One side of the town faced on to the Ticino river, the remaining three sides were protected by walls. These the French surrounded within a semicircular line of guns and trenches. Their king's camp was located within the walled hunting park of Mirabello, a country house on the north side of Pavia. The siege had not made any headway by November when 22,000 imperial infantry and 2000 heavy and light cavalry were brought from nearby Lodi under the imperial commander, Ferdinando d'Avalos, Marquis of Pescara. The be-sieging French army was now itself be-sieged.

There followed several more months of fruitless attempts to bring the French to open battle. In February 1525 the imperial mercenaries showed their customary discontent at not having been paid for several months. On 23 February, Pescara moved part of his forces camped to the west of the town, along the walls at the top or northern end of Mirabello park and during the night broke through it in several places. At dawn the following day, one detachment of troops moved to attack the house of Mirabello itself, at the north end. The bulk of the imperial infantry and cavalry began marching southwards down the length of the park towards the main French camp. As they did the French artillery opened fire but the sources vary as to how effective this cannonade was. As the imperial troops regrouped, Francis gathered his cavalry together and advanced to counter-attack. The French artillery had to cease fire as the cavalry charged. At first the imperialist cavalry were thrown back by the *gendarmerie* but as they broke through the enemy line, the French horsemen came within range of approximately one thousand of Pescara's arquebusiers who had either been initially positioned, or retreated, amidst clumps of trees and bushes at the top of the park. This natural cover also acted as camouflage and aided perhaps by the poor light of an early winter's morning, made them hard to see. Reaching this wooded and rough terrain the French cavalrymen slowed. Ahead were several blocks of imperial landsknechts which they could not hope alone to penetrate. Unable to advance but unwilling to retreat on to their own infantry now coming up the park, they halted.

In this moment of hesitation, Pescara's arquebusiers opened fire, raking the French men-at-arms with heavy shot which, at such close range, pierced armour and brought horses and riders crashing down. In the ensuing confusion Francis himself was unhorsed and the French lost the momentum of the battle. The blocks of infantry then clashed, the French began to falter, the king's Swiss mercenaries deserted the field and the situation became hopeless. Francis himself fought on but was eventually captured in the midst of this rout. The defeat was catastrophic for the French nobility with only around 400 of the original 1400 cavalrymen escaping either death or capture. There has been considerable debate as to why Francis lost the battle when at its start the numbers on both sides were relatively evenly matched. Ultimately, the French cavalry charge proved disastrous because it screened the French artillery, forcing it to cease fire just when it was needed most. Had Francis better co-ordinated the disparate elements of his army, Pescara's arqubusiers might not have had the opportunity to do their grisly work unmolested.[24]

After Pavia Charles could more or less dictate terms to his opponent. He was within his rights to dismember France, and that is precisely what Henry VIII hoped that he would do. However lacking the resources to continue the war, Charles attempted to end the dynastic disputes between himself and Francis once and for all. He demanded that Francis cede the duchy of Burgundy to him and surrender all his Italian claims. The king of France had also to give his two elder sons, Francis and Henry, to Charles as hostages until he performed the agreement. Francis was able to insist only that he marry Charles's sister Eleanor partly as a gesture of good faith, partly to prevent her from being married to the Duke of Bourbon as had been intended and partly, perhaps, to give the agreement a face-saving colour of alliance. Charles believed that the restraint he was showing in the circumstances accorded with the chivalric ethos to which Francis also subscribed. He expected Francis's gratitude in return. However that same chivalric ethos allowed and, according to some commentators including Wolsey demanded, that Francis reject any agreement inconsistent with his personal honour and duty as king of France.

Francis knew by January 1526 that he was neither as weak, nor as isolated politically as he appeared to be. Charles's dominance over Europe in the wake of Pavia seriously worried the papacy and many Italian states.

In England and in Italy the representatives of the French regent, Louise of Savoy, had worked feverishly from the moment of the king's defeat to prevent his isolation. Faced with a choice of accepting Charles's demands or remaining a prisoner and losing the opportunity to clinch a powerful anti-Habsburg alliance, Francis bowed to the inevitable. In August 1525 he made a secret declaration that he would consider invalid any concession forced from him contrary to his duty as king. He re-affirmed this immediately before signing the Treaty of Madrid on 14 January 1526. He returned to France in March and shortly afterwards concluded the Treaty of Cognac with the Pope Clement VII, Milan, Florence and Venice.[25]

In December 1527 Francis formally repudiated the Treaty of Madrid as illegal because it had required him to surrender part of the royal patrimony, contrary to the fundamental laws of France and as dishonourable because it had been agreed under duress. Charles fulminated against Francis for breaking his promises and demanded his return to captivity, but to no avail. The Treaty of Madrid is perhaps the clearest demonstration that a peace forced by one sixteenth century prince upon another of equal standing but upon unequal terms was theoretically possible, but might be illegal and would almost certainly be unsuccessful.

Although Francis had hoped that the members of the League of Cognac would force Charles's armies out of Italy for him, direct French intervention was what they had expected. He declared war on Charles in January 1528 and for a third time, poured troops and artillery into Italy. Odet de Foix, Lord of Lautrec, led several ultimately unsuccessful campaigns there between 1527–29. In February 1528 Lautrec laid siege to Naples which initially looked likely to fall to the French. However a blockade of Naples harbour by the Genoese admiral Andrea Doria was lifted when he got into an argument with Francis over pay. As supplies began reaching the city from the sea, Lautrec's besieging army succumbed to disease. The French were forced to withdraw and never returned to Naples during Francis's reign.[26]

Charles was now eager to capitalise on this success to dominate the papacy and Italy but both he and Francis lacked military and financial resources to continue the war. A truce was therefore agreed and peace negotiations began by the end of 1528. After the failure of the League of Cognac, Clement VII despaired of ever being able to play Francis against Charles successfully and decided to ally with the emperor by the Treaty of Barcelona signed in June 1529.[27]

A new Franco-Imperial peace and alliance followed shortly afterwards, promulgated at Cambrai on 5 August 1529. It was negotiated by Margaret of Austria and Louise of Savoy and is sometimes called the 'Ladies' Peace.' Under the agreement Francis was to marry Charles's sister Eleanor. He could keep the duchy of Burgundy but had to pay Charles an indemnity of two million crowns for it and as ransom for his two sons who had been in Spain since 1526. He was to withdraw his armies from Italy and surrender suzerainty over Flanders and Artois and a number of towns including Arras and Tournai. Francis was to give Charles more money and ships to help him on his journey from Spain to Italy. He was not to support the La Marck family or the Duke of Guelders in their quarrels with the emperor.[28]

With the exception of Burgundy, Charles thus obtained everything at Cambrai that he had wanted in the Treaty of Madrid. However, this time around he too made some real concessions, including releasing Francis's sons for ransom, which he had previously said that he would not do, and relinquishing claims on the counties of Boulogne, Guînes and Ponthieu. Francis's strategic position in 1529 was arguably even weaker than it had been in 1526 having yet again failed to establish French dominance in Italy and having lost several allies in the process. But at Cambrai there was a greater apparent mutuality in the negotiations between the two sides. Francis was free and in command of his own realm. He was represented by his own mother assisted by his most senior advisors with whom he was in constant communication during the negotiations. He could not claim, and probably had no reason to feel, that he had been treated unfairly. This gave the settlement at Cambrai a legitimacy which that at Madrid palpably lacked. The treaty secured an uneasy peace between Francis and Charles for six years, about the length of most 'perpetual' peace agreements of the age.

Francis honoured the letter of the Treaty of Cambrai while completely ignoring its spirit. In 1532 he became aware that the rulers of Saxony, Hesse and Bavaria, among others, had been angered by the election in January of 1531 of Ferdinand of Habsburg as 'King of the Romans', effectively the emperor's deputy and putative successor. Philip of Hesse also wanted to restore Duke Ulrich of Würtemberg to the duchy from which he had been expelled by the Habsburgs in 1519. Under the Treaty of Scheyern, signed in May 1532, Francis promised a coalition of malcontents 100,000 crowns for a war against the Habsburgs. Francis also consistently opposed the calling of General Council of the Church which Charles and the pope favoured but which the German Protestant princes and Henry VIII feared. In early 1532 he also sent envoys to Süleyman to persuade him to attack Italy, thus giving Francis the pretext to invade the peninsular, ostensibly as the defender of Christendom. When, in the summer of 1532, the sultan instead pressed home his attack on Hungary and Austria and threatened to overwhelm Vienna, Francis urged the emperor on to victory while offering personally to lead an army into Italy – just in case the Turks attacked there. Charles's response to this interesting suggestion can easily be imagined.[29]

Francis's hard work on anti-Habsburg agreements and alliances was crowned in 1533 by a marriage alliance which raised new hopes for him in Italy. On 28 October, at Marseilles, his second son, Henry, Duke of Orléans, was married to Catherine de' Medici, the niece of Clement VII. The pope, who had only four years earlier decided 'irrevocably' to ally with the emperor but who had since resented his dominance, now offered Francis another chance to organise a wider anti-Habsburg alliance like the League of Cognac. The dream of Milan and Naples in French hands suddenly revived. However, within a year Clement VII was dead and the new pope Alessandro Farnese, Paul III, proved to be an unshakeable, if sometimes frustrating, ally to Charles. Francis's intriguing momentum was brought to a sudden halt. For the next 12 months he was fully occupied with suppressing Protestant heresy at home and restructuring his armed forces.

In the spring of 1536 Francis again declared war; not against the emperor directly but against one of his allies, Charles III Duke of Savoy. Charles was also Francis's uncle and the king claimed that he had withheld lands which belonged to him in right of his mother Louise of Savoy. Francis invaded Savoy in a move principally designed to give him a stronger bargaining position in a new round of struggles over Milan. In response the emperor invaded Provence from Italy in the summer while the Earl of Nassau once again attacked northern France. The French commander in the south was Francis's chief counsellor and favourite, Anne de Montmorency. He denied Charles open battle but heavily fortified Marseilles in order to block Charles's path to the west and any possible link-up with troops coming from Spain. He ordered Aix to be evacuated and laid waste to the area around it so as to deny the emperor's troops food and water. He then established a fortified camp south-east of Avignon preventing the emperor from moving north. Having nowhere to go Charles halted at Aix and over the next month his forces succumbed to disease and hunger. Meanwhile, Francis repulsed Nassau's northern invasion and then returned south to prepare for yet another invasion of Italy. His armies, again under Montmorency, occupied Piedmont as far as Montferrat before he agreed to a truce with Charles signed in Monzon in Spain in October 1537. Pope Paul III now offered to mediate a settlement between the two antagonists. Montmorency persuaded Francis to believe that he would gain more through friendship with the emperor than all he had lost in 20 years of war. Francis reluctantly agreed to parallel talks between the pope and each of the rulers at Nice in May. In June 1538 a truce between them was agreed for 10 years. Shortly afterwards plans were made for the two enemies to meet personally.[30]

In July 1538 Charles sailed to Aigues-Mortes, just east of Montpellier and there he met Francis, exchanging words of friendship which he took as good omens for future peace.[31] More was to come. In the autumn Francis met Charles's sister, Mary of Hungary, now Regent of the Netherlands. They signed a peace treaty at Compiègne which brought to a close hostilities in the north. By late 1538 a basis for a settlement of the Milan issue was worked out. Francis's third son Charles, now Duke of Orléans, would marry the emperor's daughter or niece and be invested with duchy. Charles V's son Philip would marry Francis's daughter Marguerite. Francis would avoid interference in German affairs and join Charles on a crusade against the Turks. No formal treaty was signed between the two rulers but they reached an entente or 'understanding' on the basis of these proposals.

In the summer of 1539 there was a violent uprising in Charles's native city of Ghent over taxes and other grievances. Seizing the moment, Francis invited the emperor to get to Flanders quickly by passing through France as his guest. After careful thought, the emperor accepted the offer, arriving at Bayonne in November 1539. From there he was escorted by virtually the entire French court on a journey designed to show him the wealth and sophistication of Francis's realm. Francis met Charles at Loches and they arrived at Fontainebleau, Francis's favourite residence, in time for Christmas. In January the emperor was entertained in Paris before going on to Valenciennes where he was met by his sister. On 14 February 1540 Charles entered his home city in state and brought the revolt of Ghent to a swift end.

A swift end to the uncertainty about Milan's future is exactly what the French now hoped for. Instead, in March, Charles sent new and different peace proposals in which he resurrected the old claim to Burgundy. He now proposed that Charles of Orléans should marry Mary as planned but that they would rule the Netherlands and Charolais, not Milan. In effect Charles wanted to buy Francis's claim to Milan with territory in the north. Francis and Montmorency were stunned and appalled by these unacceptable proposals. It seemed that Charles and Francis had been thinking at cross purposes since Aigues-Mortes. All Francis's good faith and generosity had availed him nothing. Although negotiations continued for several months Francis was enraged when on, 11 October 1540, Charles V formally invested his own son Philip with the duchy of Milan. This act, entirely consistent with Charles's own sense of his authority and best interests, provoked the fall of Montmorency upon whose advice in the matter Francis had so heavily relied.

Furious at what he saw as a betrayal of trust, Francis I wasted little time in concluding an alliance with the Turks against Charles. With offers of maritime support against Charles from Süleyman, Francis declared war on 12 July 1542 ostensibly because of the murder near Milan a year previously of his envoy to the Sultan, Antonio Rincón. The king's youngest son, Charles of Orléans, immediately attacked Luxemburg but, like Robert de La Marck before him, was thrown out again within a few weeks. In the south the dauphin Henry attacked Perpignan and was similarly repulsed. After a break during the winter, hostilities were renewed in 1543 in a series of manoeuvres in which Charles took Cambrai, while Francis successfully re-occupied Luxemburg.

In the spring of 1544 an army commanded by Ferrante Gonzaga launched a massive counter-attack through Luxemburg. Charles joined Gonzaga in the summer invading northern France and reaching Saint-Dizier on 13 July. The town held out for six weeks but capitulated in August at which point he moved on through Champagne towards Paris. He came as near to the capital as Château-Thierry which he took on 7 September. The emperor was reluctant to attempt a direct attack on Paris without Henry VIII's support. Accordingly he turned north-west to Soissons preparing to link up with the English army which was just completing the capture of Boulogne. However, his money now began to run out. Francis quickly initiated peace talks with Charles and Henry. Seeing his English ally making no move to join him for the projected assault on Paris, Charles came to peace with Francis under the Treaty of Crépy of 18 September 1544.

This treaty restored the territorial status quo reached by the Treaty of Cambrai and the entente of 1538 and provided that Francis would assist the emperor against the German Protestants and the Turks. The vexed question of Milan was to be resolved by Charles of Orléans' marriage either to Charles V's daughter Mary, in which case he would rule the Netherlands, or to the emperor's niece Anna, in which case he would obtain Milan. Charles would decide the bride within four months. On the face of it this messy amalgamation of two completely conflicting proposals dating from 1538–39 seems inherently flawed. Charles was aware of the poor relationships within the royal family. Charles of Orléans was as keen as Francis to see the plan implemented but Henry feared that it would deprive him of his inheritance. Perhaps the emperor hoped to stir up a destructive enmity between them for in February 1545 he did name Anna as Orléans' bride thus promising him Milan. It seems most unlikely that Charles would ever have actually handed the duchy over to Orléans but in the event he did not have to. On 9 September 1545, the duke died and the treaty never took effect. Oddly enough given the decades of conflict between them, when Francis died in March 1547 he was actually at peace with the emperor.

THE 'CRUSADING' WARS OF CHARLES V

Despite significant victories in the 1520s over Francis, Charles V never saw the wars he fought against the king of France as his greatest achievements. Deeply conscious as he was of the Burgundian chivalric tradition and the duty upon him to defend Christian Europe, Charles remained, until his early thirties, very frustrated at his lack of personal battle experience against the Turks. It was not until 1532 that Charles first faced them at the head of an imperial army. In September 1532 Charles organised a force of Burgundian, Spanish and Italian troops and marched with his brother Ferdinand against forces of Süleyman which had besieged Köszeg, less than a hundred miles south of Vienna. However as the imperial army approached, the Turks withdrew before significant action and Charles, short of money as ever, could not pursue the retreating enemy. Charles entered Vienna on September 23 before returning to Spain.

It was not finally until 1535 that Charles found himself fighting on the battlefield and then it was not in Europe, but in North Africa. In 1534 the admiral of the Turkish fleet, Khayr al-Din, or Barbarossa, took Tunis from its hereditary lord and Spanish vassal, Muley Hassan. Charles determined to recover Tunis and ultimately to sweep the Mediterranean clean of the Turks. In the summer of 1535 he assembled a force of 30,000 Spanish, Italian and German troops and shipped them to Africa in a fleet of 400 warships and transport vessels partly supplied by Andrea Doria. He immediately attacked the fortress of La Goletta, at the port for Tunis. After a three-week siege under the fierce African sun, he commanded the artillery when the fortress was stormed on July 14. Its fall, and with it the seizure of 82 ships of Barbarossa's fleet, was the prelude to the capture of Tunis itself. Charles was in the middle of the fighting on 21 July when his army defeated Barbarossa's as it marched towards Tunis. The city itself yielded a few days later. In August Charles sailed to Sicily and then made a triumphant progress through southern Italy, spending Christmas in Naples.

The emperor took advantage of the short-lived *entente* between himself and Francis in 1539–42 to launch himself once more against the Turks in Africa. In September 1541 he assembled a huge invasion force for an attack on Algiers, hoping to reprise the glories of Tunis. However, this ill-fated expedition had to be called off almost before it began when a huge storm wrecked Charles's fleet off the African coast. He returned to Spain at the end of November.

The other enemies who Charles faced in battle were some of his own subjects. The end of the war against Francis allowed Charles finally to turn his hand against the Protestant League of Schmalkalden, first formed in 1531. Following the failure of the Diet of Regensburg in the summer of 1546 the emperor determined to crush the power of the League whose military leader was the Elector John Frederick of Saxony.

Charles entered an alliance with Maurice of Ducal Saxony in June 1546 and the following October, Ferdinand and Maurice invaded Electoral Saxony in Charles's name. Charles assembled a force of Spanish, Italian and papal troops to assist them. The papal troops were subsequently withdrawn but Charles was able to replace them with mounted forces which Ferdinand had raised in Hungary.

In 1547 the emperor personally command his army on a campaign which culminated in his most famous victory, at the Battle of Mühlberg. Much was made of it by his propagandists but it was scarcely more than a semi-disordered retreat by a smaller army in the face of a larger one. The imperial force at the time of the battle has been estimated at between 30,000 and 42,000 infantry. In April Charles marched into the south of Electoral Saxony and John Frederick, with a force of 6000 cavalry and 12,000 foot, retreated before him to just north of Meissen. He crossed the River Elbe destroying the bridge after him and intended to march north-west along the river to Wittenberg or Magdeburg, convinced that the river was protection enough from the pursuing Charles.

On Saturday 23 April 1547 Charles caught up with him and learnt that, unknown to John Frederick, the river was actually fordable at Mühlberg.

In the early hours of the following morning Charles's troops crossed the river, some in boats, some swimming, some at the ford with himself in the vanguard. He surprised the Elector's army camped some three miles inland from its banks just as preparations were underway to continue its northward march. As John Frederick began to withdraw towards Wittenberg, his rear-guard was overtaken by the imperial cavalry. He quickly rounded to face Charles's army and for some hours his infantry held a line in front of the woods of Lochau before collapsing and retreating through them. As they emerged on to the road to Wittenberg they were intercepted by the imperial cavalry. Many were killed or captured and the Elector surrendered. Charles regarded this victory as his greatest and the occasion at which he came closest to his much-cherished ideal of himself as the knightly-warrior.

For a time the Protestant military resistance to the emperor collapsed and Charles hoped to impose a final settlement of the religious controversies on the princes of the Empire. Following the failure of the Diet at Augsburg in 1547–48 in which Charles argued for a broad, conservative and temporary agreement, known as the Interim, his principal ally and still the leading Protestant prince, Maurice of Saxony, began to fear that Charles would sooner or later turn against him. In 1551 Maurice concluded an alliance with several northern German princes into which Henry II of France was drawn under the Treaty of Chambord. Henry was promised the cities of Metz, Toul and Verdun in return for money to support the rebellious German princes and a promise to guarantee Maurice his lands. By June 1552 Henry had led an army of 35,000 into Lorraine and these three towns were captured within a month.

Charles was forced to retreat out of Germany to Innsbruck and then out of Austria altogether but in October he returned with an army of 55,000 troops and over one hundred guns of various calibres to besiege Metz. As winter took hold, Charles faced the familiar problem of disease and hunger decimating his troops. In January 1553 Charles regretfully abandoned the siege and by early February was back in Brussels. Meanwhile the French invaded the Netherlands and besieged Hesdin. Amidst growing dissension within the ranks, Charles fought his last battle a little over 18 months later in Hainaut. He could not prevent Henry II's army destroying Mary of Hungary's splendid palace at Binche, but he relieved the town of Renty in Artois and pushed the French back. This was perhaps small consolation but welcome to Charles nonetheless. He returned to Brussels, where, on 22 October 1555 he resigned his sovereignty over the Order of the Golden Fleece, the first stage of his abdication as emperor.

CONCLUSION

During the first four decades of the sixteenth century warfare in western Europe, and especially in Italy and in northern France, was endemic. It was practised on a greater scale and for longer continuous periods than ever before. Armies grew larger and the equipment with which they fought increased in variety and complexity. Greater numbers were routinely killed or injured on losing sides than had been usual in the previous century. All of this was hugely expensive and provoked a wearying financial war between the protagonists. These kings raised as much money as possible from a variety of sources within and beyond their kingdoms. This money was then ploughed into warfare and almost immediately proved insufficient. More money might then be secured to sustain the campaign until this too ran out. A truce which usually became a short-lived peace was then concluded. This allowed time to reduce expenditure, build up reserves, or least to consolidate debts, to the point where new military ventures could be contemplated. The whole cycle then began again. This kind of warfare forced kings to explore new ways of raising the necessary funds which had important implications for the way they governed and administered their kingdoms.

Henry VIII, Charles V and Francis I all experienced success and failure on the battlefield. Of the three, Henry had the least direct experience of warfare and certainly of the hardships of campaigning. It was his fortune, or rather misfortune, that none of the three campaigns of note which he mounted against France lasted longer than one fighting season. As Steven Gunn has noted, Henry usually made rather ineffective war. Had his invasions in 1523 and 1544 been better co-ordinated with Charles it might have been a rather different story. He certainly felt himself to have been cheated of several opportunities to dominate France militarily. He grasped the realities of strategic planning well enough to appreciate the need to secure territory in northern France before making any larger attempt on Francis's kingdom. The king's hesitancy may have cost him greater glory in 1523 but it is unlikely, despite Wolsey's enthusiasm early in the campaign season, that Bourbon and Charles V were ever going to be in a position seriously to capitalise on the advance to Paris which Henry finally ordered. Having been left stranded at the end of that headlong dash it is not hard to see why Henry chose to secure Boulogne first in 1544 before venturing further. On the other hand, this decision looked short-sighted to his ally Charles V. The irony was that in 1544 Charles was in a much better position to co-ordinate his attack on France with Henry's and that had the English king ordered another 'plunge into the bowels of France' as Wolsey had called it in 1523, he might just have achieved his much-prized objective.

Nevertheless, Henry's establishment of the English navy, the fortification of the southern shores of England, and the naval battle which he directed from Southsea in 1545, paid real dividends. He capitalised on the defensive advantages of his island kingdom and made it an effective platform for the projection of his personal power on continental Europe. His campaigns in France won territory, albeit not much, but more importantly perhaps got him taken seriously by his two rivals. He used his position as a third military player on the field quite effectively in diplomacy. Under Henry,

England's military importance in Europe was greater than it had been for a century before him and greater than it would be in the hundred years after his death.

Francis I never achieved his chivalric dream of permanent control over the duchy of Milan and, worse still, lost parts of the realm such as Tournai and Boulogne. At first glance, he seems the least successful of the three kings at maintaining and extending his patrimony, the duty of all sixteenth century princes. He too often made ineffective war. Yet when seen in the context of Charles V's extraordinary agglomeration of territories and allies, with which he was able to surround France completely, the military achievements of Francis were considerable. Modern observers might wonder why he did not simply seek 'secure' or 'defensible' borders against his enemies and sit tight, satisfying himself with the defence of the kingdom against the Habsburg giant. This might have avoided disasters like Pavia and perhaps the frequent incursions into northern France by imperial armies but would have been inconceivable to Francis. He was a firm believer in the principle that the best defence is offence and made war on this basis on at least three fronts for 30 years, with minimal periods of respite. No king of France had ever before done this, and on such a scale. To do so, Francis had to marshal the resources of his kingdom as never before, and, all things considered, did so successfully.

In his younger days, Francis was very much of the 'derring-do' school of warfare. He was by nature impetuous and physically very brave. His cavalry charges at Marignano helped to secure victory, but that at Pavia contributed directly to his defeat. Francis learnt from his mistakes. In the last two decades of his reign, he not only invested heavily in fortifying his kingdom's borders and principal towns but practised greater restraint and shrewdness on the battlefield. He held his nerve in the face of imperial invasions in 1536 and 1544. Rather than counter-attacking immediately, he did what he could to block serious enemy advances and allowed Charles's campaigns to run out of impetus. As always in warfare there was an element of luck in this, but such restraint not only saved him precious resources but allowed him to capitalise on his enemy's predicament. In 1536 he retook all the territory which Charles had initially overrun and in 1544, Francis signed a peace treaty with Charles that split the Anglo-Imperial alliance, allowing him to turn decisively against the English army in the north-west. The loss of Boulogne was a serious blow to him, but it could have been much worse. In short he was a constant thorn in the side of Charles V. Although this brought criticism that he was hampering the emperor in his fight against the enemies of the faith, Francis considered himself justified in protecting his own kingdom and his rights above all other considerations.

Charles V's military record was long in the making but reasonably sound when set alongside those of his two contemporaries. He too had decisive personal victories as field commander at Tunis and Mühlberg. Like Henry VIII, Charles also avoided any catastrophic defeats such as his armies inflicted upon Francis at Pavia and upon his generals as La Biccoca. He had greater resources and a greater number of supportive allies than had the other two but he also had greater demands on those resources, defending such disparate territories. He used his troops, equipment and money as effectively as he could but they often proved insufficient for the task in hand. Consequently, Charles did have his share of disappointments and setbacks. The failure of the Algiers campaign and that in Provence in 1536 were deeply frustrating. The sudden losses of Metz, Toul and Verdun were bitter blows at the end of his reign.

Like his counterparts Charles felt cheated of the opportunity to accomplish his own chivalric quest. He wanted above all to lead a glorious crusade against the Turks and ultimately to liberate Jerusalem, whose king he claimed to be. Not without reason he held Francis I and the German Protestant princes primarily responsible for undermining the security of his empire and requiring him constantly to defend it. This military action exhausted both the money and men who might otherwise have been directed against the Turkish threat. The several settlements which Charles and Francis arrived at never fully addressed the underlying issues between them. Given the intense attachment to their individual inheritances it was most unlikely that they ever could.

The Habsburg-Valois conflict was renewed by the next generation of rulers with as much vigour as ever. Each side made some gains in fighting in the north between 1547 and 1559 but pressing financial difficulties forced both Henry II and Philip II eventually to negotiate. The resulting settlement between them, reached at Cateau-Cambrésis, was the most comprehensive ever achieved between the two dynasties and was maintained for the remainder of the sixteenth century. Yet the extraordinary empire which Charles created by inheritance, by dynastic marriages and diplomacy could not finally be held by military means. More than 40 years after Charles V's death, one of Spain's leading diplomats, the Duke of Sessa, assessed the difficulty of maintaining the empire which Charles had created. His analysis was one which Charles would surely have recognised and with which he would perhaps regretfully have agreed:

> ...no empire, however great, has been able to sustain many wars in different areas for long. If we can think only of defending ourselves and never manage to contrive a great offensive blow against one of our enemies so that when that is over we can turn to others ... I doubt whether we can sustain an empire as scattered as ours.[33]

4

Governors: Royal authority and the administration of the realm

> the princes's prerogative and the subject's privileges are solid felicities together and but empty notions asunder. That people is beyond precedent free and beyond comparison happy who restrain not the sovereign's power so far as to do them harm, as he hath none left to do them good.
>
> Chief Justice Fineux[1]

As well as being magnificent warriors, early sixteenth century monarchs were expected to be effective governors. The maintenance of justice was their central, God-given, duty as kings. This, together with protecting the church, they swore to do at their coronations. Doing justice was the essential and most compelling way for the royal governor to demonstrate *virtus*. The prince had therefore to be strong, had to enforce his authority in the realm, to control it and to ensure the obedience of his subjects. In their public actions and statements and in the propaganda devised by their apologists, Henry VIII, Francis I and Charles V all created the impression that having divinely sanctioned power, they had only to will something to be done for it to happen. This myth was useful in overawing their subjects and compelling their obedience. It was taken up by their successors in the seventeenth and eighteenth centuries and trumpeted in splendidly portentous phrases such as 'absolute monarchy' and 'the divine right of kings.'

'Absolutist' monarchy has often been understood as a synonym for autocracy or despotism. The Tudors and Habsburgs have been described in these terms and in France the apotheosis of this monarchy was thought to have been reached in Louis XIV whose officials, the *intendants* were alleged to have displaced the higher nobles as the real agents of government, leaving them to dance attendance on Louis in Versailles' gilded rooms. More recent historiography has emphasized that, lacking any of the institutions of modern state control, sixteenth and seventeenth-century kings were in danger of appearing, like the folktale emperor, without any clothes. In an age before effective standing armies or police forces, they still needed their people at all social levels to accept and acknowledge their authority and to co-operate in the making and enforcement of their laws. Without this, they had no capacity to maintain justice. In order to secure this co-operation, monarchs had often to accept certain practical restrictions to their power and to deal constantly with the demands of independent authorities to participate in the government, at least of their own localities.

Justice Fineux's riddle-like maxim, quoted above, perfectly encapsulates the central and paradoxical principle in Renaissance monarchy. Namely, monarchs wielded authority that was at once complete and restricted. Put more prosaically, it means that in a well ordered kingdom royal authority had to be strong, even at the risk of authoritarian rule, but always a careful balance had to be maintained between the king's power and the subjects' legitimate expectation of just rule. Sixteenth-century government was not finally about issuing 'divine right' edicts in isolation but involved a substantial amount of negotiation between the crown and the many powerful interest groups within the kingdom; the church, the nobility and gentry, the wealthy merchants and town councils, as well as lawyers and even the crown's own administrative and judicial officers.

At the same time however, the requirement upon monarchs to deliberate did not mean that they had to be 'populist' or in any sense democratic- and they were not. The basis of negotiation between them and their most powerful subjects was not whether a proposed action was popular, but whether or not it came within an agreed set of powers, rights and jurisdictions belonging to the crown whereby its freedom of executive action was established. This idea was understood in a variety of ways across Europe. It was rendered in Latin as the prince's 'plena potestas', in French as his 'puissance absolue' and in English as Fineux called it, the 'prince's prerogative.' In general terms, the prerogative allowed monarchs to determine for themselves who they would marry, against whom they would go to war and with whom they would make peace. They alone ennobled subjects and conferred other dignities upon them. They could create or change royal administrative offices as they saw fit. They could regulate commerce and coinage, grant charters to towns, universities and other corporate associations. They determined what religion their subjects practised and had the right of life and death over those who seriously breached the criminal law. They were also the final judges between their subjects in civil matters. They had control over the kingdom's armed forces and raising troops without their approval could be construed as treason. When acting under these headings the monarch's authority was final, or 'absolute', as the French jurists called it. This should never be confused with 'absolutist' or described as 'absolutism.' These words were invented by historians of the nineteenth century to ascribe despotic motives to French kings for which there is no compelling evidence. They have often been misapplied since and are best avoided in dealing with the sixteenth century.[2]

Mindful of the divinely ordained order, individual nobles, representative assemblies and the judicial courts were usually anxious to recognise their sovereign's authority while resisting any drift towards despotism. For their parts, Francis, Henry and Charles all sought to exercise their authority to the fullest extent possible, consistent with their coronation oaths. Precedent, tradition and the written law were important guides in this area but kings were not finally bound by them. They expected to be supported in this authority by their subjects. Before examining the role in governance of the representative institutions which sixteenth century monarchs could call upon from time to time, it will be useful to survey the main administrative and judicial bodies through which they routinely took advice and asserted their authority. The most important of these were the royal councils.

THE ENGLISH ROYAL ADMINISTRATION AND JUDICIARY

By the 1520s Henry VIII's 'king's council' properly so called was much smaller than the body which his father had consulted. It had between twelve and sixteen members drawn from the ranks of peers, bishops, and senior knights of the royal household. Its function was to advise the king on any matter he chose to put before it. It was also the primary executive body of the realm and joined with the king in communicating to local officials, military officers and ambassadors. The king could make executive orders or proclamations with the advice and consent of his council. Proclamations were usually issued to cover general administrative, social and economic matters, including religion, which fell under the king's prerogative. They could not touch life or limb of the subject and could not be used to create felonies. Because proclamations did not have the authority of Parliament they were regarded as inferior to statute and the common law. In 1539 a statute was passed declaring that they were to be obeyed 'as though they were made by act of Parliament for the time in them limited.' This did not mean that they could take the place of Parliamentary statutes, but clarified their legal status and enforceability.[3]

The king's council was also a judicial and investigative body which received petitions and grievances addressed to him as the realm's highest judge. In this guise it was known as the court of Star Chamber, for no more sinister reason than to describe the decoration on the ceiling of the room at Westminster where it met. It heard cases between parties, or matters referred to it by the crown, in which an allegation of interference with due process of law was the central issue. It was presided over by the Lord Chancellor and its deliberations were assisted by two chief justices. Because it was relatively speedy and flexible in its approach, getting a case before it became a popular strategy for litigants who had been frustrated in other courts. Cardinal Wolsey also used its wide-ranging power to impose fines on nobles or merchants who used their wealth and influence corruptly in matters of local justice or law enforcement. For example, in January 1525 Lord Dacre was summoned before Star Chamber to answer charges of maladministration of justice as warden of the marches in the north. This was because his onerous charge along the border with Scotland was executed at times through dealings with border raiders from both sides, men known 'to have committed felony and other misdoings.' He agreed to pay 1500 marks and was relived of his wardenships. Star Chamber also investigated violent breaches of the king's peace, punished contempt of court and perjury and enforced royal proclamations.

Because the royal council was dominated by the most powerful individuals in the realm, it was also, inevitably, a political body. For much of Henry's reign the council worked under the supervision of two royal favourites, first Thomas Wolsey and later Thomas Cromwell. Cardinal-Archbishop of York by 1515, Lord Chancellor by December the same year and papal legate *a latere* from 1518, Wolsey was *de facto* the pre-eminent churchman and the principal legal officer of the kingdom. Until the failed campaign for an annulment to the royal marriage, Wolsey enjoyed Henry's confidence as no other. He directed both the kingdom's administration and the king's foreign policy according to his own grandiose instincts. Doing so made him a wealthy man but provoked the anger of the nobles he dominated.

Cromwell was the king's chief secretary from 1531 and his vicegerent in spirituals (or deputy in church affairs) from 1536. He was also the first royal secretary to organise all the council's business. His vast correspondence shows how by threats, promises of favours and simple instructions, he ensured that royal policy was implemented on the ground. This made him invaluable to the king but his influence was deeply resented by the nobles who surrounded him. Professor Elton argued that Cromwell also instituted a 'revolution' in government which swept away the medieval form of mixed conciliar and household government and substituted a 'national' bureaucratic system with separate departments of state. The cornerstone of this revolution was the Privy Council which, Elton believed, emerged between 1534 and 1536 and became the centre of national politics, in effect a proto-'Cabinet.'[4]

However it has since been demonstrated that the changes to the king's council came later, between 1536 and 1540, and that they were really Cromwell's response to a political crisis rather than part of a fully worked out programme of administrative reform. In 1536–37 in the aftermath of Henry's break with Rome, he was accused by the leaders of the Pilgrimage of Grace, among others, of being a base-born and 'evil' counsellor who had lead the king astray. Nobles like Suffolk and Norfolk may even have orchestrated these calls and they certainly looked to take advantage of them. Cromwell saw that membership of the council had suddenly become a hot political issue. Ten years earlier, Cardinal Wolsey had drawn up plans to create a council attendant on the king comprising 20 of the principal officers of state and household. Cromwell now seized on these plans and adapted them to give the nobles what they wanted while trying to safeguard his own influence with the king.[5]

Under the Act of Precedence of 1539 there were deemed to be eleven 'great offices of state' in England. Six of them were 'noble' offices, derived from military and royal household arrangements of the central middle ages. They included those of the Earl Marshal, Lord Admiral and Great Chamberlain and these could only be held by a peer. The remaining five were the 'administrative' offices of Lord Chancellor, Lord Privy Seal, Lord Treasurer, Lord President of the Council and the Principal Secretary. All but the last could only be held by those of the rank of baron or above. Under a proclamation of early 1540, those who held these offices automatically became members of a new royal council. Within the ranks of the new body, 'administrative' positions outranked the 'noble' positions and councillors also became the highest-ranked peers in England, regardless of how recently, or how long ago, they had been ennobled. In order to safeguard their status, the highest aristocrats were given both an 'administrative' and a 'noble' or household office. Thus the Duke of Suffolk became Lord President of the Council and Lord Great Master, chief of the king's household.

Dr Starkey has shown how, far from splitting what became known as the 'Privy Council' from the royal household in the way Elton described, these reforms actually pulled the two closer together. The position of Cromwell himself, the supposed architect of the 'revolution,' illustrates the close connection between the two. In 1539 Cromwell, who was Baron of Wimbledon and the king's secretary, was made Lord Privy Seal. In that year he also became 'chief nobleman' of the king's privy chamber making him Henry's principal body servant. These positions gave him great political clout but, as a mere baron, he still lacked the status of his aristocratic rivals on the newly constituted royal council. That is why on 18 April 1540 he was made Earl of Essex and Lord Great Chamberlain at a stroke. This promotion to magnate status enabled him hold both an 'administrative' and 'household' office of the highest rank, allowing him to operate on equal terms with his rivals.

It seemed that Cromwell had beaten his enemies by joining them. But within three months they had capitalised on Henry's unhappiness in marriage to Anne of Cleves to bring the new earl down on charges of supporting religious radicals in Calais. On 10 August 1540 the new council was given its own secretariat and began its official existence. Throughout the mid 1540s it met regularly in the private apartments of the king. Not surprisingly, more members of the aristocracy were prompted to seek conciliar and court offices in order to safeguard the status of their titles. Thereafter the aristocracy was formally entrenched at the heart of Henry's regime and denied any commoner the sort of influence over the king that Wolsey and Cromwell had enjoyed. This reinforced the king's ties with the aristocracy serving him, but it also served the peerage's wish to maintain its central role in the government of the kingdom.[6]

The peers of the council took an active part in maintaining law and order within their areas of influence and on the national scene. In war some commanded the different main sections of the royal army. Apart from along the border areas with Wales and Scotland and in Ireland, there was no English equivalent of the provincial governors of France or the Netherlands. However in time of civil unrest or external threats, privy councillors like the dukes of Norfolk and Suffolk could be appointed temporarily as lords-lieutenant with power to command the levies of armed men in the counties. Permanent lords-lieutenant were not appointed until 1585.

In addition to the royal council sitting in Star Chamber, Henry VIII's realm had a considerable number of judicial tribunals, the most important of which sat at Westminster Hall during the four legal terms of the year. The court of King's Bench was the court of instance for writs of the Crown. It had jurisdiction in all civil and criminal matters in which the king was concerned. It also had the power to correct errors in other courts, issuing writs to bring such cases before it. The Court of Common Pleas was the oldest of the common law courts. It heard all civil cases between parties relating to title to land. The Exchequer Court heard cases concerning the collection of the king's revenues from his feudal estates.

In addition there was a large group of courts exercising the king's 'equitable' jurisdiction. The most important was Chancery, which judged civil cases but allowed litigants to avoid the standardised and hidebound pleading procedures, the 'forms of action', used at common law. It sought to adjudicate on the merits of each case and arrive at a common sense outcome for the parties. This made it a popular court in which to litigate. Delays rapidly built up in the 1520s under Chancellors Wolsey and More. The Court of Requests performed a related function for those who were too poor to sue at common law. This court heard petitions or 'poor men's causes' and judged cases according to equity. These considerations also made it a popular court in which to fight civil cases, but its primary concern was with infringements of rights, particularly of the customary rights of tenants on manorial lands. It routinely dealt with allegations of sharp practice by landlords, such as enclosing of common land and rack-renting.

In the 1530s a range of new financial courts of record capable of enforcing their own orders and adjudicating disputes, was established. The first was the Court of Augmentations set up in 1536 to deal with all new income from crown lands and specifically that from monastic lands. The Court of First Fruits and Tenths was established in 1540 to administer ecclesiastical revenues raised for the king under Reformation legislation of the 1530s. By 1542 the Court of Wards and Liveries was responsible for all the feudal revenues owed to the king.

Twice a year 12 judges from the courts at Westminster Hall made 'circuits' of the counties, holding assize courts (from Old French *aseeir* 'sit at') in over 70 towns at which they heard more serious civil and criminal cases. These circuits encompassed the whole kingdom, except for the shires of the palatinate counties of Chester and Durham which had their own judicial arrangements. The work of the judges of assize complemented and completed that of the Justices of the Peace. These were gentry or noble landowners empowered to meet four times a year, at 'quarter-sessions' to try cases involving land, debts, felonies and misdemeanours. JPs also regulated local markets, weights and measurements, prices and wages in conformity with national legislation. They were empowered to raise armed men within the county for its defence or to maintain law and order. They were also prominent in the special commissions of enquiry or 'oyer et terminer' which, like their Yorkist predecessors, the Tudors empanelled regularly to investigate particular problems, such as instances of corruption or civic disturbances in the counties.[7]

Much of the work carried out by Tudor JPs had, until the fifteenth century, been done by sheriffs. Under the Tudors the sheriffs' role was significantly diminished but they still retained some important functions. In Henry VIII's reign there were 28 shrievalties in England covering 38 counties. Each sheriff served annually and was either a prominent local landowner and/or a courtier close to the king. His responsibilities included summoning juries, serving royal writs, especially those for elections to parliament, and overseeing the execution of sentences. He was assisted by a legally trained deputy, the undersheriff, and his officials, the coroners and escheators. There were between four and six coroners in each county who investigated criminal matters relating to murder and suicide and other felonies. Escheators were responsible for the king's rights over feudal lands in each county. They were appointed annually and reported to the Lord Treasurer.

At the lowest level of administration were the manorial courts which possessed jurisdiction over contracts made within the power of the manorial lord and over civil debts worth less than 40s. They also held an ancient criminal jurisdiction over trespass, assaults not occasioning bloodshed and damage to crops by animals. By the sixteenth century they had little if any judicial clout and were instruments of local agricultural administration. Their officers, the bailiffs and constables, assisted all other royal officials at a parish level.[8]

This system of gentry administration worked well enough in lowlands England but not at the margins of the kingdom. Traditionally, powerful magnates were appointed as 'wardens of the marches', to administer the counties along England's borders with Scotland and Wales. These men, such as the Percy earls of Northumberland, were largely independent lords whose military power had been a major factor in the Wars of the Roses. Wary of relying on such 'overmighty subjects' the Tudors preferred initially to rely on a combination of lesser lords and on special regional councils with wide civil and criminal jurisdictions.

The Council of the North was first established in 1525 when Lord Dacre was dismissed from the wardenships of the West, Middle, and East marches, covering Westmorland, Northumberland and Cumberland. It was first under the nominal presidency of Henry's natural son the Earl of Richmond and later under Bishop Cuthbert Tunstall of Durham. It never proved very effective in administering the crown's holdings in the north and in 1537 it was re-established after the defeat of the Pilgrimage of Grace as a judicial and administrative body with no responsibility for the king's lands.[9]

The early Tudor administration of Wales through marcher lordships was complex and often ineffective. Of the various lands of the principality, some owed direct loyalty to Henry, others only indirectly through the lords who held them. This created a jungle of conflicting and competing legal jurisdictions and although most areas were nominally under English sovereignty, the English common law did not apply. Wolsey had issued ordinances designed to impose some order but neither these, nor establishment of the Council in the Marches of Wales in 1525 as Princess Mary's council, had resolved the problems. Henry's need to enforce the break with Rome throughout his dominions prompted a resolution. Between 1529 and 1543 Wales was progressively united judicially and politically to England. The principality and marcher lordships were reorganised into 12 Welsh shires. English common and statue law were introduced and royal officials along the English model were appointed. The Welsh counties were organised into four judicial circuits and county sessions were held twice a year. The Council in the marches of Wales was once more reconstituted. It had wide civil and criminal jurisdiction, acting as a local Star Chamber, although in no sense derived directly from its Westminster namesake. Based at Ludlow, it supervised the Welsh shires as well as Herefordshire, Shropshire, Worcestershire, Gloucestershire and Cheshire.

There was in addition a short-lived Council in the West. It was established after Henry Courtenay, Marquis of Exeter, was convicted of treason in 1538. He was brought down for his support of Princess Mary and resistance to Cromwell. Courtenay's lands in Devon and Cornwall were then administered by the Council under the presidency of Lord John Russell. Although he became the dominant noble in the south-west during the mid-Tudor years and established his family's fortunes there, the Council itself was no longer in existence by 1547.[10]

THE FRENCH ROYAL ADMINISTRATION AND JUDICIARY

In France the king made law by edicts or *ordonnances* which he did not have to pass through a representative legislative body as did the king of England.

Yet, just as the legislative power of the English monarch was at its most ample in Parliament, so in French legal theory, the king's legislative power was most secure, most 'absolute,' when he acted with 'good counsel'. The difficulty lay in defining exactly what 'good counsel' was beyond a notion that the king should confer with the great and the good of the kingdom. It could be interpreted very narrowly to mean only those whom the king chose to consult, or widely to include the judges of the Parlement of Paris, the highest law court in France, who scrutinised all royal edicts before they were enforceable. At the start of the sixteenth century this imprecision was reflected in the fact that the royal council was technically a very large body comprising hundreds of men of importance throughout the realm, all of whom bore the title *conseiller du roi*. However it never met as a body and well before Francis 's reign the king's advisors were actually drawn from a much smaller group of powerful individuals.

The French conciliar organization was rather more complex than in England with a number of different bodies assisting in discrete, although often overlapping, aspects of the king's authority. Each had its own particular staff, procedures and times of meeting. The largest of these was the *Grand Conseil*, an exclusively judicial body. It could hear cases brought directly to it or on appeal from lower courts and from the Parlement of Paris. The council that dealt with the routine administration of the kingdom was the *conseil privé* or *conseil des parties*. It met in the afternoons and not usually in the king's presence. When required, his financial and legal specialists, the *gens de finance* and *maîtres des requêtes*, assisted in its deliberations.

The French equivalent of what in England was eventually the privy council, was the *conseil étroit* or 'narrow' council. Under Francis I it comprised roughly 12 of his immediate relatives, the highest princes of the realm and his favourites. In addition to its political function it could act as a judicial body, hearing matters referred to it by the *Grand Conseil* and itself referring cases to that body. Within the *conseil étroit* there was an even smaller group of no more than three or four of the king's most trusted advisors. It met him each morning and was thus known as the *conseil du matin* or, after 1526, as the *conseil des affaires*. Anne de Montmorency, René de Savoie, Philippe de Chabot Lord of Brion, the Chancellors Duprat and Olivier and, later in the reign, Cardinal François de Tournon were its main members.[11]

Carrying out the orders of these powerful bodies was the royal administration under the Chancellor of France, the chief administrative and judicial officer of the realm. He held the Great Seal and supervised the use of other seals which authenticated all the king's documents. The king's secretaries drew up royal acts and ordinances, together with accounts and financial orders. They maintained the records of the king's various councils, countersigned his letters and his instructions to ambassadors or provincial governors. The secretaries were also the king's advisors. Men such as Florimond Robertet, Nicholas de Neufville, Jean Breton and Guillaume

Bochetel developed expertise in a number of fields of royal business and by the 1540s the most senior of them were wealthy and influential men in their own right, full members of the king's *conseil privé*. Their families were closely inter-related and concentrated among themselves enormous financial power and political influence. Francis I's royal secretaries became the forbears, in many cases literally, of the 'secretaries of state' who emerged in the latter half of the sixteenth century and of the royal ministers of the seventeenth century.[12]

The most important royal representatives in the localities were the provincial governors. By the start of Francis I's reign all 11 provinces of France had a governor who was appointed personally by the king. They were designated royal councillors and their broad duty according to one letter of provision signed by Francis was 'to represent our person in all affairs of the said province.' As *lieutenants-généraux* of the king, they had quasi-regal status and were usually drawn from the wealthiest and most prestigious families in the province. The governors were important power brokers who were expected by their contemporaries to represent them effectively to the king and to secure from him offices and pensions within his armies and administration. They fostered close associations with important individuals, families and corporations within the province. Governors were also major players in the national and international politics of the realm. Anne de Montmorency, the Great Master of the royal household was governor of Languedoc between 1526 and 1544. Philippe de Chabot, the Admiral of France, was also governor of the politically sensitive duchy of Burgundy between 1526 and 1543. Under Francis, governors were not allowed to nominate their successors but in several cases, such as the Bourbons in Picardy, and both the Chabannes and Trivulce in Lyonnais, he did allow several members of one family to succeed each other as governor. This had the advantage of maintaining continuity within the provincial elite but it was only long after Francis's reign that such families began to establish dynastic holds on provincial governorships.[13]

At the provincial level the judicial and administrative systems ran alongside each other. Below the provincial governor was the *bailli* or *sénéchal*, who was invariably a nobleman and the principal means of communication between the royal regime and those in his immediate locality. There were approximately one hundred *baillages* in France at the start of Francis I's reign. Each *bailliage* grouped together a number of smaller units called variously, *châtellenie*, *prevoté*, or *vicomté* consisting of a castle and its dependant lands and parishes owned by its lord or *châtellain*. They had seigneurial courts staffed by magistrates who heard civil and criminal cases concerning those whose low social status did not entitle them to appear in higher courts.

Baillis had wide military and judicial functions, encompassing most of those, which, in England, were entrusted to the JPs and judges of assize. They kept registers of all those in their *baillages* who owed the king military service, summoning them at the king's command and in response to any local unrest. They also supervised munitions and fortifications, published royal ordinances, supervised local commerce and municipal elections in their areas. The *bailli*'s judicial responsibilities were exercised by a legal expert, the *lieutenant-général*, who was himself assisted by a large group of lawyers and officials. The *baillage* court had wide original and appellate jurisdictions, judging cases involving nobles and royal servants as well as ecclesiastical benefices and hearing cases on appeals from *châtellenies*. Because of their high standing among the French nobility, *baillis* were routinely employed by the king away from their localities and were often at court. For example, Jean de Dinteville, the *bailli* of Troyes, was a *maître d'hôtel* or steward in the royal household. He was also frequently an envoy to England and appears in that capacity in Holbein's famous 1533 painting, *The Ambassadors*.[14]

From the *baillage* courts appeals lay to the provincial law courts, the Parlements. There were five at Francis's accession: Dijon, Grenoble, Aix-en-Provence,Toulouse and Bordeaux. Francis made the *Echiquier* of Rouen in Normandy a Parlement in 1515. The equivalent body in Brittany, sitting at Rennes, was the *Grand Jours*. These provincial bodies had developed from courts which had once administered the great territorial lordships prior to their incorporation into the realm of France. Their judges now exercised royal judicial authority but always remained alert as to how the king's legislation sat with the long-standing legal traditions of the locality.

The Parlement of Paris was the oldest and most prestigious sovereign court in the kingdom. It heard cases on appeal from all over northern France, apart from Normandy and Brittany, as well as from central France as far south as Lyon. Nevertheless, it had to contend with the rival authority of a number of other high courts whose jurisdiction in financial matters broadly paralleled that of the Exchequer court in England. One was the *Chambre des comptes* which heard cases relating to the king's finances and collection of his revenues. Another was *Cour des aides* which decided matters relating to the payment of taxes while the *Cour des monnaies* considered cases involving counterfeit currency and devaluation of the coinage. Mention has already been made of the wide jurisdiction of the *Grand Conseil*.

The Parlement of Paris also had an original jurisdiction as the protector of the fundamental laws of France and the competent authority to adjudicate between the office of kingship and the individual who exercised it. The Parlement checked all royal legislation against its interpretation of these laws. Only when it had approved a royal edict was it registered, and so given effect. It could refuse to register a particular piece of legislation and remonstrate with the king over it. The king could insist that it be registered by issuing one or more *lettres de jussion*. If the Parlement still resisted, he could come in person to hold a royal session, later called a *lit-de-justice*; a special meeting at which he resumed his full powers as the kingdom's highest judge under God to insist that the legislation be registered. At this point the Parlement had to capitulate. This is exactly what happened in 1518 when, after two years of wrangling, the Parlement still refused to ratify the Concordat of Bologna which Francis had agreed with Pope Leo X and which had been promulgated in 1516. On 24 July 1527 Francis held another *lit-de-justice* at which he retrospectively ratified all Louise of Savoy's decisions which the Parlement had challenged during the king's absence in Spain the previous year. In all these controversies, the crown's judicial officers asserted that nobody could question the king's exercise of his authority. As Chancellor Poyet told the Parlement of Rouen in 1540 'once the prince has decreed them [his laws], one must proceed; no one has the right to interpret, adjust or diminish them.' In fact most legal theorists echoed Claude de Seyssel's view that at the very least the king's 'absolute' power was 'bridled' by his religious duty as the 'most Christian king' and the fundamental laws of France. Nevertheless, the Parlement certainly had a hard time under Francis as it strove to defend what Professor Shennan has called 'the paradoxical principle' at the heart of French (and indeed English) constitutional theory. Namely, that royal sovereignty and its limitations existed together and that one did not diminish the other.[15]

The judges of the Parlements were customarily ennobled on the grounds that administering royal justice entitled them to higher than ordinary status. Their offices were also venal, meaning that they could purchase them and on payment of further money to the king, even pass them on to their sons. Many *parlementaires*, such as Jean and his son Odet de Selve, members of the Parlement of Toulouse, rose to prominence as jurists and diplomats for Francis I. The *parlementaires* constituted a formidable social and political oligarchy in the regions where they worked, jealously asserting their rights and privileges against other powerful groups including town councils, provincial assemblies and royal governors.[16]

The ability to purchase a royal office had existed well before 1515 but became institutionalised under Francis. Venality of judicial and fiscal office subsequently became one of the distinguishing characteristics of *ancien régime* France. A prospective office holder had to satisfy his intended colleagues of his qualification for the position, which normally included university education. Offices were keenly sought among those qualified and who were eager to gain, for themselves or their sons, the social and financial advantages royal offices entailed, chiefly exemption from direct taxation. Faced with increasing costs, the king created more of these offices and thus a market in crown service. For example, 40 new councillorships were created in the Parlement of Paris between 1522 and 1543. There were 11 *maîtres des requêtes* in 1515 and 18 by 1547. Creating more offices helped the king's immediate needs but created longer term difficulties. Those office holders already in post resented the proliferation of new-comers as tending to diminish the status, and value, of their offices. Secondly, the king may have had more officers in name, but having sold those offices once, he then had no direct control over their subsequent sales. Purchasing them again should their holders prove incapable was not always easy given the tight financial circumstances he was always in and which had compelled him to create venal offices in the first place. Contemporaries such as Seyssel and Rabelais frequently satirised the corruption and pretentiousness of administrative nobles. Office holding strengthened the numbers of lawyers involved in royal government but not necessarily its effectiveness.[17]

THE NETHERLANDS AND SPAIN, ROYAL ADMINISTRATION AND JUDICIARY

Like Francis I, Charles V made law by royal edicts. He was also expected to take counsel from his leading nobles and judicial officials and to honour the promises he made at his accession to respect the existing customs and privileges of his many different subjects. Charles considered that the best way to do this was to deal separately with each of his realms. He had ten different councils alone to advise him on his Hispanic, Italian and American dominions. In Spain he was formally advised by the councils of Castile and Aragon which also had judicial roles. There was also the Council of Finances established in 1522 to devise a yearly budget and to control all Charles's income and expenditure. In 1526 a new Council of State was established as the supreme advisory body for all Charles's Iberian dominions. However, the emperor preferred still to use those already existing and separate councils in Castile and Aragon. The Council of State did assist Empress Isabella and Prince Philip whenever they acted as regents. These various councils were all staffed mainly by middle-ranking noblemen assisted by legal specialists, the *letrados*.

In the Netherlands, Charles ruled through regents. The first was his aunt, Margaret of Austria. The regent's powers were prescribed in a series of public and private documents drawn up under the emperor's instruction. A public ordinance gave her extensive power to act as Charles's representative and was designed to consolidate her position against possible opposition. The 'instruction' and 'restriction' were private documents and were more narrowly prescriptive. They detailed specific procedures the regent was to follow in administering her charge. They reserved certain matters for the emperor himself and in general directed the regent to behave in any situation, not finally as she thought best, but as she believed Charles himself would act.[18]

Margaret had her own council although in practice she tended to rely on the advice of favoured individuals. This caused some resentment among Flemish and Dutch nobles. Margaret died in 1530 and Charles's sister Mary succeeded her as regent. Mary was advised by three 'Collateral Councils' based at Brussels. The first was the Council of State, an executive board for the Netherlands, on which sat twelve, mainly Flemish, nobles. The second was the Council of Finance which operated like its Spanish counterpart. The third was the Privy or Secret Council. Like its French cousin, it was staffed by prominent administrators and dealt with routine judicial and administrative matters.

Charles's authority in the Holy Roman Empire and the Habsburg hereditary lands was exercised by his brother Ferdinand acting in a variety of different legal capacities. In Austria and the Tyrol Ferdinand initially ruled as Charles's lieutenant but with very limited authority. He could not negotiate with local representatives without referring everything to his brother. Between 1522 and 1525 the emperor conceded to Ferdinand, first secretly and then publicly, the possession of the Habsburg hereditary lands. This decision augmented Ferdinand's authority and enabled him to deal directly with local nobles and to build among them significant personal loyalty to him. It was Ferdinand who laid the foundations of what was to become the Austro-Hungarian empire. In 1521 he married Anne of Hungary, the sister of King Louis II. At Louis's death in 1526, Ferdinand was elected to the crowns of Hungary and Bohemia.

In the Holy Roman Empire Ferdinand also ruled initially as the emperor's deputy and chair of the *Reichsregiment*. This was an executive committee with representatives of the emperor and the German princes, including the seven electors, which administered the *Reich* in his absence. The emperor Maximilian had hoped that it might be used as an instrument of royal authority but its princely members were determined that it should operate to restrict his freedom of action. Charles resented its existence but had been forced to accept it 1519 as part of the deal he struck with the electors to secure the imperial title. He confirmed its authority at the Diet of Worms in 1521. Under these arrangements Ferdinand could do nothing unilaterally and for a decade until Charles's return to Germany in 1530, the *Reichsregiment* prevented any co-ordinated German action being taken against the Turkish threat in the east or against Luther's supporters.

In 1531, following his coronation as emperor the previous year, Charles finally persuaded the seven imperial Electors to take the constitutionally unwarranted step of electing Ferdinand as 'King of the Romans' and thus his recognised successor. Although this decision ran contrary to Charles's own dynastic instincts, which were to keep the title for his own son Philip, he also needed an effective ruler in Germany at a time of increasing religious and political unrest. There is some evidence that in 1546–47 he contemplated asking Ferdinand to renounce the imperial succession in favour of Philip but rumours about this caused such resentment that the idea was quickly abandoned. Ferdinand's election enhanced his personal authority in the German lands and the *Reichsregiment* lapsed. No 'limitation' was issued when Ferdinand was granted powers of government in the empire in 1531. Thus his power was, in theory at least, more extensive than that held by Charles's regents in the Netherlands and Spain.[19]

Apart from, and in a sense over, all Charles's regents and their councils was the emperor's own Council of State, which travelled with him on his endless peregrinations around Europe. It was broadly the equivalent of the English Privy Council. Initially it comprised only Charles's Burgundian aristocrats but, during the 1520s and 1530s, Spanish and Italians grandees were gradually brought into it. Its principal sphere of activity was advising the emperor's on foreign relations, and whether or not to go to war. The Council of State also advised on appointments to governorships and vice-regal positions throughout the empire. Charles insisted upon handling major appointments himself rather than delegating this responsibility to his regents. This sometimes frustrated his regents who were deprived of the opportunity to reward deserving subjects quickly with royal offices and pensions.

From 1521 the Council of State was dominated by the imperial Grand Chancellor, Mercurino di Gattinara, who co-ordinated the various secretariats which reported to the council. A Spanish secretariat handled correspondence and legal papers relating to Spain, Italy and the Mediterranean. A French secretariat dealt with ambassadors in France, with matters arising in the Netherlands and with correspondence relating to German affairs. Gattinara did more than any other to convince Charles of the importance of his imperial destiny and the need to master Italy and the French king. He tried unsuccessfully to make all the emperor's councils and secretariats work harmoniously under him towards this aim but was defeated by the sheer diversity of administrative traditions within Charles's dominions. Although capable and vastly experienced, Gattinara's insistent didactism rather wearied the emperor as he matured and their relations were not always close.[20]

As in England after Wolsey, it was the royal secretary, or rather secretaries, who succeeded Gattinara as Charles's principal advisors. In Spain, Francisco de los Cobos, the Secretary of the Council of Finances, supervised the emperor's affairs in Castile, in Italy and in the Americas. Like many of his French counterparts, he became wealthy on the strength of royal service. He took a share of the profits of customs on imports of silver bullion given to him by Charles. In 1539 he acted as regent in Spain and four years later, when prince Philip was regent for his absent father, Cobos was his chief counsellor. Charles advised his son of Cobos, 'no one knows as much about my affairs as he and you will be glad of his service' but also warned Philip against allowing him undue influence or letting him pass his privileges on to his relatives. Meanwhile, Nicolas Perrenot, the Lord of Granvelle, Charles's secretary for the Franco-Burgundian territories, also rose to prominence. By the mid 1530s the emperor trusted him implicitly. He described Granvelle to Philip as his best guide in international policy' and advised his son to keep him close, 'for he can instruct you on many things.'[21]

In the kingdoms of Castile and Aragon the royal administration did not reach into the localities in quite the same way as it did elsewhere in Europe. The great majority of the land in Charles's Spanish realms was owned by a relatively small number of aristocrats. Here the strong tradition of nobles exercising power directly on their lands with limited reference to the monarchy continued under the emperor. Charles relied for the maintenance of law and order in large parts of his kingdoms on these nobles and the clergy who had their own courts. In Castile he also looked to the urban militia groups, the *Hermandades* or 'brotherhoods' to keep law and order in their local areas. In towns across both realms, there were elected magistrates, the *alcaldes* and town councillors, the *regidores*, who conducted the business of government and heard judicial cases at first instance. They also supervised trading in the town and it was from their ranks that the towns represented in the Cortes drew their delegates. These offices were jealously contested among faction-ridden oligarchies of prominent families but the crown strove to influence these elections, letting it be known who its favoured candidates were.

In an attempt to enforce royal authority and to increase the crown's influence in urban areas in Castile, Queen Isabella had also appointed local governors based in a significant number of towns. It was the responsibility of these *corregidores* to ensure that royal edicts were obeyed and to supervise the administration of the town council. They also ensured that the town's walls were repaired, its markets properly maintained and its streets cleaned. They exercised judicial functions, among the most important of which was to hear complaints against aristocrats whose lands lay near or next to towns. They frequently attempted to expand their holdings at the municipality's expense. Some *corregidores* were very effective in combating these encroachments with the support of the royal council. Nevertheless, towns with *corregidores* were still a minority and have been described as 'a small chain of islands in an ocean of aristocratic estates.' *Corregidores* had always to proceed cautiously because the crown also depended on the goodwill of powerful aristocrats. In the years immediately prior to Charles's accession, the reputation of *corregidores* declined. Many used their positions to profit personally or were absent from their posts for long periods. They were often figures of hate during the revolt of the *Comuneros*. After the revolt was suppressed Charles renewed the system of *corregidores.* He increased their salaries and social status in order to discourage profiteering. He also cracked down on absenteeism and insisted that they had sufficient legal training to do their jobs effectively.[22]

As was the case in France, England and the Netherlands, in Castile and Aragon the judicial system was interwoven with the royal administration. The elected magistrates, as well as the *hermandades* and the *corregidores* all referred civil or criminal matters on appeal to a higher judicial body known as the *audiencia.* The Castilian *audiencia* was established permanently at Valladolid by Isabella in 1489 and supervised justice in the north. After the re-conquest of Granada, a similar body was set up there for the south and subsidiary courts were also established at Seville and Santiago. Each of the three kingdoms within the crown of Aragon also had its own *audiencia.* The sovereign councils of Castile and Aragon also acted as the supreme courts in the same way as their French and English counterparts. In addition, the Cortes of Aragon maintained a standing committee, the *Diputación*, whose role was to ensure that laws were properly enacted having regard to traditional liberties of the kingdom. There was also an hereditary official, the Justiciar who supervised royal officials to guard against abuses of these liberties. The kingdoms of Valencia and Catalonia each had their own *Diputación*.[23]

In the Netherlands the systems of administration and justice paralleled those in France but there was great variety in the names and duties of different officials. As in France, the most important provincial officials were the governors, or *stadholders*. All provinces of the Habsburg Netherlands apart from Brabant, which lay near to Brussels, had governors. Like their French counterparts, these men were all drawn from the high nobility and had dual roles of representing the emperor's authority in their province while also assisting him in the wider affairs of the Netherlands and the empire beyond it. They were the military commanders of the province, responsible for its defence and upholding law and order. With a few exceptions, they also had the right to nominate candidates to municipal offices during annual elections to them, the so-called 'renewal of the government.' Under Charles, half the appointments to *stadholderates* were concentrated among seven families: the Croys, Nassaus, Lalaings, Egmonts, Lannoys, Berghes and Montmorencys. Chief among them was René de Châlons, the Prince of Orange and holder of the possessions of the Nassau family in the Netherlands from 1538. In the 1540s he was governor of Holland, Zeeland, Utrecht and Gelderland. He was also one of Charles's principal favourites and foremost military commanders. He was killed by canon ball shrapnel in front of a grief-stricken emperor at the siege of Saint-Dizier in 1544. His family later played a prominent part in the revolt against Philip II.[24]

The main provincial officials were the *drosten* or *baljuws*, the equivalents of the French *baillis*. The lowest royal officer was the *schout* or sheriff who, in towns and most rural areas, was responsible for maintaining law and order. In rural areas the *schouts* reported to *baljuws* and in urban areas they worked with, but were not responsible to, the town council – the *raad* or *vroedschap* headed by the burgomasters. Appeals from these officials and the town courts lay to the provincial high council, or *Hof* which acted as an administrative centre and judicial court. It also enforced Charles's fiscal orders in the localities. The councillors and judges of these courts were increasingly drawn from the ranks of trained legal officials rather than from the military nobility. Above the provincial courts was the central supreme court of the Netherlands, the Great Council or *Grote Raad* which sat at Mechelen.[25]

THE EXTENT OF ROYAL AUTHORITY

Francis, Henry and Charles were all active legislators who extended the royal writ further than their predecessors. In ordinary circumstances, their laws were effectively promulgated and the regime of each king maintained reasonably good levels of public order. Criminals were convicted and punished and civil cases adjudicated by due process, however devised. Yet for all the undoubted developments in administrative and judicial competence observable in the early sixteenth century, monarchs often still had difficulty in securing immediate or full compliance with their commands.

The failure of the so-called Amicable Grant in England shows how a royal regime could not necessarily depend on the co-operation of its subjects when there was no clear agreement that it had a right to demand something. In the spring of 1525 Cardinal Wolsey tried to raise a voluntary grant of money to Henry so that he could capitalise on Francis I's defeat at Pavia in February by launching another invasion of France. Coming as it did on the heels of the taxes already agreed by Parliament in 1523, the demand caused widespread resentment. Commissioners were sent out in April to levy this extra-parliamentary tax of a sixth on goods of the laity and one third on those of the clergy. The inhabitants of some areas of the country simply refused to pay, pleading relative poverty. Others, such as those in East Anglia, contributed small amounts and in parts of Suffolk there was even a small-scale uprising. The nobility and gentry in the localities evidently had no appetite at that moment for war with France nor for giving the king more money themselves, nor yet for screwing it out of their own tenants. Without their support Wolsey had to abandon the scheme. Instead he negotiated a peace settlement with France which, as he later proudly proclaimed to the king's councillors, gave Henry 'more treasure out of France yearly than all his revenues and customs amount to.' The French never paid anything like the amount Wolsey suggested but they did contribute significantly to Henry's income and, doubtless to the relief of his loving subjects, he did not again ask for extra money to go to war for another 20 years.[26]

Another striking instance of the limits on royal authority comes from France usually described, under Francis, as the most obedient realm in Europe. In August 1539 the king issued the Ordinance of Villers-Cotterêts. With 192 clauses it was one of the longest and important of the reign. It was aimed at improving the judicial system. Among its more important orders were that all legal documents were to be written in French rather than Latin and that registers of birth and death were to be kept in all parishes. Confraternities, associations of masters and workers in particular trades formed for religious and charitable purposes, were to be banned. They were thought to be a focus for social and religious unrest and a strike among print workers in Lyon in April 1539 was probably what prompted the banning order.

As Professor Knecht has noted in presenting evidence from the region around Nantes, there are strong indications that the edict's provisions were not implemented throughout the whole of France, or at least not immediately. Latin continued to be used in legal documents in many areas well into the eighteenth century. In the Nantes region, the births and deaths continued to be recorded in the manner they had been since the early fifteenth century. Parish clerks conformed to the new ordinance only insofar as it did not clash with established practice. Each year, registers were supposed to be sent to the nearest *baillage* court but in the Nantes region there is no evidence that this was done. The order for the abolition of confraternities was widely resented and ignored. A number of them had received concessions to operate again within 18 months of the edict's promulgation and there is ample evidence of their existence 20 years later. The dilatory response to the ordinance of Villers-Cotterêts is one instance of how far practice could lag behind the theory of the king's 'absolute' authority.[27]

Monarchs were also faced not just with reluctance to comply with their instructions, but outright rebellion over grievances such as tax demands, religious changes or the more usual unrest over food shortages. In these circumstances they were necessarily dependent upon the nobility to contain unrest. In most instances of civil riot and disorder the nobility did intervene to curb at least the worst excesses of violence while officers of the regime bought time in negotiations. Popular uprisings often petered out as quickly as they began and most were expressions of localised grievances or problems. If a coherent set of demands were formulated among rioters these could become the basis of negotiation, or abandoned as part of the process of finding a solution with the authorities. At heart, most sixteenth century rebels were reluctant ones. Aware of the enormity of the crime of rebellion and the drastic penalties the king could in theory impose, they were usually anxious to raise their grievances, while assuring the sovereign of their ultimate loyalty and looking for a settlement.[28]

This did not always happen of course. The revolt of the *Comuneros*, in Castile in 1520–21 was no 'little local difficulty' but a large-scale revolt in Castile in which Charles almost lost his kingdom. Ferdinand and Isabella had tried to work with the great nobles, respecting their traditional and major role in governing the localities in return for an acknowledgement of royal authority in central government. They continued to give leading nobles sizeable pensions and positions of military command. Much of their success also came from doing as Charles VIII and Louis XII did in France, that is, directing noble aggression against a common external enemy. The re-conquest of the Moslem kingdom of Granada was begun in 1482 and it fell to the Spanish a decade later. New titles were created and lands were given to nobles in the conquered territory, no longer from the royal patrimony.

Charles arrived in Castile in 1517 with a large Flemish entourage, speaking no Castilian and just as much Catalan (the dominant language in the crown of Aragon). He packed his popular, Castilian-born, brother Ferdinand off to Germany and appointed his entourage to a host of offices in the Castilian administration. He demanded subsidies from the Cortes of Castile while ignoring its request that he remain in the country and learn the language. The revolt broke out in May 1520 shortly after Charles had left for

Germany. It was led by the town of Toledo and sustained by the middle ranks of society, both noble and non-noble, in 14 of the 18 towns represented in the Castilian Cortes. Its long-term causes centred firstly, on tensions between the towns and the high aristocracy and secondly, on dissatisfaction among textile manufacturers and workers about the export of wool which deprived them of raw materials for their trade and the opportunity to build up an indigenous textiles industry.

Towns were divided between each other and within themselves over support for the revolt but, by July, a *junta* had been formed which demanded the dismissal of Charles's Flemish councillors, a reduction on the rate of royal taxes which the towns paid, and regular meetings of the Cortes. By September it was threatening to take over the functions of the government and to depose Charles. Fortunately for the absent king, the high nobility refused to countenance the revolt. Summoning their retinues of armed men, Fadrique Enríquez and Iñigo de Velasco, the Admiral and the Constable of Castile respectively, formed an army which defeated that of the *Comuneros* at Villalar in April 1521. During the following six months the revolt was snuffed out and by the time Charles returned in 1522 the crisis was over. The aristocracy had not intervened in defence of the king from any great personal loyalty, but because their own interests were threatened by widespread disorder and because they wanted to maintain the advantageous relationship with the crown established under the Catholic Kings.[29]

In 1538–39 Charles V faced a revolt in his home city of Ghent. It centred on the craft guilds' objections to extra taxes levied for the war against Francis three years earlier. The revolt caused real destruction and instability in Ghent, reaching its height in the summer of 1539. Charles was perhaps fortunate that by the time he arrived in Flanders in January 1540 with 5000 troops, the revolt had lost impetus and the town was ready to submit. In May 1540 by an ordinance known as the *Concessio Carolina* he imposed an exemplary punishment. He deprived Ghent of its privileges, removed the craft guilds from any role in its government and imposed a huge fine on the citizens. Twenty-five of the rebel leaders were executed and a new fortress was built in the middle of the city. Charles was very fortunate that at the time of the unrest he was at peace with Francis. Apart from allowing him to travel through France to Flanders in the autumn of 1539, the brief *entente* between them dissuaded Francis from stirring further trouble in Flanders and allowed the emperor to assemble sufficient troops there to overawe the populace.

Three years earlier Henry VIII had also faced a serious revolt. In October 1536 a series of popular uprisings, known collectively as the Pilgrimage of Grace, broke out. Centred in Lincolnshire and Yorkshire, they were prompted by a range of economic grievances, aristocratic resentment of Cromwell's influence over the king and anxiety provoked by the initial dissolution of monastic houses in the north. The rebels included a few nobles like Lord Darcy and gentlemen like Sir Robert Constable together with local town leaders and farmers. The 'Pilgrims' assured the king that they were loyal subjects who only wanted to protect him from heretical 'evil counsellors' about him who had introduced misguided religious changes. By November they numbered 30,000. Faced with an uprising on this scale, the royal regime was unprepared and feigned conciliatory intent while it summoned peers and gentry to arms.

By December a royal army had been formed under the command of the Duke of Norfolk. He met with leaders of the rebels at Pontefract. They were promised pardons, the calling of Parliament and consideration of their grievances if they disbanded, which they quickly did. Had the rebels pressed on and gathered more support among a majority of English nobles anxious about the recent political and religious upheaval, they could have severely tested the Tudor king's grip on the crown. Henry was saved by their loyalty. A second wave of unrest early in 1537 was met by a regime more prepared and it was put down with determined severity. The leaders of the unrest were eventually tried for treason and executed and the dissolution of the monasteries gathered pace.[30]

In the autumn of 1542 Francis I faced the most serious popular revolt of his reign. It was also about taxes, namely the salt-tax or *gabelle* and it broke out in the county of Poitou in the west of France. The king had made several changes to the system of selling salt designed to increase its tax yield. He and the town council of La Rochelle had also disagreed over the way the council was meeting its responsibilities to the king. Unlike Henry VIII who studiously avoided going anywhere near the rebels in 1536–37, in December 1542 Francis entered the lion's den. With the support of the local nobles, and having raised the local men-at-arms, he entered Poitou, detained the leaders of the rebellion and came to La Rochelle. By now the town was anxious to settle its differences with the king. Its councillors admitted rebellion and threw themselves upon his mercy. In an elaborate ritual, staged on 1 January 1543, he censured the rebels for disrupting the realm when he was at war against the emperor. Then, drawing a pointed contrast between himself and Charles at Ghent three years earlier, he pardoned them without imposing any drastic penalties. He had little real choice in the circumstances anyway but within a few years had effectively re-imposed the advantageous sale arrangements. His authority was also finally preserved due to the loyalty of his subjects and the crown's readiness to compromise at least in the short term. Had force been required to suppress the revolt militarily, it would have seriously impaired his war effort against the emperor.[31]

CONCLUSION

Henry VIII, Charles V and Francis I were all obliged by the legal and constitutional traditions of their realms to consult at least their more powerful subjects about decisions which affected the kingdom. Each of them developed the institution of the royal council that he had inherited from his predecessor, striving to make it a more effective instrument not just of consultation but of royal authority. Apart from cutting out dead wood of supernumary councillors, they concentrated real political power in smaller bodies answerable to them directly. Each made their councils, alongside the royal household, the primary focus of the royal affinities they built among nobles. The concentration of political power in the *conseil étroit* in France and especially in the hands of the aristocrats who staffed the Privy Council in England are the best examples of this trend. All three monarchs were keen to extend their authority to the geographical margins of their kingdoms and to consolidate the primacy of their authority as kings and feudal lords, often in the face of local resistance or indifference. Structural changes were introduced to the judicial and administrative systems they inherited, designed to increase the effectiveness of royal officials.

The increasing complexity of government meant that there was also a somewhat contrary impulse, towards the creation of subsidiary councils to deal with discrete aspects of the king's authority or particular regions of the realm. This was particularly true of Charles V's immense empire. In Spain his councils were staffed, not by magnates, but by lesser nobles and the *letrados* whose positions depended directly upon the king. In the Netherlands the councils established for Margaret of Austria and Mary of Hungary as regents of the Netherlands did employ lesser nobles as administrators but they were also designed to give the Flemish and Dutch nobility a means of sharing in the government of the absent overlord. The number of different councils may have reflected the reality of Charles's widespread dominions but it was still rather discomforting to the emperor. Try as he might, he simply could not hope to bring to all his dominions the degree of personal supervision he was able to give to Spain from the mid 1520s and which he believed was appropriate for all of them. As Professor Koenigsberger has observed, despite the immense administrative talent at his command, Charles V still wished to take all major decisions personally. This made it difficult for local governors and viceroys always to act effectively, especially in times of military emergency. Charles therefore appeared to have had the personal control he wanted and which he thought necessary to secure the personal loyalty of his subjects, but at the cost of lost opportunities and administrative and financial inefficiency.[32]

The Tudor monarchy's control of the central areas of England was built upon the efforts of its Yorkist predecessors and it was here that the administrative system outlined above functioned best in ordinary circumstances. The role of JPs at the crown's agents in the localities was established by 1500 but much expanded under Henry, particularly in appointments to county commissions. Henry VIII's incorporation of Wales into English legal administration was in part at least prompted by a wish to extend that kind of control to the margins of realm and to make regional customs and laws subject to royal authority and judicial procedures. Yet Henry had still to rely on a combination of powerful marcher lords, councils and garrisons to control the dangerous territory on the borders with Scotland and with those areas in Ireland beyond English control. Taken together with Wales, these three areas comprised over half the land area of the Tudor state; an area upon which its grip was often quite tenuous.

Both Wolsey and Cromwell strove to cultivate an ethos of crown-controlled magistracy among the nobles and gentry of England. Wolsey's role in extending the reach of the king's justice, particularly through Star Chamber, was important in this regard and his capacity for administrative innovation is only now emerging from the long shadow once cast by Elton's Cromwell. The idea of a Tudor 'revolution in government' is no longer tenable but Cromwell did work diligently to improve the royal administration. He did so more by shortening and clearing traditional lines of communication between the crown and the localities than by replacing them with a self-sustaining administrative system detached from the person of the king.

Francis I was certainly authoritarian and there was no shortage of rhetoric demanding complete and unquestioning obedience to him during his reign. There is ample evidence of his limited patience with the Parlements and he did at times lay down the law in no uncertain terms to his officials and his subjects more generally. Edicts like that of Villers-Cotterêts, show Francis's determination that royal law would be superior to local customary law and traditions throughout his realm. Nevertheless, it is also clear that the rhetoric of his authority often reached further than this practical power and there is no evidence that Francis ever aimed at financial or administrative centralisation of the kingdom *per se*. His realm was three times the size of Henry VIII's principal dominions of England and Wales and had roughly five times the population. Whereas Louis XIV had one royal official for every 250 members of the population, Francis only had about 7–8000 administrators in total or one for every 2–3000 inhabitants. Given these statistics, it was impossible for the royal regime to secure obedience to the king at all times and in every place within the realm. Political statements about the king's all-embracing authority which should never be challenged were usually made by him or his legal officials precisely when that authority had been questioned by the Parlement or by one or another of the many privileged groups or institutions in his kingdom. Of necessity he ruled by a mixture of intimidation and bargaining, giving certain concessions in one area while insisting on obedience in another. He played sections of society off against each other as need arose, trying at all times to maximise his personal authority while respecting sufficiently the legitimate aspirations of the nobility, who were the subjects upon whom he most closely depended.

Considering the size of their various dominions, especially France and Iberia, in an age before modern communications, the sophistication of the royal administrative systems outlined above is impressive. All three kings worked closely with their legal advisors and financial experts to remove failings in judicial or administrative systems whenever they were detected.

They insisted as far as they were able upon exercising the fullest extent of their royal prerogative but sixteenth century royal government was as much characterised by compromise and negotiation as by the issue of summary commands and the rhetoric of an all-powerful monarch to whom total obeisance was due. In order to demonstrate the veracity of this statement and before any final conclusion can be drawn about the effectiveness of the government of these Renaissance monarchs, consideration must be given to the representative institutions, to taxation and to religion in the political life of their respective realms.

5

Governors: Revenue, representation and religion

> ... the prince is created for the subjects (without whom he cannot be a prince) to govern them according to right and reason and defend them and love them as a father does his children ... if he acts differently and instead of protecting his subjects endeavours to oppress and molest them and to deprive them of their ancient liberty, privileges and customs and to command and use them like slaves, he must be regarded not as a prince but as a tyrant.
>
> The States-General of the Netherlands[1]

In the monarchies of early-modern Europe, kings were expected to rule justly and effectively. Individuals at all social levels expected rulers to use their executive powers to maintain the realm's security and internal stability. As the States-General of Netherlands reminded Philip II, they were also to respect the lives, property and traditional rights of their subjects. In order to meet all these requirements, monarchs had to take advice beyond that given by their councils and to involve a wider cross-section of the merchants, artisans, gentry and nobles of the realm in the business of government. Doing so tended to encourage a broader basis of co-operation, or coercion, than that provided by their own officials and the nobles of the royal affinity. This was the function of the representative assemblies, the estates or parliaments, most of which had been established by the fourteenth century and some much earlier still.

The greatest demand of government was for money; lots of money. Monarchs were entitled to financial assistance from their subjects in the form of direct taxation, for expenditure incurred directly in governing and defending the realm. Nevertheless, it was also widely held that the subjects' consent to taxation was necessary and giving a collective consent to proposed taxation was one of the prime functions of representative assemblies. For a monarch to attempt to levy direct taxes without this prior consent was not only difficult practically but invited accusations of unjust, even tyrannical, government.

Although common throughout sixteenth-century Europe, representative assemblies were very differently composed and organised and had widely differing relationships with the rulers who summoned them. Some national institutions such as the Polish parliament were active participants in government. Others, such as the Estates-General of France seem to have functioned primarily to defend sectional interests against the claims of the monarchy. Some assemblies, such as those in Valencia and Catalonia, represented only a small proportion of the subjects within a composite monarchy while others were provincial assemblies whose consent bound only discrete parts of an individual kingdom. To varying extents, all these assemblies were also involved in defending, or changing, the most important laws of the realm. Among the most active in this respect was the English parliament.[2]

THE ENGLISH PARLIAMENT AND ROYAL INCOME

The initiative for summoning and dismissing (proroguing) the English parliament lay entirely with the king but its acts were taken to be those of the sovereign and the whole realm together. This was the legal doctrine of the 'king-in-parliament.' Henry prided himself on his use of Parliament. He called it more frequently and kept it sitting for longer periods than either Henry VII or Elizabeth I. He summoned nine Parliaments in his 37 years as king, five of them in the last 18 years of his reign. The legislation they passed to sanction the break with Rome and to enact the Henrician Reformation is amongst the most important in England's history. Never an actor to miss a winning line, Henry solemnly articulated his view of its place in his government to the chief officers of the English Parliament of 1542:

> And further, we be informed by our judges, that we at no time stand so highly in our estate royal, as in the time of Parliament, wherein we as head and you as members, are conjoined and knit together into one body politic.[3]

This sounds very egalitarian – almost democratic. It isn't. Henry meant not that his authority was somehow dependant upon Parliament for its legitimacy, but that when acting in and through Parliament, the king's highest consultative and judicial body, his pre-existing authority was amplified to its fullest extent.

The Parliament consisted of the king himself, the House of Lords and the House of Commons. Those who sat in the Lords did so as the sovereign's peers and chief counsellors with a right to 'consult warn and advise' him. The strict definition of an individual's nobility was the receipt of a writ of summons to sit in the Lords. It was perfectly possible for the king to summon the Lords without the Commons as the 'Great Council', something that Henry did on several occasions, including January 1537 in response to the Pilgrimage of Grace. The Commons was a representative body because, in theory at least, every community of the realm sent spokesmen to it when summoned. Only those of knightly status, resident in the counties or the chief burgesses resident in the boroughs were eligible for election to the Commons. MPs were primarily concerned with the interests of property owners, the only people entitled to vote for them but they were supposed to represent all those living in their constituencies. Thus the 'Commons' referred not to ordinary working people, but to men of gentry status. Henry enlarged the Commons by forty constituencies, most created in the 1530s as the regime sought greater control over the localities in England. Twenty-four parliamentary seats were allocated to the shires created in and bordering the principality of Wales as part of its incorporation into English legal jurisdiction.

The county palatinates of Chester and Durham were also brought into the parliamentary fold, as was Calais. Rather than the 'ungracious dog hole' it had once been described as, the 1536 Act enfranchising Calais described it as one of 'the principal treasures' of the realm of England. This contrasted sharply with the position of Henry's two other continental cities, Tournai and Boulogne. Although there were representatives of the former at the parliament of 1515 when matters affecting the city were dealt with, the bulk of the evidence suggests that neither it nor Boulogne were actually enfranchised for the English parliament under Henry VIII. They were legally regarded as part of his possessions as 'king of France' rather than constituent elements of England.[4]

The English monarch's revenues were augmented through recourse to Parliament. His 'ordinary' income came from the crown's estates, from profits of justice, from sale of wardships and from customs. The revenues of tonnage and poundage, from wool and wool fells and leather were, strictly speaking, Parliamentary votes of indirect taxes, but as they were conferred on new monarchs automatically, they were in practice part of his regular revenues. The income from ordinary sources diminished significantly during the fifteenth century. Henry VII invested much time and effort in recovering the full amounts to which he was entitled but by Henry VIII's reign the crown's ordinary income was insufficient for its purposes.

As Sir John Fortescue reminded his readers, the king was entitled to call upon Parliament for help with his 'extraordinary' expenditure. This was mainly for warfare and defence. It was traditionally raised through the Parliamentary grant of a 'tenth and fifteenth' of landed income. However, by the fourteenth century this had become an agreed and fixed sum paid through quotas on all the different counties. It no longer reflected the true wealth of the country. Perhaps Wolsey's greatest contribution to Henry's domestic government was further to develop taxation by directly assessed 'subsidy', first initiated in the fifteenth century. Subsidy taxation was based not on fixed quotas but on the wealth of individuals, assessed on oath by royal commissioners. In England, unlike in France, Spain and the Netherlands, the nobility was liable to pay tax. Subsidy assessment tightened the screws on nobles and wealthy gentry but Parliament, in which such people had their voice, still determined the frequency and rates at which direct taxes were levied. Not surprisingly, Wolsey found it difficult to secure by directly assessed subsidies more than was possible by traditional tenths and fifteenths. Nevertheless, he established the principle that the burden of taxation should fall on those in the kingdom most able to bear it.[5]

Assessments were made in 1522–23 and after strenuous negotiation, a subsidy was voted by Parliament in 1523 roughly on the basis of two shillings in the pound on goods and lands payable over four years. Further subsidy acts were passed in 1534, 1540, 1543 and 1545 each payable over two to three years. This regularity of parliamentary subsidies has sometimes been seen as another aspect of the Tudor 'revolution in government' whereby Parliament accepted that voting supply co-operatively was part of its 'national' responsibilities. However it had always so regarded taxation, provided that it had been requested on a legitimate basis. The Henrician regime was usually careful to make the traditional link between taxation and the defence of the kingdom, even if it was increasingly treated as merely an aspect of good government and the maintenance of the realm. When the connection with defence was not made clear as happened in 1532, the demand for a subsidy was refused.

The amount estimated to have been raised by direct parliamentary taxation over the course of Henry's reign has been averaged at £48,000 annually between 1512–17 and £89,000 between 1541–46. To these figures must be added various extra-parliamentary levies and forced loans raised to supplement the subsidies. These often secured a third or a half as much again as subsidies, so that for example, extra-parliamentary lay taxes in 1542 came to just over £112,000. The biggest single source of Henry's income was the English church. In addition to the traditional and periodic payment of clerical tenths as agreed by the provinces of Canterbury and York, Wolsey used his power as papal legate to impose the subsidy system on clerics. He compelled subsidies of between five per cent and ten per cent of clerical income in the years 1523 to 1528. This yielded as much as £120,000 for the crown. Another subsidy of £118,000 payable over five years followed in 1531.

Limited as it was under Wolsey, the clergy's power to resist royal taxation was destroyed in the break from Rome. From 1534 a fine of the first year's value of each benefice now came to the English crown. These were the 'first fruits' and amounted to about £5000 annually. Clerical tenths were also made a permanent tax on the basis of the *Valor Ecclesiasticus*, the valuation of church property and income carried out in 1535. From 1540 clerical subsidies were also revived so that annual income from the church, averaged approximately £47,000 between 1535 and 1547. To this should be added the proceeds in sales and rents from lands seized at the dissolution of the monasteries which have been estimated at a little less than £50,000 per year at their height between 1539 and 1543.

Impressive though these figure are, the detrimental effect of inflation and the costs of war ultimately proved too great. Henry also had to raise loans in London and Antwerp at high rates of interest and finally to debase the coinage in order to fund his last war and remain solvent at the end of his reign. Debasement raised profits estimated at £1,270,000 between 1544–51. This measure was effective for Henry's short-term aims but undermined the stability of crown finances in the reigns of his children.[6]

The royal finances were collected, disbursed and accounted for through a complex mix of treasuries and officials. The Exchequer was the realm's chief accounting office. Its two major components were the Exchequer of Receipt, responsible for collection and disbursement of revenue and the Exchequer of Account which audited the accounts and enforced payment of outstanding debts. The Exchequer's procedures were slow and its accounts could not readily give an accurate indication of how much money the king had at any given moment. It made payments by assignment of debts owed to the crown rather than in cash. Like their Yorkist predecessors, the early Tudors wanted a more flexible system which gave them cash in hand and more accurate short-term accounting for the daily needs of the crown. Under Henry VII the Exchequer continued to collect revenues raised by parliamentary taxation, but all 'ordinary' crown revenues were paid to a royal household official, the Treasurer of the Chamber, who effectively acted as the king's banker. Payments out of the Chamber Account were authorised by the king and Henry VII checked the books meticulously. Payments included those to ambassadors and the expense of the royal household itself. By the end of his reign, this system of 'Chamber finance' was used to collect and disburse the bulk of crown revenue. Its operation was formalised in 1515 with the creation of two general surveyors of the crown responsible for determining and collecting the revenues to be paid into the Chamber account.

Henry VIII wanted the flexibility in his personal finances which had been the original intent behind the creation of the Chamber account. The larger, more routine, expenses of the household continued to be paid through the Chamber but with the rise of the Privy Chamber, the king's fluctuating personal expenses were now handled by one of his closest courtiers. William Compton and Henry Norris after him, operated what began as a 'sub-branch,' as it were, of the main Chamber account, known eventually as the king's 'Privy Purse.' Initially it paid relatively small sums on Henry's daily needs but by the early 1530s it was disbursing considerable sums on his directly 'monarchical,' as opposed to administrative, expenses. These included gambling debts, payments for his building programme and for personal plate and jewels. From June 1529 the Privy Purse ceased to draw money from the Chamber at all. It now drew directly upon stores of ready cash kept in a number of treasuries in Henry's palaces, especially in Whitehall, known collectively as the 'Privy Coffers.' They were themselves replenished from sources personal to the king such as the twice-yearly payments of his

French pension and the funds brought into Henry as part of the break with Rome. During the 1540s they were sustained by the profits of sales of monastic lands and yields from clerical subsidies. Between 1542 and 1547 the Whitehall treasury received a total of £240,000 which helped Henry to fund his last, and most expensive, war against Francis I.[7]

Meanwhile the older 'Chamber system' underwent a series of changes designed to cope with the new and expanding areas of royal revenues. The new financial courts established in the 1530s worked under the supervision of the Privy Council but were independent of Exchequer and the General Surveyors who continued to administer those revenues of which they had control since 1531. By the end of the century, through a series of haphazard changes and reforms, the Exchequer had regained its prominence in Tudor finance. With more flexibility, if not always greater efficiency, in its receipt, disbursement and auditing procedures, it reclaimed most of the functions exercised by the semi-autonomous courts created in late 1530s.[8]

THE FRENCH ESTATES AND ROYAL INCOME

As we have noted previously, the king of France made laws entirely on his own initiative and authority. He was expected to consult his realm in making these laws, but they did not depend for validity upon the consent of a national representative body. The French representative institution was the *Etats-généraux*, or Estates-General, of France which had come into existence in the early fourteenth century, not long after the English parliament. It was structured around the three separate estates of the realm; nobility, clergy and commons. The representatives of the first two estates were elected by the nobles of each *baillage* and by the clergy. Those of the third estate were drawn mainly from the wealthy citizens of towns. After 1484 they were also chosen from assemblies in each of the realm's *baillages*. The French king alone determined when and for how long the Estates were summoned.

The king's laws and his demands for taxation could be presented to and discussed by the delegates to the Estates. While their legal force did not depend upon its assent, in matters of taxation particularly there was a notion in medieval French government that such assent was desirable. It might also be helpful in ensuring that the realm actually paid up. The king would declare his needs to the Estates and they would in turn present their *doléances* or grievances about his government. He might, or might not, then redress them in a reforming edict. The Estates were perhaps most useful to the monarchy in times of emergency. For example, in 1439 Charles VII had used the Estates-General to obtain the kingdom's consent to the *taille personelle*, a hearth tax levied to support his *ordonance* companies. It was originally a temporary impost but as the *ordonance* companies were not subsequently disbanded, the *taille* continued to be levied without further assent of the Estates-General.

Francis I, who enjoyed high prestige at least among his noble subjects, declined to summon the Estates-General at all during his reign. This might be interpreted as evidence of an all-powerful king trying to destroy the institution through neglect. However it is more likely that the Estates were not summoned because in ordinary circumstances in the past they had not proved very helpful to government anyway. While, in theory, they were summoned to find ways and means of helping the king, the delegates' main objective was usually to preserve the privileges of the social group that they represented. Differences in language and customs among French people, their loyalty to provincial bodies and suspicion of those in far-distant parts of a large kingdom meant that consensus among delegates was often hard to achieve. As fifteenth-century monarchs had discovered, even when a vote of taxation was agreed by the national assembly, it had often to be renegotiated at the provincial level and frequently raised less than had actually been granted to the king.

Both Louis XII and Francis I found other ways to consult more widely beyond the royal council when they felt it necessary. Each summoned selected representatives of the towns to meet with them on economic or currency matters. Numerous towns throughout France were self-governing under royal charters. They negotiated directly with the crown over tax, often trading concessions in the amounts levied for defensive works undertaken from which the king could derive a benefit. Taxation was not the only reason why kings consulted their realms and Francis could also invite selected representatives of the three estates to a special meeting known as an 'Assembly of Notables' where major issues were discussed. He called such an assembly in 1527 to sanction his repudiation of the Treaty of Madrid in the hope that this would justify his decision before the international community.[9]

Francis may have been able to do without the Estates-General but he was required to summon the provincial estates. A majority of French provinces, located in the centre and north of the realm, did not have their own assemblies and were called *pays d'élections*. They were grouped into four *généralités*, each of which was further subdivided into *élections* where royal officials, the *élus*, assessed and collected the tax. Those provinces with their own assemblies were known as *pays d'états*. They had to be consulted before new taxation had any effect within their borders and the king depended upon them to collect it as well. The six main provinces with their own estates were Normandy, Brittany, Languedoc, Provence, Dauphiné and Burgundy. All lay in peripheral areas of the kingdom and were those more recently incorporated within it. The provincial estates used their power to tax to pay the salaries of the royal governor and his lesser officials and the troops located in their provinces. They also raised taxes for their own purposes, voting money to repair bridges and roads, to build hospitals and to aid in poor relief.

Many of the provincial estates were still quite robust institutions under Francis. The Breton estates in particular was deeply conscious of the pre-existing customs of the duchy which only slowly accepted Francis' direct authority over it between 1515 and 1532. While the provincial estates could not refuse outright a request for royal taxation, most, like that of Langedoc, bargained strenuously over the amount, tried to insist that it was conditional upon the king redressing grievances and also arranged its assessment and collection within the province. The king was equally robust in his dealings with provincial estates. When he summoned them, Francis insisted that grant of supply came before, not after, redress of grievances. Moreover, as David Potter has pointed out, because of a wide range of historical accidents and customs it did not always follow that *pays d'état* were better able to resist royal taxation. Some provincial estates, such as Normandy, had proved inept at raising the agreed taxes themselves and so royal *élus* operated within the province. The provincial estates could also be asked to ratify royal decisions or treaties signed with foreign princes.[10]

The costs of Francis I's many military campaigns resulted in a massive and near-continuous crown deficit from the early 1520s which he could not fund from traditional 'ordinary' sources of revenue. The main tax was the *taille* of which there were two kinds. The *taille réelle*, a land tax payable by all persons in certain regions of the kingdom, and the *taille personelle*. The clergy, nobility and a range of other social or professional groups and some major towns were exempted from the latter so it fell largely on unprivileged commoners. To the *taille* were added *crues*, surtaxes levied theoretically for specific purposes such as fitting galleys out in 1534 but in practice also a permanent part of taxation. The *taille* and its *crues* was the most profitable tax and the income from it doubled over the course of Francis's reign, from 2.4 million *livres* per annum in 1515 to 4.6 million in 1544–45.

Francis also relied heavily on indirect taxation. *Aides* were dues payable on a range of consumer goods and levied principally in the towns. They were resisted strongly in most areas and some provinces such as Burgundy and Provence paid none at all. The second major indirect tax was the *gabelle* a sales tax on salt. Income from it reached 700,000 *livres* per annum. It was not imposed uniformly across the kingdom. Burgundy for example paid at a lower rate than the rest of France and Brittany had no *gabelle* at all. In 1543 Francis extended the scope of one tax, the *solde des gens de pied* which was levied on walled towns. Each was required to pay for contingents of between 500 and 1000 infantry soldiers. It was levied even in peacetime. Total annual amounts collected by all these imposts were relatively small at about 1.6 million *livres* in 1515, rising to 2.8 million in 1547.

The shortfall in cash from taxation revenue led the king to meet his immediate costs through forced loans from towns, from wealthy individuals, from French and foreign bankers and his own financial officials. Francis also relied heavily on the Church for financial support. The Concordat of

Bolgona signed with Leo X allowed Francis to levy a tenth on the clergy, a practise he repeated fifty-seven times throughout his reign, collecting between 18 and 20 million *livres* in the process. Beyond taxation and loans, the most important expedient which Francis adopted was the creation and sale for profit of noble titles and of royal judicial and fiscal offices. Whereas Henry VIII debased the coinage in an effort to meet his debts, Francis, his critics argued, debased the status of his own officials and gave away a measure of crown control over its servants.[11]

Francis inherited a complex fiscal administration based, like the English one, on the traditional distinction between 'ordinary' and 'extraordinary' revenue. Four *trésoriers de France* were responsible for the ordinary revenue. Alongside them were four *généraux des finances* responsible for extraordinary revenue. Each was responsible for a *généralite*, itself divided into *élections* in which the *élus* operated. Like the Exchequer in England, these officials paid crown debts by assigning revenues owed to it in the localities. They did not usually deal with cash collection or payments. The complexities of this organisation, its inherent slowness and the scope for evasion, meant that there was often a wide discrepancy between what was theoretically owed to the crown in tax and what it actually collected.

In a series of reforms dating from March 1523, Francis established new central treasury under an official called the *Trésorier de l' Epargne*. After a number of initial difficulties and adjustments to his role, it was decreed in June 1524 that he was to be responsible for revenue from the king's domains and that from taxation. Another official, the receiver of the *parties casuelles* was to supervise all other sources of irregular income such as loans and that from the sales of offices. The intention behind these reforms, just as with those instituting 'Chamber finance' in England the previous century, was to increase the king's control over his finances, to increase his stocks of ready cash and give him a kind of current account from which to pay his immediate expenses. In practice not all the revenue that was supposed to reach the *Epargne* did so but the king was at least given a clearer idea of how much money he had and greater direct control over it.

Under the edict of Rouen of 1532 this process was taken a step further when it decreed that all royal revenue apart from that from the *parties casuelles* was henceforward to be paid into the coffers of the *Epargne* now to be based permanently at the Louvre. Like Henry VIII's 'Privy Coffers', this treasury was intended to give the king an ample supply of cash to be used mainly in war against Charles V. Once more reality lagged somewhat behind the theory but a substantial cash reserve was built up. The final stage in Francis's fiscal reforms came under the edict of Cognac in 1542 when the kingdom's four taxation *généralités* were subdivided into sixteen districts called *recettes-générales* each under a receiver empowered to collect all the king's regular revenues and the old distinction between 'ordinary' and 'extraordinary' revenues was done away with. The treasurer of the *Epargne* was now at the head of a single financial administration.[12]

THE CORTES IN SPAIN, THE STATES OF THE NETHERLANDS AND ROYAL INCOME

Charles V had to deal with a wide range of representative bodies, all with strong traditions of independence and ways of proceeding which he did his best to respect but not without frequent and bitter wrangles over their support. In the Holy Roman Empire there was the imperial Diet or *Reichstag* and the kingdoms of Sicily, Sardinia and Naples also had representative assemblies on the Aragonese model. In the Netherlands, Charles's Regents negotiated with the States-General. In Spain there were the *Cortes* in Castile, in Aragon and Valencia and the *corts* of Catalonia.

In 1517 the *Cortes* of Castile, like the Estates-General of France, theoretically comprised three estates or *brazos* representing the nobles, the clergy and commons. However the 'commons' actually comprised only 18 towns of the kingdom, each of which sent two representatives, the *procuradores*. The clergy and nobles only attended the *Cortes* twice in Charles's reign, in 1527 and in 1538. In the latter year the *Cortes* refused to agree to the *sisa*, a new tax on articles of basic necessity and Charles dismissed the noble and ecclesiastical houses, never summoning them again. This reduced still further what limited representative quality the *Cortes* had. Thereafter it was a small body of 36 men who were comparatively easily manipulated or coerced to do the emperor's bidding. The *Cortes* of Castile was the most compliant of the Iberian estates, raising an average 350,000 ducats for Charles annually in subsidies or *servicios* over the course of his reign.

The *Cortes* of Aragon, like those of Valencia and Catalonia, remained a much stronger body than its Castilian counterpart. It had a similar tricameral organisation, the 'commons' representing 22 towns of the kingdom. It strenuously guarded the *fueros* or ancient privileges of the realm, one of which was that no tax could be levied unless voted for unanimously by the whole *Cortes*. This happened infrequently so that it never raised more than an average of 100,000 ducats annually for Charles.

The representative institutions in the Netherlands were far more developed than those of Castile and Aragon or indeed those in France. Each of the 17 provinces had its own States, drawn from the nobility, clergy and commons. As in Castile, the estate of the commons was represented by towns which were themselves dominated by mercantile elites. The Habsburg regime negotiated directly with each province for taxation and delegated the task of raising it to the provincial assemblies and cities. The States-General was the meeting of representatives of all the provincial estates. Its voting system was complex and reflected the particularism so characteristic of the political elite of the Netherlands and which suited both individual provinces and the monarchy. There was little scope for co-ordinated action by the States-General because resolutions had to be passed by a majority of representatives from each of the provinces and by a majority of the States-General as whole. In these circumstances, the States-General was usually convened merely as a convenient way for the crown to communicate its needs to the provinces. The government's financial requirements were set out in a 'general proposition' before the real bargaining began with a 'particular proposition' delivered to the delegates of individual provinces.

The Netherlands experienced increases in rates of taxation which outstripped population growth and inflation rates across the length of Charles's reign. These increases were not steady but fluctuated with periods of war and peace. Estimates of the subsidies, called *aides* or *beden* voted to the emperor during the 1540s by the States-General of the Netherlands put the figure at an annual average of 345,000 *guilders*. He also imposed indirect taxes on goods and services in the towns. Most of Charles's income in the Netherlands was raised through public loans or *renten* in which people invested and which paid annuities. The provincial states or the States-General stood surety for the loans. Their deputies and the town magistrates were drawn, not from the landed nobility, but from the urban patriciate. They invested in this public debt at good interest rates and Charles passed a significant debt for interest on to Philip. As was the case in Holland, the material and political fortunes of such people became progressively linked with those of the Habsburg regime and assisted in maintaining social and economic stability. As Professor Israel has observed, with its prosperous towns and cities and acquiescent assemblies, the Netherlands was 'a formidable adjunct to Habsburg primacy in Europe and the world more generally.'[13]

Like his English and French counterparts, Charles had both ordinary and extraordinary revenues and expenditure. Like theirs, his expenditure always exceeded his income due primarily to the vast costs of war. In Castile the king's 'ordinary' revenue, derived chiefly from his landed estates and indirect taxes. The principal royal tax was the *alcabala*, a levy of ten per cent payable on all financial and property transactions, including those by nobles. It accounted for between 40 and 45 per cent of the total ordinary income. It was often paid through a fixed lease or *encabezamiento* in which the Cortes or a particular municipality agreed to pay a fixed sum representing the value of the tax yield to the crown for a certain number of years and then collect the tax itself. The advantage to the crown of this system was that is got a steady supply of income but the proceeds of the tax once collected were often higher than the agreed fixed sum. The 'profit' was then kept by the body raising the tax.

The king also earned income through a range of tolls and duties imposed on a number of commodities, including oil, Grenadan silk and Castilian wool and precious metals. Like the king of France, Charles enjoyed a monopoly on the production, storage and sale of salt, exercised through tax farmers. There were also monopolies on the production of mercury and on the trade in slaves from Africa. The king benefited from the *servicio y montazgo*, a long-established tax on the seasonal movement of grazing animals, predominantly sheep, and on their pasturing. Its total impost was negotiated annually with the powerful wool producers' corporation, the *Mesta*.

The king's 'extraordinary' revenue came from parliamentary *servicios* and special levies on the Church raised by papal concession to assist in Charles's efforts against the Turks and the Lutherans. These were the *cruzadas*, and clerical *servicios*, the proceeds of which accounted for twenty per cent of revenues. There was also the income derived from the lands of the three Castilian crusading orders which were taken into royal control in 1522. Charles also had steadily growing income from the Americas. By the mid 1530s the emperor's income from American silver and other metals averaged 252,000 ducats a year. All these sources of income raised total crown revenues in Castile estimated to have been one million ducats in 1522 rising to four million by the start of Philip II's reign.[14]

Significant though such sums are, they were dwarfed by Charles's expenditure. He is estimated to have spent 2 million ducats alone on the war against France in 1551–52. He raised more money through a range of expedients. Like Francis I, Charles V created administrative offices for sale and imposed extra charges on the purchasers for the right to pass them on to their successors. The offices of town councillors or *regidores* were purchased readily by the economic elites of the municipalities so perpetuating the power of local oligarchies. Offices in the central administration were also sold but, in contrast to France, judicial offices did not become venal under Charles. Entry to *hidalgo* status could also be purchased but it was not until the seventeenth century that higher titles of nobility were sold. Charles also sold lands from the royal domain to raise money. He imposed 'free' or rather forced loans on his aristocrats and clergy, just as his counterparts elsewhere did.

He also borrowed money from Spanish, German and Italian bankers using a contract known as an *asiento*. It was a legal instrument prescribing when, where, in what currency and at what exchange rate a loan would be advanced. This made it a useful way of raising money in the areas where it was wanted, thus avoiding the need to transport large amounts cash over long distances with all its inherent dangers. It also specified what the interest on the loan would be and how it was to be repaid. Interest rates on *asiento* loans rose from 17 per cent in the 1520 to a staggering 48.8 per cent by 1551–52. Another form of loan was the *juro* (meaning 'I swear') in which, in exchange for cash, Charles assigned, over a longer term, some of the revenues owing to the crown. These loans had low rates of interest but good security. The problem was that as Charles increased the number of *juros*, and assigned more of the ordinary revenues of the crown to his creditors, he had less capital with which to service his debts. For example, from 1525, the revenues of the Castilian crusading orders were assigned to the German bankers, the Fuggers. Initially they were to hold these revenues for three years but in fact held them for over a century and they became the foundation of their enormous Spanish business. *Juros* absorbed 36.6 per cent of revenues in 1522 but 65.4 per cent by 1543.[15]

The Spanish financial administration was as complex as any in Europe. The main accounting office for Castile was the *Contaduría mayor de Hacienda*, the rough equivalent of the English Exchequer of Receipt. It was presided over by two main officials the *contadores mayores* who checked receipts and expenditure and organised the recovery of money owed to the king. They were assisted by eight lesser officials, each responsible for a different component of the king's finances. Tax collection, the payment of salaries of royal officials and maintenance of the king's debts were all organised through these officials. Alongside the *Hacienda* was the *Contaduría mayor de cuentas*, the Castilian equivalent of the *Chambre des comptes* in France or the Exchequer of Account in England. This body audited the accounts of those responsible for collecting or disbursing the royal revenues, checking payments against the ordinances authorising them. When satisfied that the money in question had been collected or paid out properly, it issued a quittance to the official responsible. The king could also appoint special commissions from time to time to investigate any problems with the handling of his revenues or in particular areas of the kingdom.

This complex financial administration was typical of its time in that it could not always overcome delays or quickly discover problems in the system which impaired its efficiency. It was also ponderous and jealously guarded its rights and responsibilities. Like Henry and Francis, Charles therefore established a new executive body to advise him on his revenues. In 1523, the same year that Francis I set up the *Trésor de l'Epargne*, Charles established the *Consejo de Hacienda* or Council of Finances. However, unlike the *Epargne* or the Chamber Account in England, this was not a new treasury or accounting system but a body charged with reducing inefficiency and fraud in the existing system and investigating new ways and means of raising revenue. At the start of each year it drew up an annual report on the king's revenues and projected expenditure. It pressed the *Contaduría mayor de cuentas*, to speed up its work especially for the king's military needs. The Council of Finances enforced payment of fines and sold goods and rights confiscated by the crown. The Secretary of the Council of Finances became Charles's most powerful official in Spain during the 1530s and his remit, directly or indirectly encompassed most of the administration in Spain.[16]

THE CROWN AND THE CHURCH

The monarchs of England and France and the Holy Roman Emperor all played an important role in the religion of their respective realms. Their temporal power was sanctified by God through the church which was closely involved in the public manifestations of monarchy. They also exercised extensive powers of patronage over the higher echelons of the church hierarchy and churchmen were prominent in the administration of their realms. So far as may be judged, at their accessions Francis I, Charles V and Henry VIII, all had a personal faith of a conventional sort. Even as they assumed power however, the religion of their childhood was being challenged as never before.

Numerous studies in the last decade have demonstrated that throughout Europe, at all social levels, there was a widespread commitment to Catholic doctrine, rituals and practices. Yet all was not well. Many popular pietistic movements such as the Brethren of the Common Life in the Netherlands called for a return to the values of the gospels in the daily lives of all people. Charles, Henry and Francis had some sympathy with these views. They patronised moderate reformers like Erasmus and Jacques Lefèvre d'Etaples (c1450–1537) but all rejected the views of Luther and Calvin as disruptive of the social order and as threats to their personal authority as sanctified princes.

Henry VIII and the English Church

Of the three kings it was Henry VIII who had the longest spiritual journey but even he did not travel that far. His enthusiastically conventional Catholicism as a young man was expressed most eloquently in his 1521 publication against Luther, the *Assertio septem sacramentorum*, or 'Defence of the Seven Sacraments' for which he received the papal title 'Defender of the Faith.' Nevertheless, the king was jealous of his authority and Diarmaid MacCulloch has detected an ambivalence about the power of the clergy even in the young Henry. This was sharpened to a fine edge by the failure of his campaign for papal annulment of his marriage to Katherine of Aragon.

The central issue at the heart of Henry's break with Rome was his lack of a son with whom properly to secure the Tudor succession. Across the Channel sat his keenest rival, Francis I, with an heir, a spare and one left over. Daily by his side was Anne Boleyn whose comparative youth and charm promised the resolution to this royal crisis of masculine confidence. By 1527 the king had convinced himself that his marriage to his brother's widow had contravened divine law, Pope Julius II's dispensation for the match notwithstanding. He therefore determined to rid himself of Katherine. To Henry's thoroughly Catholic mind it was simply a matter of Pope Clement VII correcting the prior error by annulling the marriage. Henry could then marry legitimately for the first time and, with Anne, have the son over whom England longed to rejoice. But for the power of Charles V, Clement would probably have complied with this request. Unfortunately for Henry, imperial troops sacked Rome in May 1527 just as his demand for an annulment was formulated. For several years thereafter, Clement lived under the emperor's protection and virtually as his prisoner. Charles, whose own son and heir was also born in 1527, was resolutely opposed to any public rejection of his aunt Katherine. Within three years what had begun as polite request from an English king to the pope, became a determined campaign to rid England of all papal authority.

Henry's unwillingness, or inability, to see his desire for an annulment other than in spiritual terms created enormous problems and opportunities for those who concerned themselves in England's relationship with the Almighty. It was Anne Boleyn and her client scholars, men such as Edward Foxe and Thomas Cranmer, who persuaded the king of the theological and political virtues of a moderately 'evangelical' approach to faith; one which emphasised knowledge of scripture as central to belief. With them, Henry explored a range of writings such as William Tyndale's *Obedience of a Christian Man* and Christopher St German's *Doctor and Student*. Although Henry eventually reviled Tyndale's translations of the Bible, his arguments, like St German's, tended to reduce significantly the sacramental role of the clergy, whence it had formerly derived so much of its psychological, legal and financial power. This Henry found useful, although there is no evidence that he ever doubted the importance of the priestly office. Henry's advisors also roused his own sense of his princely dignity on more directly political issues. In a number of texts, the most important of which was the *Collectanea satis copiosa*, they showed by reference to English historical chronicles and a number of medieval conciliarist tracts why Henry's was a national, imperial, kingship. He was such a king as should not, indeed could not, tolerate the jurisdiction in his realm of any external power.

During 1531–32 a steady stream of translations and commentaries of Erasmus' writings together with English tracts was produced under the patronage of Anne Boleyn and Thomas Cromwell. This material was intended to support Henry's quarrel with Rome. It railed against clerical privilege while insisting upon England's doctrinal orthodoxy. Between 1530 and 1534 control over the English church was gradually invested in the sovereign, initially to put pressure on Clement VII and ultimately on the basis of Henry's 'imperial' status as articulated in the preamble to the Act of Supremacy of 1534. The first major step was taken in 1531 when the clergy represented in the Convocation, or clerical parliament, agreed to pay a huge fine for having recognised Wosey's legatine authority before the king's. It was to be paid to Henry as the 'sole protector and supreme head of the English church' with the proviso, insisted upon by Convocation, that this was 'so far as Christ's law allows.'

In March 1532 the Act in Conditional Restraint of Annates was passed which temporarily halted payments from English benefices to Rome. This was followed in May the same year by the formal Submission of the Clergy, under which Convocation agreed not to meet without Henry's permission and that no new canon laws were to be passed without the king's scrutiny. In September 1532 Henry signed a new defensive alliance with Francis I against Charles V. In October he and Anne met Francis at Calais and Boulogne and they were secretly married early in 1533. By the end of

February she was known to be pregnant. Now the clock began running against Henry. Doctors confidently predicted a boy and at all costs he had to be born legitimate.

Despite growing unease and opposition both inside and outside its ranks, Parliament passed the Act in Restraint of Appeals in March 1533. This prevented the king's 'great matter' being referred to Rome henceforward. Meanwhile, acting on Henry's imperial authority as set out in that Act, Thomas Cranmer, made Archbishop of Canterbury (by the pope) on the death of William Warham late in 1532, held an inquiry into the king's marriage. It was scarcely a surprise when, in May 1533, he pronounced it invalid and it was annulled. Katherine could not appeal against this decision without breaking the law. Anne Boleyn was crowned queen on 1 June 1533 and her daughter Elizabeth was born at Greenwich on 7 September. Having crossed his personal Rubicon, and despite the sex of the child, Henry pressed on in completing the break with Rome. In the first session of the 1534 Parliament the Act of Succession and the Act for the Submission of the Clergy were passed. The first affirmed Anne as queen and Elizabeth's legitimacy. It made it treason to deny the king's title or to slander his marriage. The second confirmed the submission of the clergy of 1531 and among other things, entrenched Henry's control over canon law and licensing of priests.

In the second session of the 1534 Parliament came the defining Act of the Henrician Reformation, the Act of Supremacy. This time with no qualification, Henry was declared to be 'the only supreme head in earth of the Church of England.' This was supported by the Treason Act which came into effect in February 1535 and made it a capital offence to deny Henry's title or to impugn his authority over the church. Subjects were required to swear an oath affirming the royal supremacy. It was this oath that Bishop John Fisher and Sir Thomas More refused to take and they were both tried for treason and executed in the summer of 1535.[17]

With the break from Rome completed, apparently with no immediate adverse reaction from Europe, Henry slowly became more confident that he could indeed supervise the practise of religion in his own kingdom. His advisors now tried to influence the sort of settlement Henry would adopt. Between 1535 and 1537, under Cromwell's vice-gerency and Anne Boleyn's fall notwithstanding, the reform of the tenets of the faith developed along Lutheran lines. The Act of Ten Articles passed in 1536 reduced the sacraments from seven to three (Baptism, Penance and Communion) and made the Bible, the Nicene and Apostles' Creeds the basis of faith. In a concurrent set of injunctions, Cromwell begun attacking the church customs associated with pilgrimages, with praying for the dead and keeping candles, or 'lights' burning on altars and before statues of saints.

Conservative bishops and nobles reacted adversely and Cranmer chaired a committee charged with clarifying the essential matters of doctrine. Henry took a keen interest in its deliberations, making marginal comments and often rather pedantic corrections to the working papers Cranmer sent to him. Its findings echoed the spirit of the Ten Articles and were published late in 1537 as the *Institution of a Christian Man*, or the 'Bishops' Book.' It recovered the four sacraments missing from the Ten Articles but lessened their importance. It also stressed the role of the priest as preacher to which Henry made no objection when reading the book prior to its publication. The Bishops' book was followed in November 1539 by the *Great Bible*, the official bible in English. With Cromwell's assiduous supervision it enjoyed steady sales at least in urban areas in the south. The frontispiece depicted Henry handing down the purified word of God to his bishops and ministers who interpreted it to a grateful people.

To the disappointment of evangelical enthusiasts that is as far as doctrinal reform went under Henry. In 1539 Cromwell chaired yet another Parliamentary committee appointed to pronounce definitively on the doctrinal issues so heatedly debated over the previous three years. The committee took its lead, not from the chairman, but from the king. Its findings were conservative and orthodox. They were enshrined in the 'Act for abolishing diversity in opinions', known usually as the Act of Six Articles passed in 1539. Transubstantiation was confirmed and its denial was made punishable as heresy. Communion in both kinds was deemed not necessary to salvation. Priests were not able to marry and vows of chastity should be observed. Private masses should continue and auricular confession, about which Henry had his doubts, was determined not to be required by divine law but yet 'expedient and necessary to be retained.'

Scarcely had Cromwell finished this work than he lost Henry's favour as a consequence of the king's unhappy marriage to Anne of Cleves which he had advocated. This allowed his conservative opponents, especially the Duke of Norfolk and Stephen Gardiner, the Bishop of Winchester, back into favour. It also deafened the king to Cromwell's pleas when, in June, he was arrested on suspicion of supporting sacramentarians in Calais in direct contravention (so his enemies said) of the 1539 Act. He was quickly tried and executed for heresy and treason. With Cromwell's death, the momentum towards a more Protestant reform since 1534 was halted.

The edifice of English doctrinal Catholicism may have remained virtually intact under Henry, but the walls of the monasteries did not. Henry viewed their dissolution as the necessary consequence of his removal of papal authority from the realm. He could not let remain within it religious orders like the Benedictines, Franciscans and Dominicans whose highest echelons were powerful in Europe and worked closely with the papacy. Financially hard-pressed as ever, Henry could not resist the prospect of their wealth, revealed in the *Valor Ecclesiasticus*, when the reasons for taking it seemed so compelling. Their communities were broken up and their land seized by the crown. Most of it was then sold into private ownership. This 'privatisation' of the English church produced an unprecedented financial windfall for the king and his favourites but the loss of the livelihood and the social welfare services traditionally provided by the monastic orders. It was deeply resented among many people of all social orders and was the major factor in provoking the Pilgrimage of Grace in 1536.

By the 1540s as he grew older and suffered yet another matrimonial disaster with Catherine Howard, the Supreme Head took solace in a new definition of himself as a king who was also priest and prophet in the Old Testament tradition. He saw himself, and was portrayed publicly by his propagandists, as an English king David or Solomon courageously and wisely guiding his people between the twin dangers of slavish adherence to Rome and adoption of the Lutheran heresy. His personal faith at this time in his life has been described aptly as 'a ragbag of emotional preferences.' He seems to have favoured a basically Catholic world view shorn of certain unscriptural elements, chiefly the belief in purgatory, the intercession of saints, the need for auricular confession and of course, monasticism. The blessings of Henrician Catholicism, if it may be so described, were extolled in *The Necessary Doctrine and Erudition for any Christian Man*, published in 1543 and known as the 'King's book.' It confirmed in its essentials the religion as prescribed under the Act of Six Articles. It was in effect Henry's conservative answer to the 'Bishops' book' of 1537. To his own satisfaction at least, he had had the last word in the doctrinal controversies of the previous decade.[18]

The religious conservatives held sway during the last eight years of Henry's life. Nevertheless, he kept a significant number of evangelicals like Cranmer, Sir Anthony Denny the chief Gentleman of the Privy Chamber, and Jane Seymour's brothers in positions of power close to him. In early 1546 there was some discussion between them and the king about altering religious ceremonials, such as creeping to the cross and even an extraordinary statement made in August to Cranmer and the visiting Admiral of France that Henry and Francis I had agreed to abolish the Mass in their realms. Bishop Gardiner silenced all this with a timely warning that any such change would jeopardise an alliance with the emperor which he was then busy negotiating. Nevertheless, it was the evangelicals who won the final battle fought over Henry's death-bed for control of his son's regency council. In the end, significant though Henry's impact on the practise of religion had been, it was only under Edward VI and Elizabeth I that the doctrine of English Protestantism was developed.[19]

Francis I and the French Church

As he told Henry VIII on at least one occasion, Francis I felt no need to break away from Rome in order to assert his power over the French church. There was a legal tradition in France dating back to the late thirteenth century, that the king of France was 'emperor in his kingdom' and that the secular and ecclesiastical institutions were responsible primarily to the king, not the papacy. This tradition, known as Gallicanism, had been given legislative force in 1438 in a royal edict known as the Pragmatic Sanction of Bourges. This had sought to limit papal power over the French church by prescribing that all episcopal and abbatial appointments were to be by election. The pope's role would be simply to confirm the elected candidates. It also abolished the payment of annates to the papacy. The edict was ostensibly one in favour of church reform, apparently designed to ensure that the best candidates for benefices would be chosen and instituted free from potentially corrupt papal, or royal, interference. Not surprisingly, the papacy continually pushed for its abrogation.

In fact the elections to major benefices under the Pragmatic Sanction were constantly subject to interference from both lay and clerical Frenchmen. They were characterised by protracted lobbying, legal suits and sometimes violence as leading noble families in the locality of each abbey or cathedral fought to secure the election of its candidate for any available position. The crown also favoured certain candidates, opposed others and often simply imposed its nominees on chapters. By 1515 it was effectively in control of most appointments.

While the king of France was clearly able to use the Gallican doctrine to his own advantage, he had also to deal with the pope as a political figure. Alliances with the papacy could be vital in securing and advancing his interests. So it was in December 1515 when Francis agreed the Concordat of Bologna with Leo X. In return for the pope's recognition of his conquest of Milan earlier that year, Francis agreed, among other things, that henceforward bishops, abbots and priors was to be nominated by the king but instituted to their benefices by the pope. The Concordat effectively abrogated the Pragmatic Sanction. It also seemed to anticipate the resumption of annates. In fact, as historians have subsequently found, and as Chancellor Duprat argued at the time, although Francis theoretically recognised papal primacy in the Concordat, it actually strengthened royal control of ecclesiastical appointments.

Nevertheless, the Parlement of Paris saw the Concordat as a threat to the French king's traditional independence, while the Faculty of Theology of the University of Paris, the Sorbonne, feared for the privileged access its graduates had to benefices under its influence. In 1516 the Parlement refused to ratify the Concordat. It took a long campaign of insistence, even intimidation, by the king, the chancellor Duprat and leading nobles of the kingdom before the Parlement finally registered the Concordat on 22 March 1518 and even then it indicated that it had done so only under duress. Thereafter the Parlement watched Francis's religious policy closely.

Francis's relations with the Medici popes Leo X and Clement VII were generally peaceable. From the mid 1520s he made genuine if spasmodic efforts to persuade Clement VII to annul Henry VIII's first marriage and to reconcile the Lutherans to the Catholic faith. By the 1530s he was supporting Lutheran princes and followed this with several alliances with Süleyman, to the general scandal of Christendom. The king's high ecclesiastical politics made full use of his good relations with the Holy See and the crown's patronage powers under the Concordat of Bologna. Of the 243 bishops elected between 1516 and 1555, approximately 70 per cent were nobles, either of old noble families or those recently ennobled and about 20 per cent were foreigners, virtually all Italians. The high aristocratic families like the Guise and Bourbon were well represented among the major benefice holders but Francis also appointed to the episcopacy a considerable number of men of lower rank. Many, such as Jean du Bellay, proved themselves able administrators and diplomats. He was Bishop of Paris and a frequent ambassador in Rome and England. He became a cardinal in 1535 and was a substantial patron of learning and the arts.[20]

Francis's use of high ecclesiastics in his government was entirely traditional but it caused concern to a circle of reformist thinkers centred on Guillaume Briçonnet (1470–1534), the Bishop of Meaux. This group included Lefèvre d'Etaples and Gérard Roussel and it argued that many bishops and abbots were too preoccupied with politics and with the concerns of land-owning. Neglect of their pastoral responsibilities was setting a bad example for those under their authority. The Meaux circle urged the French clergy at all levels to devote itself conscientiously to the care of souls, to fight popular superstition and denounce the suspect preaching of orders such as the Franciscans. These criticisms provoked resentment and allegations that they were tainted by Luther's heresy which extended even to Francis's sister, Marguerite, who was a patron of the Meaux circle. During the 1520s the king had a difficult balance to strike between support for such reformers and the suppression of Lutheran heresy in a political climate where the distinction between them was often hard to make.

Francis's attitude to dissent hardened after the 'Affair of the Placards' on 18 October 1534. A group of radicals posted broadsheets attacking the Mass on the doors of churches in Paris and in the royal château at Amboise. This action, together with a few isolated acts of iconoclasm, caused widespread outrage. Here was something upon which the king and the Parlement could make common cause. Genuinely outraged and anxious to be seen observing his coronation oath to uphold orthodoxy, Francis supported an immediate and wide-ranging investigation into heresy over the following six months. This secured the conviction and punishment of nearly one hundred supposed Lutherans and the hurried departure from the kingdom of many others, including Jean Calvin (1509–64) who fled to Geneva. A significant number of exiles went to Strasburg in the Rhineland and there joined a growing community of French reformists led by Martin Bucer (1491–1551).

Despite its suddenness, the extent and nature of this reaction should not be exaggerated. Francis never tolerated Lutheran ideas in the 1520s, but 'Lutheran' was then a blanket term of abuse which covered a multitude of varying beliefs. There was a great deal of unorthodoxy and uncertainty of belief around, but much of it was still identifiably Catholic rather than avowedly Protestant in nature. In the wake of the Placards, the demarcation lines between erroneous understanding, legitimate criticism of the church and more extreme doctrinal heresy appeared to be somewhat clearer. There was a marked increase in the numbers prosecuted for heresy after 1540 when, under the edict of Fontainebleau, royal judges were given wide powers to repress dissent. This was matched with a drive to ensure orthodox teaching among the population generally. Where Henry VIII's regime produced six defining articles of faith, the Sorbonne produced twenty-five which received royal endorsement in 1543. In the same year the first French Index of banned books was promulgated.[21]

Luther's ideas made some impact on the lower clergy and among certain sections of the urban population but did not gain much demonstrable support among the majority of French people, especially in rural areas. Ecclesiastical historians have sought in vain for a dominant form of Protestantism, or even a strongly Protestant social stratum, across France during the 1530s and 1540s. Where groups attracted to Lutheran ideas have been found, such as among the print workers of Lyon in the 1530s, they were characterised more by internal division than a coherent set of beliefs or a capacity to advocate religious change among those in their localities, much less before the royal regime. Luther's ideas, at least as they were disseminated in France, focused on the deficiencies of Catholic doctrine and practice, but for those satisfied (as most people were required to be) by Catholicism's apparent monopoly of access to God and its explanation of his purposes, they offered no compelling credo to set against that of the established church.[22]

Jean Calvin's writing began to circulate in France in the late 1540s and early 1550s, much of it printed in Geneva and sent through the annexed duchy of Savoy. It presented a more integrated explanation of the nature of humanity and its salvation which was fundamentally different to that of the Catholic church. Its organisation was also more open and inclusive than that of the hierarchic church and was highly effective in drawing converts. Francis I's authority as king was never seriously troubled by Calvinist dissent, but neither he nor his successor were able completely to suppress it. Calvinism always remained a minority religion in France but by the late 1550s, its adherents were sufficiently numerous and sufficiently elevated socially to influence more people than Luther's followers ever could. This allowed the Calvinists to exploit, and indeed to exacerbate, the crisis of royal authority into which France was plunged after the death of Henry II in 1559.[23]

Charles V and the Church in his empire

Summarising the available evidence of the emperor Charles's personal religion, Hans Schilling has recently argued that his piety was genuine. He saw both his personal and public life as emperor governed by the demands of his duty to God and his ancestors. This was made clear at the Diet of Worms in April 1521 when Charles condemned Martin Luther as a heretic. Charles recalled that all his forbears had been 'defenders of the Catholic Faith, of the sacred customs, decrees and usages of its worship' and that to be otherwise himself would be 'to the eternal dishonour of us and our descendants.' Thus began the emperor's long campaign to preserve Catholic orthodoxy throughout his dominions.

The spread during the 1520s of radical religious and social ideas was due in no small measure to Charles's absence from Germany after 1521. The German princes were unenthusiastic about helping an absentee overlord and many were sympathetic to Luther's anti-clerical views. A vigorous propaganda war against the pope was conducted through the printing press and personal communications. Widespread social and political unrest generated by the new religious ideas and by grievances against princely overlords culminated in the Peasants' War of 1525–26. Charles's mercenary troops returning from Italy and those of the Swabian League slaughtered over 70,000 peasants before order was restored. Faced with the dynastic rivalry of Francis I, the need to establish his authority in Spain and to check the advance of Süleyman, Charles simply could not return to Germany early enough to impose his will upon his subjects directly. In the aftermath of the Peasants' War, the Diet of Speyer in 1526 recognised the right of local governments to determine religion in their areas on an interim basis until a General Council of the church could be called. Hopes were high of a resolution at the Second Diet of Speyer held in 1529. However the Catholic majority of delegates called for the enforcement of the Edict of Worms and no agreement was reached.

During that summer a minority issued a 'Protest' against this view and were thereafter known as 'Protestants'. By the time Charles returned for the Diet of Augsburg a year later the confidence of those supporting Luther had grown considerably. All sides felt that a settlement on their terms could be achieved but when the pope refused to call a General Council, none was forthcoming. Charles instead demanded a complete capitulation by the Lutherans princes. Seven princes and two cities responded with a documented statement of belief subsequently known as the Confession of Augsburg. A majority of these Protestants then formed the defensive League of Schmalkalden early in 1531. Thereafter, an identifiable force opposed an emperor who lacked troops, local support and who was pressed by a host of commitments elsewhere.

During the next 16 years there were successive attempts to reconcile the Protestants with the Catholic church. In 1545 the Council of Trent was finally convened but immediately prorogued when the Protestants refused to recognise its legitimacy. Only after Francis I died and Süleyman was distracted with problems elsewhere in his empire, could Charles finally take on the Schmalkaldic League. His victory at Mühlberg in April 1547 was followed by yet another diet at Augsburg and here Charles imposed a conservative Catholic 'interim' settlement until the Council of Trent could re-convene. The Protestants had lost the battle but eventually won the war against Charles. They rejected the 1548 Interim of Augsburg and with the help of Henry II of France, forced Charles to a reasonably favourable truce, the Peace of Passau. This suspended the Interim of Augusburg but no concessions were made by him on the essentials of Catholic doctrine. Charles's failure to recapture Metz in early 1553 broke his health and signalled the end of any attempt to impose a religious settlement by military or any other means on the Germans. Two years later the final diet of Charles's reign, at Augsburg in February 1555, was presided over by his brother Ferdinand because the emperor could not bring himself to endorse the inevitable loss of religious unity. The Religious Peace of Augsburg, formally recognised the protestantism of the 1530 Confession of Augsburg as a legitimate denomination in the Christian faith in the Empire. For Charles, this settlement was a humiliating statement of failure and its adoption was a major factor in his decision to abdicate.[24]

In Spain Charles inherited the most religiously and culturally diverse realm in Europe. Prior to the re-conquest of Granada in 1492, Jews and indigenous Spanish had lived in an uneasy co-existence with each other under Moorish authority. After the re-conquest, the Jews were formally expelled from the whole of the peninsular as part of the Catholic Kings' efforts to create an orthodox, homogeneous society. Yet Jewish and Muslim ancestry, beliefs and customs permeated every level of Spanish society. The majority of Jews were forcibly converted to Christianity and were known as *conversos*. Those fewer Muslims who converted and remained in Spain were called *moriscos*. Both groups remained the object of intense official suspicion while also being well represented in the ranks of the universities, the lawyers and among the nobility. The Inquisition was introduced in Castile in 1480 primarily to search out 'false' converts, who continued to practise their traditions privately.

Among the ecclesiastical elite, the consciousness of 'alien' cultures in Spain, prompted the reform of the Spanish church which pre-dated Luther and which went hand-in-hand with the vigorous persecution of dissent. Both these impulses were embodied most notably in Francisco Jiménez de Cisneros. The founder of university at Alcalá soon renowned for its biblical scholarship, Cisneros was also archbishop of Toldeo and Inquisitor General from 1507. He was Charles's first regent in Castile between 1516–17. He encouraged interest in the biblical humanism of Erasmus and promoted further reform of the Church in Spain and beyond. By the 1520s the higher echelons of Spanish clergy were among the best motivated and educated in Europe. It was no coincidence that Spaniards such as Domingo de Soto and later Ignatius of Loyola were at the forefront of the Catholic resurgence against Protestantism.[25]

During the early 1520s Erasmus's writings continued to enjoyed widespread popularity in Spain and with emperor himself. However, as the religious controversies gathered pace elsewhere in Europe, the openness to reform which the Spanish high ecclesiastical authorities had shown, began to diminish. In 1520 Adrian of Utrecht replaced Cisneros as Inquisitor-General and extended the Inquisition's enquiries beyond suspect *conversos* to those tainted with Lutheran ideas. A number of lay groups, which practised forms of devotional mysticism and a less formal type of Catholicism, also came under suspicion. Despite their rather vaguely defined beliefs, the *alumbrados* or 'enlightened' were identified as heretical and the movement as whole was suppressed. By the end of the decade the Inquisition increasingly branded any deviance at all from strict Catholicism, including even the moderate reformism of Erasmus and his Spanish followers, as 'Lutheranism'. Throughout the 1530s a steady stream of prosecutions was launched against some of the most esteemed biblical scholars, even those with close connections to the royal court such as Alonso de Virués, one of Charles's own chaplains.

The steadily more repressive attitude of the king and the Inquisition during the 1540s was lamented by many of Spain's leading intellectuals, including members of such vehemently anti-heretical orders as the Dominicans and newly-founded Jesuits. They sought in vain to have the Inquisition distinguish Erasmus and other moderate reformers from Luther. In 1547 the first Spanish index of banned books was published, students were discouraged from studying abroad and no books could be imported without licence. Even from his retirement at Yuste in the mid 1550s, Charles continued to urge the harshest penalties upon those found guilty of heresy and the Inquisition's remit was widened still further in the reign of Philip II.[26]

Meanwhile in the Netherlands the Habsburg regents maintained a less onerous but still vigilant watch on heterodoxy. The Burgundian lands had no history of an active 'territorial' church associated closely with the monarchy such as existed in Spain and France and which was being developed in England. There was also a stronger tradition here than elsewhere of religious experimentation and tolerance. Luther's influence remained modest, largely because most Dutch and Flemish people remained committed to a church much influenced by Erasmus and his followers. It was not identified with an oppressive external force, such as the papacy, in the way the Church was in those parts of Germany which embraced Luther. Nevertheless, the regime took immediate steps against any who expressed support for Luther. In Brussels in July 1523 two Augustinians were burnt for heresy.

For a period in the 1530s the much more radical force of Anabaptism, which posed a threat not just to religious belief but to the structure of society, did attract a number of adherents in some cities, especially Amsterdam. It was vigorously suppressed and its sympathisers went underground in Netherlands by the late 1540s. During the 1540s the authorities in the Netherlands, as elsewhere, published lists of banned books and increased the number and intensity of investigations of suspect material. In the end however, rather as in France, it was Jean Calvin who had the greater influence in the Netherlands. Philip II's reorganisation of the episcopal structure of the church in the Netherlands, as part of an attempt to secure his dominions against the threat of Calvinism, indirectly led to increased Calvinist influence. His heavy-handed implementation of his religious policies contributed significantly to the slow but steady alienation of many Dutch nobles, the radicalisation of politics and eventually the revolt of the Netherlands against Habsburg rule from the mid-1560s.[27]

CONCLUSION

In taxation, as in religion and legal administration, the metaphor of the realm as a body whose various parts worked harmoniously together under the king as head was a cliché in constitutional theory well before 1500. It was usually employed by royal propagandists insisting on the body's obedience to the all-knowing head. In reality it was equally true that the head could not live without the body. The body politic was represented formally, but not exclusively, in the various estates and parliaments which Henry, Francis and Charles convened when they wanted money, the life-blood of government.

Their subjects recognised their duty to support the monarch but were reluctant to pay more than necessary and were alert to demands for taxation which had no precedent. Royal dealings with representative assemblies, and other independent corporate bodies from whom money could be had, or whose assent to laws imposing taxation was required, were usually insistent and not infrequently high-handed. They have in the past often been taken as evidence of the crown trying to extend its power for doctrinaire reasons. Pressing necessity is a better explanation for this behaviour than conscious policies of 'centralisation.' The personal ambitions of these three kings to be great warriors and to maintain splendid courts forced them into making continual demands for more money. They also strove to tighten up their fiscal administrations to ensure that the maximum yield from taxation reached the royal coffers. In the area of religion, too, kings were driven by necessity. Ensuring conformity to the faith among their subjects was a duty imposed by God and a mark of their effectiveness as kings. Toleration of dissent was unthinkable, even if, for a variety of reasons, the dividing line between orthdodoxy and heresy was not always easy to draw.

Historians of Francis I's reign tend to divide themselves into those who stress his authoritarian nature and 'centralising' tendencies, and those who emphasise the 'contractual' or 'popular' nature of the monarchy. The same broad contours of debate can be found among historians of Henry VIII's reign and those studying Charles V. The former group tend to highlight clashes between the monarch and national assemblies, provincial estates or other corporate bodies especially over the arrangements for taxation. They point out that in the majority of cases the kings got their way, eventually. The latter focus on the fact that kings needed to negotiate with these bodies in the first place and that they frequently had to settle for less money than initially hoped for or had to abandon attempts to extend the scope of taxation because of the difficulties in obtaining the co-operation of those required to pay it. The failure of the Amicable Grant in England in 1525 is a good example of this. It is not fudging the issue to say that depending upon the individual monarch, both schools may be right according to different times and circumstances. To call Renaissance monarchy 'contractual' does not necessarily imply that the parties to it were equals or that they always worked well together.[28]

Most disputes between Francis I and the Parlements or Estates were about whether the king's wishes or actions came within the royal prerogative, the terms of the 'contract'. Both sides argued their cases according to their own interests and the reality often lagged behind the theory. The king did push for greater scope in his powers, the local corporate bodies resisted this in the hope of getting him to reduce his demands or take them elsewhere. The king had the right to be obeyed when acting within his prerogative and nobody could dispute that regulating religion, improving administrative efficiency or raising revenue for the defence of his kingdom were within his powers. Francis cannot be called 'popular' in the modern sense and never sought to be. However the informal ties of patronage between the king and his nobles, built up through granting favours, promoting families and generally acting as a 'good lord' to them, generated among them goodwill towards the royal regime. The support of those with influence in the localities, in representative institutions and Parlements could be invaluable in avoiding disputes in the first place and finessing the majority of those that did arise to a satisfactory conclusion. When direct confrontation with the king did occur it was usually because of a breakdown in communication along 'the usual channels'. The evidence shows that when he persisted in his demands, the king's will triumphed more often than not but it is still important to recognise that he did have to negotiate with a variety of corporate bodies. Francis could not and did not unilaterally impose his will upon a passive kingdom.

A broadly similar pattern is observable in Charles V's relations with the many different representative bodies in his empire. Those in his Italian dominions, in Aragon, Valencia and Catalonia raised enough to cover the costs of their own defence and administration but contributed little to the maintenance of the empire as a whole. It is often noted that in Castile there was little tradition of resistance to demands for royal taxation. So much is true, but neither was there a tradition of innovation in tax matters as there was in England, and even in fifteenth century France. Charles did indeed dominate the *Cortes* of the kingdom. He summoned it more frequently than his predecessors and it voted him more subsidies but, representing as it did only eighteen towns and cities, it could not properly speak for the kingdom as a whole. On the only occasion that Charles summoned all three *brazos* and asked them to agree to the *sisa,* as a way of helping to deal with his massive expenditure, he was met with solid resistance. So although his power over it was clear, Charles could not use the *Cortes* as a forum through which to appeal to his subjects for financial assistance on a different basis from what was traditional.

In principal however, Charles worked for an effective relationship with the *Cortes*. Unlike Francis, he summoned the national representatives on average every three years. This was primarily to ensure a steady income from the subsidies it voted, but he also listened to its petitions and approved many of them. It also took on the administration of tax collection so that in time it associated itself more with the policies and problems of the monarch. Charles's relations with the church were also on the whole co-operative. Both in contributing to the king's financial requirements and in vigilance against heresy, the church in Spain helped to sustain Charles's vision of himself as the secular leader of Christendom in the peninsular and beyond.

Unlike the Castilian *Cortes*, the English Parliament could legitimately claim to represent the 'political nation' effectively. Its evolution was assisted by and, in turn assisted, a strong monarchy. The English Parliament was constitutionally an integral part of governing in the way that most continental assemblies were not. The king's problems were more immediately felt to be the kingdom's concerns and, provided always they were requested in the interests of the realms defence or at least its 'good government', subsidies were voted by the Parliament without too much trouble. Consequently, of the three kings, it was Henry VIII who had the greatest success in directly taxing his subjects, especially the clergy. The kingdom's wealth was more accurately assessed and taxed under him than it had been under any of his immediate predecessors and than it would be under his daughter Elizabeth.

The Parliament's acceptance that the king's concerns were its own was most fully demonstrated in Henry's matrimonial and religious affairs. Never before had it been told that it had the power to make laws recognising the annulment of one royal marriage and the validity of several successive ones. English kings had long claimed a power to supervise clerical as well as lay affairs within their kingdoms but in making himself Supreme Head of the English church, and claiming to have spiritual authority in it, Henry extended the royal prerogative significantly. There was resistance in the English Parliament to this dramatic step and Henry overcame it by the usual monarchical methods of persuasion and intimidation. His regime played upon a degree of anti-clericalism among the common lawyers, well represented in Parliament, and encouraged their ambitions to assume some of the lucrative business traditionally handled by the ecclesiastical courts. Casting himself as the indifferent arbiter, he promised to protect the churchmen from these demands while equally solemnly assuring his lay subjects that he would curb the pride of priests and prelates. He isolated opponents and silenced them by the threat of, or actual, execution under laws which widened the definition of treason beyond precedent. All this was done by a Parliament made tractable through its careful management by the king's ministers and members of the royal affinity. It was a Parliament apparently anxious to prove its loyalty to a king whose reign, it was constantly assured, had fostered domestic security and England's fame abroad.

The robust statement of the duties of a king towards his people quoted at the outset of this chapter was addressed to Philip II when the States-General renounced its obedience to him. To those who framed it, his authoritarian response to the spread of Calvinism in the Netherlands had ridden rough-shod over the traditional privileges and duties of the Dutch nobility. Philip had failed as their king in a way his father never had. Charles had faced rebellion in Spain and Flanders, but like his contemporaries in England and France, he also maintained a balance between his own demands and those of at least his more powerful subjects. He insisted upon their obedience but was always careful to respect their traditional privileges sufficiently in order to sustain their loyalty to him. His monarchy, like that of Henry VIII and Francis I, was at once authoritarian *and* contractual.

6

Patrons: Government, politics and the royal court

> The world had such a hope in his virtues and such an opinion of his magnanimity and such a conceit of his judgement and wit, that every one confessed, that of very long time there was none raised up to crown with a greater expectation. He was made the more agreeable to the fancies of men by the consideration of his age ... his excellent feature and proportion of body, his great liberality and general humanity ... But especially he pleased greatly the nobility to whom he transferred many singular and great favours.
>
> Holinshed's *Chronicles*[1]

This description of a young king taken from a sixteenth century English source is like many which greeted royal accessions in the early 1500s. It highlights an imposing physique, an attractive personality and magnanimity towards the nobles as desirable qualities in a ruler. It is a description of Francis I of France but was written 30 years after his death. Francis, like Henry VIII and Charles V, helped to shape this definition of successful monarchy. At the start of the sixteenth century the members of the nobility throughout Europe remained acutely conscious of the traditional connection between ownership of land, service in war and social status. As the apex of the social and political hierarchies, monarchs had therefore not only to be successful warriors, wise peacemakers and just governors, they had also to be effective patrons of the nobility.

In *The Governance of England* Sir John Fortescue enunciated the first principle of effective royal patronage. He wrote that the king must 'exceed in lordships all the lords of his realm and there should none grow to be like him which thing is most to be feared in the world.' He wrote against the background of considerable unrest among nobles in England during the middle decades of the fifteenth century known as the Wars of the Roses. That series of political manoeuvres and military battles between the houses of York and Lancaster was provoked by the weakness of the regime of Henry VI. It was fought by magnates, such as Richard, Duke of York and Richard Neville, Earl of Warwick, who drew to themselves members of the lower nobility and gentry who were anxious for financial and personal security at times of political uncertainty and falling incomes on landed estates. These sizeable followings, known as 'affinities,' were, in reality, private armies whose members wore the livery and badge of their master and served only his private interests. In the contest between these 'overmighty subjects', the English crown became a football kicked and scrabbled over in a series of short reigns until, so legend has it, Henry Tudor literally picked it up after the Battle of Bosworth in 1485 and clung on to it.

In France and Spain during this time, great territorial magnates also took advantage of domestic and foreign policy problems faced by the monarchy to establish or extend their hold on land and power. In Spain between 1464 and 1480 successive groups of nobles challenged the Trastámara dynasty, disputing the succession of Henry IV and the legitimacy of his heirs in turn. A series of wars ensued before the marriage of Ferdinand, the heir to Aragon, and Isabella, the heir to Castile, in 1469 consolidated the Trastámara's authority and prestige. In France, aristocratic discontent with Louis XI provoked a conflict in 1465 known as the 'War of the Public Weal' in which he nearly lost the crown. Charles the Bold, the Duke of Burgundy, stirred further trouble in and beyond France in the 1470s until he was defeated and killed in battle at Nancy in 1477. After Louis XI's death in 1483, another Valois prince, Louis of Orléans, led a revolt in alliance with the Duke of Brittany against the regime of the Beaujeu family which dominated King Charles VIII during his adolescence. Louis was reconciled to the king in 1491 and then succeeded him, as Louis XII, in 1498.

These dynastic conflicts and tensions showed how important it was for monarchs to ensure that they were personally fit for the job, that their resources were adequate and that they were supported by at least a majority of the nobility. As Fortescue saw in England, 'overmighty' subjects were created by 'undermighty' kings and this was a situation which Henry VIII, Francis I and Charles V were determined to avoid. All were fortunate that their immediate predecessors had been reasonably strong monarchs who had rebuilt or sustained the wealth of the monarchy, cajoling, enticing or intimidating most of the great magnates, and many lesser nobles, into co-operation with the crown. Rather than trying to destroy the greater nobles, without whom they could not function, they had harnessed the legitimate aspirations of the whole nobility to govern while ensuring that the crown had decisive influence in the government of the localities.

There were two broad models of strong leadership which their predecessors had followed in achieving this position. The first was a cool, dignified and business-like monarchy in which the king impressed his nobles with the regality of his person and office, keeping a close eye on them through legal and financial officials, while maintaining a slight but carefully measured separation. The sovereign's dress, lifestyle and his court's entertainments were not extravagant but sufficiently regal and colourful to command respect. Access to him was open but carefully managed while good service was rewarded but never routinely. Such an approach, when backed with the growing financial and legal competence of the crown, warned some nobles and reassured others that a challenge to the monarch was unlikely to succeed. This was style of kingship practised by Henry VII, by Ferdinand and Isabella in Spain and by Louis XII of France. It was also favoured by the mature Charles V.

In complete contrast was the model of ebullient, participatory kingship most clearly associated with the early sixteenth century. Here the monarch identified himself fully with the aspirations of his nobles. Distance between himself and favoured subjects was reduced and enthusiasm for him was generated by exciting activities which he initiated. The king's dress was as extravagantly expensive and spectacular as his court's entertainments. His manner invited those who sought power to distinguish themselves to him by appealing to his personality and providing advice or other services which increased his authority in the realm. It also spawned rivalry between advisors and this style of kingship had its critics, not least among courtiers themselves. As many of them found to their cost, this ebullient style did not always deliver what it seemed to promise, rewards for all in full measure. This was the model of kingship adopted by the younger Henry VIII and by Francis I.[2]

Nevertheless a balance had always to be struck Dignified monarchy could easily become too distanced and ineffective. The laudable husbanding of crown resources could descend to parsimony or greed which caused anxiety among nobles. Most English noblemen living in the last years of Henry VII's reign believed that they had witnessed exactly this shift, and this perception helps to explain the paeans of praise which greeted his son's accession. Similarly, lordly extravagance could become mere prodigality. Therefore a balanced approach towards the nobility in which no individual was allowed to become too powerful while the power of the nobility as a whole was sustained under royal patronage was best. Although often difficult to achieve in practice, this was what being a good royal patron was all about.[3]

ROYAL PATRONAGE IN ENGLAND

The central aim of politics in Tudor England, as in all European monarchies of the sixteenth century, was to gain the favour of the monarch. With favour came influence and power. Securing that influence meant appealing to Henry VIII's personality which was expressed most fully in the life of his court. Henry was determined to be obeyed and, ideally, loved by his noble subjects. At first all was youth and joy. Edward Hall's account of the first years of the reign describes the colourful 'May-day' world of a late-medieval tapestry. Led by an 18-year-old sovereign determined to enjoy himself, the English court joined in a seemingly endless round of hunting, hawking and tournaments. These entertainments were often followed by banquets which impressed all comers with their scale and colour. Banquets usually concluded with a display of 'largesse' in which the king deliberately played the part of the patron by throwing money to the court or allowing his courtiers and foreign ambassadors to tear the costly decorations from his masking apparel. Hall describes such an invitation in February 1511 when the king's servants and other 'common people' also joined in, stripping him to his underwear. The royal guard was summoned to restore order but Henry, ever the showman, turned a tricky moment to 'laughing and game,' giving it all away 'for honour and largesse.'[4] It was all too good to last – and it didn't. Nevertheless Henry's spontaneous personal style in his youth and the early splendour of his court attracted European attention. Under Wolsey's guidance, this royal flair for entertainment proved useful in England's international relations. More immediately, it appealed directly to the instincts of the nobility and gentry and drew to Henry the men and women who would play major roles in his government.

Whereas his father and his youngest daughter both restricted the size of the English peerage, Henry VIII increased it over the course of his reign although by Continental standards it remained quite small. There were 51 peers at his death in 1547, nine more than at his accession and half the 34 barons then living owed their titles to him. Of the 17 peers of the rank of viscount or above, 11 were created by Henry. He respected the ambition of nobles to distinguish themselves in battle and Thomas Howard's victory at Flodden in 1513 was rewarded the following year with his restoration to his father's title of Duke of Norfolk while his own son became Earl of Surrey. Sir Edward Stanley became Lord Monteagle after commanding the left flank of the royal army at Flodden. The extraordinary creation of Charles Brandon as Duke of Suffolk in 1514 was due to his friendship with the king born largely from his skills in the tournament. The former esquire had first been ennobled in 1513 as Viscount Lisle when Henry made him marshal of the royal army for the invasion of France.

Ten years later there was another brace of promotions, most in preparation for Henry's second war against France. Sir Henry Marney was made a baron and Lord Privy Seal in February 1523 but died shortly afterwards and the barony passed to his son. Sir Arthur Plantangenet was created Viscount Lisle in April and Henry also made barons of three officers in the pale of Calais: Sir Maurice Berkely the lieutenant, Sir William Sandys, the treasurer and Sir Nicholas Vaux, the lieutenant of Guînes. Later in the 1520s a number of ennoblements were made as part of Henry's campaign to secure the succession and the security of the Tudor dynasty. Thomas, George and Anne Boleyn were all successively ennobled and received grants of land between 1525 and 1534. They were followed in 1536–37 by Jane Seymour's brothers and in 1540 by Thomas Cromwell, made Earl of Essex. All had played their parts in finally providing Henry with a legitimate male heir by 1537. In the last decade of his reign, Henry's appointments continued to be focused on those who had distinguished themselves to him personally through service in military, diplomatic and legal spheres. These included men such as William Fitzwilliam, created Earl of Southampton, Baron Russell and Sir John Dudley, made Viscount Lisle in 1542.[5]

Henry VII had worked hard to increase the size of the crown's estates relative to the amount of land held by magnates. He also established a formidable legal machinery to keep the nobles in check while creating a royal affinity in the localities among the lower nobles and gentry. This was sustained through the judicious distribution of money and royal offices, gifts and other benefits. All these measures slowly restored the crown's dominance as landholder. Narrowly defined, the crown's annual landed income averaged £40,000 at Henry VII's death. It fell to around £25,000 by 1515 as Henry VIII reversed his father's attainders and granted annuities and offices as early evidence of his 'good lordship.' Nevertheless, this figure still dwarfs the incomes of even the greatest magnates. In 1524 the Earl of Northumberland was assessed for tax on landed income of £2920 per annum and the Duke of Norfolk for a similar amount although his estates were actually worth around £4000. The average taxable income of English peers was £800 in 1523–24 but this amount underestimated new landed revenues.

Despite his very different style of government, Henry VIII was more his father's son than is often realised. This was particularly true in his dealings with the nobility. After 1515 he alienated very little crown land permanently to nobles and when he did, grants were concentrated on a few families whose status substantially depended upon his favour. As his reign progressed, Henry conceived of 'good lordship' as upholding the dignity of the nobility in general and encouraging peers to express their authority and status in serving the crown, rather than handing out land and cash to curry favour with the peerage generally. He also maintained his father's tight controls on military retaining. He licensed individual peers to muster troops and his ministers prosecuted those who did not disband at the expiry of these licences. During his reign most peers had to work hard to maintain their estates. He did assist some who had fallen on hard times but, as the unfortunate career of Richard Grey, third Earl of Kent shows, such assistance was not automatic. Grey alienated most of his estates, worth some £1500 in annual income in the 1480s, in gambling debts or in disadvantageous deals with grasping courtier administrators. His half-brother Henry Grey succeeded to the title but little else in 1523. Due partly to enemies his predecessor had created at court and partly to his own irascibility, Henry Grey received little help from Henry VIII. His father had helped Richard Grey because the king felt he needed to keep him in place as part of the political landscape of Kent. With a stronger royal affinity in the county by the 1520s, Henry VIII seems to have taken the view that it was not his responsibility to bail out peers whose poverty, albeit at one remove, was self-induced. Grey did not succeed in restoring the family's fortunes.[6]

More typical of the peerage as a whole and more useful to Henry VIII was Henry Bouchier, Earl of Essex. He had comparatively small landed estates but they were unusually well concentrated in Essex and Hertfordshire. His annual income from royal annuities and offices, including the constableship of Windsor Castle, was more than £150 by 1514, but he had not received any land from Henry VIII despite being part of the king's first circle of intimates. He was 20 years older than the king and, as he began to feel his Tudor middle age, he gradually reduced his regular attendance at court. For the next 20 years he managed his estates effectively and administered seigneurial justice within his jurisdiction reasonably well. His income was assessed for tax at £850 in 1534, slightly below the average yearly income of the peerage at the time. He maintained the ancestral seat at Stanstead Hall in Halstead and had a household of 50 servants. Bouchier served the king as and when required. He mustered troops from his affinity, inspected defensive works in the county and served as a Justice of the Peace and crown commissioner in Essex. Despite some minor disputes he worked harmoniously with his fellow peers, especially with John De Vere, fifteenth Earl of Oxford whose income was triple Bourchier's. Lacking the wealth of such men, Essex could not play power politics on the national stage and contented himself with managing his own affinity, comprised largely of lower gentry and yeoman families. He supported them in disputes, used them in the administration of his own lands and was respected in the county.[7]

The principal noble families at the end of Henry's reign were certainly not all the same ones as at his accession. In Buckingham's place as the single duke of the realm stood the short-lived Henry Brandon, the son of Charles, Duke of Suffolk. The Duke of Norfolk had been attainted in the weeks before the king's death. Nevertheless, Helen Miller's detailed study of the early Tudor nobility concludes that the king was careful to balance the creation of new peers with the promotion to higher ranks of established ones and that therein lay his success as patron of the English elite. He needed no individual noble, but he needed and respected the nobility. As we have seen, during the 1540s the high nobility came to monopolise the most important offices in the royal council as well as those in the royal household and in the localities. Helen Miller summarises Henry's attitude to the nobility thus: 'By his readiness to increase its size he demonstrated his belief in its value. By refusing to make an excessive number of grants he preserved its status.'[8]

With the increased size of the royal demesne and the royal affinity, Henry also extended his direct patronage of the gentry in the counties and of burgesses in towns. A greater percentage than ever before of the estimated 1200 to 1500 gentry families in England became landowners and tenants under the direct control of the crown. More opportunities were created to appoint stewards, bailiffs and other officials on demesne lands. Like his father, Henry insisted upon exclusivity so that his officers served no other locally dominant lord. He also increased their numbers on county commissions and among the ranks of the JPs. He and his ministers rewarded good service with prestigious offices in their households and in the higher echelons of the administration.

From the late 1530s the dissolution of the monasteries provided further opportunities for Tudor gentlemen. Not only did it create a myriad of greater or lesser offices within new institutions of the royal administration such as the Court of Augmentations, it also provided new lands seized from the monasteries and available for lease or purchase from the crown. Some men with legal training, such as Sir Richard Rich and Sir Thomas Audley, profited from enthusiastic service in these new posts to buy up large tracts of ex-monastic lands, to establish themselves as men of consequence and to make their way into the peerage.[9]

As Steven Gunn has noted, prospective rewards of various kinds gave ambitious individuals the incentive to involve the king in local affairs in the hope of distinguishing themselves by serving his interests. By its nature, royal control emanating from Westminster was more compelling but still less direct than that which had been exercised by the great magnates in the previous century. For this reason it might actually be preferred by gentlemen seeking to assert their independence from such territorial heavyweights. Whereas in the early fifteenth century service in the household of a great noble was a high ambition for such county gentlemen, increasingly under the Tudors it came to be seen merely as a stepping-stone to service in the king's household or was rivalled by the prospect of service in the household of a minister such as Wolsey. Yet any idea that these developments signified an alliance between the 'middling sort' and the crown to destroy the power of high nobles should be rejected. Although they could not perhaps command the dedicated and exclusive service among the upper gentry that they once had, peers such as John De Vere and even Henry Bouchier, retained the highest offices in land, had a real capacity to advise the king and remained important connections between the monarch and his realm.

THE COURT OF HENRY VIII

During the reign of Henry VIII the household of the king became both a political boxing-ring and a clearing-house of royal patronage in a way that it had not been under his father. Henry VII had jealously guarded his personal space as part of his policy of keeping nobles at what he believed was a respectful distance. The king's private apartments were known formally as the 'Privy Chamber' although they actually consisted of a number of rooms, chiefly the 'Presence Chamber' where he ate and received important dignitaries and the 'Bedchamber' where he slept. Within this space the first Tudor king was attended only by low ranking and therefore politically insignificant servants. His personal space was his own and in it Henry could work on his papers unmolested by courtiers. The privy chamber was politically neutral ground.

This changed dramatically under Henry VIII. He was attended in his personal apartments by his own friends who were anything but politically neutral. The first of them were companions drawn from the noble families of his father's regime and from those with whom he jousted in the first years of his reign. They included the afore-mentioned Henry Bouchier, Earl of Essex, and Sir Henry Guildford, later Master of the King's Horse and Comptroller of the Royal Household. By 1518, with Henry in his mid-twenties, they were in turn succeeded by even younger companions known as the king's 'minions'. Men like Sir Francis Bryan, Sir Nicholas Carew and William Carey now attended the kings as he dressed, ate and through most activities of his day. They could also be sent on important assignments by him. In 1518, following a French model, Henry created for them the office at court which was eventually formalised in 1526 as 'Gentleman of the King's Privy Chamber.' The significance of this office was that it gave the king's personal companions exclusive access to him in places where most people had none. Most courtiers only saw him when he chose to be in the public areas of the palace or when they were summoned to him. The more important might attend him regularly as he dined in his 'Presence Chamber,' when he hunted and when he travelled between palaces. In a political system where royal approval was the mainspring of the patronage machinery, but where the king himself was not always easy to find, free access to him was highly prized.[10]

Access to the king's private apartments became the key to power in Henry's reign. Those who had it introduced family and friends at court. As the career of Sir William Compton shows, with access came offices, pensions and gifts from the king and a rapid rise in fortunes and social status. Compton was Henry's 'groom of the stool', the servant who looked after the king's personal possessions, money and most private needs including attending him on his close stool. He amassed many royal offices and with the profits from them, he built a fine house at Compton Wynates and founded the fortunes of the earls of Northampton. At Compton's death in 1528 the king had to ask Wolsey just how many offices and gifts he had given to his favourite because he had completely lost count.[11]

These developments unsettled Cardinal Wolsey who had enjoyed unrivalled influence with Henry since 1513. He was the first to see the worrying potential of the new office. As Lord Chancellor he had regular audiences with king, taking his barge to Greenwich or riding in state to see Henry at one of his country houses. However the pressure of business during the law terms and Henry's hectic schedule of pleasures during the summer meant that it was not always easy for Wolsey to be with the king. Moreover, wherever Henry was, so were his privy chamber servants and Wolsey did not like it. During the decade after 1518 Wolsey tried various strategies to remove them altogether or to reduce their numbers so as to minimise their influence upon Henry. Under the Eltham Ordinances of January 1526 their formal status was recognised, but they were forbidden to 'intermeddle' in Henry's affairs and had to occupy themselves only in maintaining the king's comfort or representing him abroad when called upon to do so. They were temporarily cowed but the flattering treatment they received as ambassadors in France and elsewhere, together with the support of Henry's inamorata, Anne Boleyn, emboldened them against the cardinal. In 1527, while entangled in negotiations in France and with the problem of the king's first marriage looming ever larger in his mind, Wolsey fretted about the renewed ascendance of those in the privy chamber. He did so with good reason. In 1529 he fell from power partly because of their conniving.[12]

The word 'faction' first came into English usage in 1509, the year of Henry VIII's accession. It was an ironic coincidence that in his funeral sermon for the king's maternal grandmother, Margaret Beaufort, Bishop John Fisher stressed how she was able to discover any 'factions or bands' among her servants and resolve conflicts between them. Her son had some similar capacity; her grandson evidently did not. Professor Ives described the fully evolved Tudor faction as:

> a web of personal ties, an alliance to secure spoils, but a political axis as well, seeking to promote particular politicians and particular policies.[13]

Although there has been scepticism among some historians about the usefulness of the concept of faction in Henry's reign, it is difficult to find an alternative concept which so neatly defines the kinds of personal alliances observable among his courtiers from the late 1520s. Confronted with the forceful but insecure personality of Henry VIII and amidst the crowded surroundings of the court where rumour and gossip were endemic, it made sense for people to work together to promote one of their number and through their rise, to achieve wider aims. However, once such a promotion was secured or a desired shift in royal policy accomplished, the need to co-operate ceased and new groupings could form. Some individuals had greater influence with the king than others and so became leaders of factions. The real objectives of such leaders were rarely shown overtly. Instead they used the king's ambitions and anxieties as the means to increase their own influence with him or to diminish that of others. The most recurrent, and therefore most profitable, royal dilemma was of course the question of the succession and the king's matrimonial career.

From the advent of Anne Boleyn in 1527 factional politics was the norm at Henry's court. She rose with the support of a faction of gentlemen of the privy chamber who wished to remove Wolsey as the king's great favourite. Her own aim was to displace Katherine of Aragon as queen and she duly succeeded, partly by destroying Henry's faith in Wolsey. From 1527 she and her relatives and friends among the privy chamber staff worked to deny the cardinal precious access to the king, while poisoning Henry's mind against him. Although crowned queen in 1533, she ultimately failed to secure her position by producing Henry's longed-for male heir. Her subsequent fate has been much debated by historians. Despite the strenuous objections of George Bernard, and Retha Warnicke's attempt to substantiate contemporary allegations of witchcraft against Anne, the account of her fall presented by Eric Ives and supported by David Starkey remains the most carefully argued and convincing. Anne was brought down by Thomas Cromwell, the man with whom she had been allied as an advocate of evangelical church reform. By 1536 he was fearful of losing his own influence with the king as Anne became increasingly alienated from her husband. To save himself, Cromwell hijacked a plot that had been hatched by a faction of aristocrats and religious conservatives to unseat Anne by dangling Jane Seymour in front of the king. He used the flimsiest of evidence of supposed adultery with which to secure her conviction and execution, together with half the privy chamber staff, on charges of treason.[14]

During the four years after Anne's death, Cromwell's credit with Henry was unrivalled. He maintained it by the ruthless removal of all those whose influence with the king threatened his own. He rode out the storm of the Pilgrimage of Grace before, in 1538–39 turning on his erstwhile allies, those political and religious conservative courtiers who supported Princess Mary's restoration to the succession. He planted charges of conspiracy and treason on a group whose main victims included the Marquis of Exeter and Sir Nicholas Carew, one of the king's closest friends since his youth. At the height of his power, Cromwell ran the king's administration and the royal affinity alongside a substantial one of his own. For a short time, he also ran the court. During the later 1530s the space within royal palaces available to king and closed to most courtiers began to grow rapidly. At Hampton Court and especially at Whitehall, Henry built a series of 'privy lodgings' which extended well beyond the formal 'Privy Chamber'. By the 1540s it was possible for him to move around several acres of royal apartments and even to come and go from them without ever being seen in public. In this secret world Cromwell operated as Wolsey never could. He stacked the privy chamber with his own men, thus neutralising its potential against him. By 1539 he was 'chief nobleman' of the privy chamber and in 1540 he was briefly Lord Great Chamberlain, responsible for the king's ceremonial and his entire private service.

Yet it was not enough. Despite his efforts in reforming the Privy Council, Cromwell could not finally master it. In June 1540 he was spirited away from the council board and from the king by sudden arrest, his own preferred technique. He followed where he had sent so many before him, convicted and executed on charges of treason. In his wake a rough equilibrium established itself between those Cromwell appointees in the privy chamber and his opponents in the council. Although the 'old' nobles and religious conservatives seemed to have won the day, towards the end of the king's life they were eclipsed. Led by Sir Anthony Denny, Henry's last chief gentleman of the privy chamber, a faction of 'new' nobleman including Jane

Seymour's brothers entrenched themselves against the conservatives. Stephen Gardiner lost Henry's favour over a dispute involving ownership of lands. An attempt by the Duke of Norfolk and his son to position themselves as the dominant players after Henry's death was foiled and a successful counter-conspiracy brought the Earl of Surrey to the block on charges of treason. Only Henry's own death saved Norfolk. Finally, as the king lay dying at Whitehall in late January 1547, the key members of this faction doctored his will so as to give themselves control over the council and person of the young Edward VI.[15]

ROYAL PATRONAGE IN FRANCE

Like Henry VIII, Francis I was fortunate that his immediate predecessor had done much to restore the security and prestige of the monarchy. From the start Francis made it clear that he would provide still more opportunities for the nobles. He would rule in their interests, provided always that they were co-operative. His would be a kingship of participation more glamorous than Henry VIII's. Gossiping Venetian ambassadors noted how in the earliest days of his reign, Francis had little time for 'government.' He would meet his council each morning for as short a time as possible. Then, referring business to his mother and to his former governor, the lord of Boisy, he would charge off with his friends and his dogs in pursuit of stags and boars, often not returning until dusk. Greying brows furrowed over this apparent dereliction of duty, but the younger members of the nobility were thrilled. There were also frequent banquets and entertainments whose splendour equalled anything seen in England since 1509. Within months of his accession, Francis was planning another French invasion of Milan.

It has been estimated that by c.1560–80 there were about 25,000 families in France who claimed the status of nobility. This was still a tiny fraction of a population of around 15 million but a vast number compared with the nobility of England. Although they were ranked according to title, all nobles were theoretically equal members of the realm's second estate. Nobles were made primarily by birth into a family of noble lineage or *ancienne race*. They were entitled to bear arms, were exempted from direct royal taxation, and were known as 'sword' nobles. In addition, the king could ennoble people for services rendered, in return for payment and by the late fifteenth century some royal legal offices customarily conveyed nobility to their holders. The importance and social status of those who were later known as 'robe' nobles, because of the long gowns worn by administrative officials, has become one of the great socio-political controversies of sixteenth-century French history. However, unlike in England where each noble promotion and disgrace had an impact on the composition of the peerage, in

France it was only change at the very highest levels that created seismic shifts in the political landscape.[16]

Francis I was a reasonably successful patron. He did not please every noble and alienated even some of the most powerful, but in general he esteemed and utilised the nobles in ways that enhanced their personal honour and their material wealth. Naturally it was to the upper echelons that he had most to direct his skills as patron. It was from these ranks that Francis appointed the great officers of state, his chief courtiers, his military commanders, provincial governors, main councillors and the leading clergy of his realm. At the top of the hierarchy were the king's three sons and other princes of royal blood. Until the mid 1520s the most powerful of these princes was Charles, Duke of Bourbon. He was Constable of France, the kingdom's chief military officer and controlled a vast domain of lands in central and eastern France. Following his wife Suzanne's death in April 1521, Bourbon became involved in a complicated legal dispute with the king and Louise of Savoy, both of whom laid claim to substantial parts Suzanne's lands. In August 1523 the Parlement of Paris ordered the sequestration of Bourbon's lands and a few months later Francis upbraided Bourbon over rumours that he was about to marry Charles V's sister. Angered by the legal case and Francis's treatment of him, Bourbon planned a revolt and plotted with Charles and Henry VIII to carve up France between them. He renounced his allegiance to the king in September 1523 but, lacking wider support among the nobility, his attempted coup failed. He fled France and entered the service of Charles V but was killed during the Sack of Rome in 1527. His lands were forfeited to the crown and parcelled out among Francis's relatives and close associates. Despite the disgrace of the head of the clan, the numerous other members of the Bourbon family continued to enjoy the king's trust and favour, holding the governorships of four provinces.

Next in hierarchy were the *princes étrangers* who were sovereign princes of territories outside France but who swore allegiance to the king of France and who were naturalised Frenchmen. The most important of them in the early sixteenth century were members of a cadet branch of the house of Lorraine. Claude de Lorraine was naturalised by Louis XII in 1506. Francis I made him Duke of Guise and a peer of France in 1527. He was governor of Champagne from 1524 to 1543 and then succeeded Philippe de Chabot as governor of Burgundy. His brothers and sons were prominent in the church and in military establishment under Francis. The Lorraine/Guise family became one of the most powerful in the kingdom with a vast *clientèle*. It contracted marriages into the Bourbon family and Claude's daughter, Marie, married James V of Scotland in May 1538. The family played a leading role in the reign of Henry II and in the Wars of Religion that followed his death in 1559.[17]

The *haute noblesse* or high nobility, were those not of royal blood but who still had substantial estates, status and influence in the realm. These families typically disposed of annual incomes of 100,000 *livres* or more.

They included the Gouffier, Montmorency, and La Trémoille. These families wanted to protect and enhance their wealth and status in the localities where their lands lay and in the kingdom as a whole. They were able to do so by prudent management of their estates, by careful marriages, by service in war and by co-operating with the monarchy in the expectation of high office and rewards.

For example, the La Trémoille family had suffered considerable misfortunes in the fifteenth century. It recovered its wealth in the sixteenth by consolidating its holdings in the provinces of Berry, Poitou and Saintonge in central and western France. These estates were managed carefully, supervised by gentlemen of the La Trémoille *clientèle*. The family asserted its seigneurial rights over tenants and against other families in court cases in Brittany and in Paris. From an estimated 15,000 *livres* in 1484, landed revenues rose to approximately 40,000 *livres* between 1517 and 1542. Louis II de La Trémoille's independent landed wealth was supplemented by some 375,000 *livres* in pensions, gifts and offices from Francis I. He was *lieutenant du roi* or deputy governor, in Brittany. He held the honorary post of *premier chambellan* to the king and was a knight of the Order of Saint Michael. His only son Charles was killed at Marignano in 1515 and after his first wife's death a few years later he married the very much younger Louise, Duchess of Valentinois, the daughter of Cesare Borgia. Louis II was killed leading his ordinance company, fighting alongside the king at Pavia in 1525. At his death his lands passed to his grandson, François II.[18]

Below the highest level of the nobility came the *moyenne noblesse* who held comparatively modest estates but whose annual income still measured several hundreds or thousands of *livres*. It was from this echelon that the great families, such as the Bourbon and La Trémoille, recruited their followings. Obligation and reciprocity were vital elements in patron–client relationships which were always conducted in the language of faithfulness, or *fidélité*. Clients assured their patrons of exclusive service and devotion and were promised financial rewards, protection and support in return. They might have to serve for a long time before these rewards were forthcoming but there were often real emotional bonds based on shared experiences which held patrons and clients together. Often these bonds were formalised in marriages. Yet it is also clear that self-interest was important in these relationships and that were not totally exclusive. Clients had considerable freedom of movement between patrons especially at times of political opportunity or tension when the *grands* competed with each other to increase their *clientèles*. One individual could change patrons or sustain different kinds of relationship with a number without necessarily incurring dishonour. Typically the sons of client families would complete their social and military education as a page or *gentilhomme* in the household of their parents' patron. From here they would move on usually to the patron's ordinance company. Those who showed promise might be preferred to a still greater lord's household or directly to royal service, holding offices in the king's household or his military establishment. It was from this broader group of nobles that the majority of *baillis*, town governors and military captains were chosen.[19]

The experience of the Noailles shows how a family could profit by careful planning and exploiting noble patronage networks. By Francis I's reign the family had built on series of advantageous marriages in the fifteenth century to consolidate its land holdings in the Limousin area. With the wealth of these lands, its members contracted still more advantageous marriages and by the 1520s the Noailles had married into the client group of the La Tour family, *vicomtes* of Turenne. François de La Tour was in turn related by marriage to Francis I's favourite, Anne de Montmorency. Antoine de Noailles fought with François de la Tour in Italy in the mid-1520s and under his influence was appointed as a table servant to king Francis from 1529. He then served the king in his home region, first as captain and then mayor of Bordeaux and also *lieutenant-général* of the province of Guyenne. The Noailles thus became a direct link between the king and the provincial nobility of Limousin. During the Wars of Religion they served the Bourbon family. Backing the winner, they were elevated to the aristocracy and attained the highest ranks of royal military and administrative service under Henry IV. Finally, in 1663, their rise was complete when created dukes and peers of France by Louis XIV. The Noailles were certainly exceptional in the speed and degree of their success but were entirely typical of their social group both in their ambitions and strategic use of the patronage system.[20]

THE COURT OF FRANCIS I

Writing in the 1580s the legal commentator Jean du Tillet observed that under Francis I members of the nobility, like Antoine de Noailles, were keen to serve the king in his household, despite being paid relatively small wages, 'so that in peace his court was magnificent and in war, his entourage very strong.'[21] The court of Francis was indeed larger and more sophisticated than those of his predecessors although the process of enlargement had begun under them. His household proper, as compared to those for his wife and children, had 40 categories of servants, the more prestigious of whom were nobles. The household had three major departments. These were the chapel under the *grand aumônier*, which served the king's spiritual needs; the chamber under the *grand chambellan* whose officers attended to the king's personal requirements; and the *hôtel* under the *grand maître de France*, the Great Master, with its various sub-departments responsible for lodging and feeding the royal entourage. Its officers included household stewards or *maîtres d'hôtel*, as well as the *panetiers*, *échansons* and *valets tranchans* who served the king his meals. The department of the *écurie* looked after the king's horses and messengers. The *vénerie* and *fauconnerie* were responsible for his hunting hounds and birds respectively together with the other accoutrements of the chase. There were also four companies of royal guards; the Scots, the Swiss and two companies of one hundred men-at-arms, the *gentilshommes de la maison.*

Unlike their English counterparts, French courtiers expected that their king would live 'publicly,' in other words that they would see him, and perhaps be spoken to by him, daily. This obligation was met formally by the ceremonies of his rising and retiring, the *lever* and *coucher* when substantial numbers of courtiers would assemble in the outer royal apartments to greet the king. They might also see him as he went to Mass or moved about the court and when he hunted. Again in contrast to England, French royal tradition also allowed Francis comparatively little personal space. Whereas Henry VIII eventually built himself vast warrens of royal lodgings, in most of Francis's palaces his private apartments had only three principal rooms. These were a reception room or *salle*, a *chambre* or bedroom and small study known as a *retraite* or *cabinet*. At Fontainebleau he also had a gallery in which to walk and entertain guests and his rooms usually had a private staircase, such as the one at Saint-Germain-en-Laye, which gave out on to the royal gardens.[22]

There were many foreigners, especially Italians, at Francis's court and he favoured Italian styles of dress and dance. Women played an important role in his court. His sister and mother were major influences upon him as well as patrons of art and learning in their own right. Their households, like those of Queens Claude and Eleanor, provided places for young noblewomen to serve and complete their social training. These same women appeared at the court's regular social events. All significant royal occasions were marked by tournaments and feasting at which the king showed ostentatious generosity. At tournaments gender roles were well defined and the women's were largely passive. They were expected to watch with a mixture of appropriate concern and adoration while the men performed. In the banquet afterwards things were more relaxed. Men and women could literally get closer together and women played a more active role in the courtly conventions of erudite discussion as well as in the serious business of gossip, sexual attraction and matchmaking. Francis's enthusiastic participation in the court's life enhanced his reputation among his subjects and foreign observers alike.

Shortly after his accession Francis created a new office at his court which enabled him to focus this royal munificence very precisely on those whose outlook he shared and whose company he enjoyed. This was the position of *gentilhomme de la chambre du roi* or 'gentleman of the king's chamber.' The significance of the new office was that it allowed its holders to be close to the king not just at his formal appearances, but at all times of the day when they were on duty. They became the king's closest personal servants. Under the supervision of the *premier gentilhomme*, these officers attended the king as he rose, washed and dressed. They escorted him to Mass and then accompanied him throughout the day. Because of the opportunities for influence and favour this proximity created, the office quickly became most prestigious. Each *gentilhomme* generally served for three to six months a year and when not at court was employed in the king's army, as an ambassador or in supervising the localities. Their habitual proximity to the king gave them a status which enhanced their authority and effectiveness in working for him. In international relations especially, the *gentilshommes de la chambre* became esteemed representatives whose knowledge of their master was highly prized by those to whom they were sent. It was of course this office which provided the model for the equivalent office of 'Gentleman of the King's Privy Chamber' in England. Henry first gave his 'minions' this office in September 1518 when a French embassy which included six or more *gentilshommes* was on its way to London for the signing of the Treaty of Universal Peace.

Francis had 21 *gentilshommes* in 1518, most of whom had known him before he became king. One was Charles du Solier, Lord of Morette, a *gentilhomme de la chambre* for the entirety of Francis's reign. He first accompanied the king on his conquest of Milan in 1515. Thereafter Morette was busy meeting and greeting Italian nobles drawn to the court of their new overlord. In 1518–19 he was held as hostage in England for Francis's performance of his obligations to Henry under the Treaty of Universal Peace. He was later a frequent ambassador to England, Spain and the Netherlands. He also commanded a French fleet in the Mediterranean during the campaign for Naples in 1528 and in the 1530s was granted the lands and/or revenues of several lordships. Although exceptional in length, Morette's career and the range of tasks on which he was employed in it were typical of those who were gentlemen of the chamber.[23]

Alongside the great princes, the *gentilshommes de la chambre* became the core of the king's affinity. They included the members of dozens of high and middle ranking noble families and several were provincial governors. Sons, nephews, brothers and cousins often followed each other in holding this office. The most important of these men was undoubtedly Anne de Montmorency, the king's favourite for most of his reign. He was *premier gentilhomme de la chambre* and *grand maître* from 1526, and Constable of France from 1538. He was also the governor of Languedoc. Though only a baron, Montmorency's favour with Francis allowed him to build a vast client network of his own. The more offices, pensions and other rewards his nominees were granted, the greater became his reputation at court and beyond and the more prospective clients he attracted. From this larger pool he promoted protégés who backed his policies, safeguarding his position. His client network eventually rivalled those of the great princes of Bourbon and the Guise. It fed and helped to sustain the king's affinity.

David Potter has shown how close were the connections between the court and a number of Picard families, such as the Heilly and the Humières. In 1526 the Heilly family supplied the king with his most famous and powerful mistress, Anne, made Duchess of Etampes a decade later. The Humières were related to the Montmorency clan through the marriage in 1525 of Charlotte d'Humières to François de Montmorency, Lord of La Rochepot, the brother of the *grand maître* and briefly the provincial governor of Picardy in 1537. Alongside other prominent clans like the Créquy, these families secured senior appointments, and pensions, not just in the province but in the royal *chambre*. They assisted the king in the administration and defence of Picardy through their own client groups. In turn, their court connections and influence helped them to advertise and extend their *clientèles*.[24]

Anne de Montmorency favoured a policy of peace with the emperor. Between 1529 and 1536 and again from 1538 to 1541 he was able to secure it. During peacetime pressure for places at court increased and the court grew larger in the 1530s and 1540s. There were for instance over 60 *gentilshommes de la chambre* by 1540. Consequently the court lost something of the relaxed quality of the earlier years. It became more formal in its hierarchical divisions and in its routine. As he grew older Francis spent more time close to Paris. He also spent more time away from most courtiers, at Fontainebleau and at his hunting lodges, retreating with smaller groups of favourites and dallying with his 'privy band' of women. During the 1530s English ambassadors reported the emergence of factions around Montmorency and his rivals, especially admiral Chabot and Francis the dauphin. The latter's hostility towards the *grand maître* stemmed from his years as hostage for his father in Spain, for which he blamed Montmorency. Meanwhile his younger brother Henry grew apart from his father and closer to Montmorency. Ambassadors also reported the steadily growing influence of Francis's mistress.

Francis tried to balance these factions, so as not to give one individual or group too great an advantage over another. In most cases, and in contrast to his English contemporary, Francis was not vindictive towards those courtiers whom he no longer favoured. Rustication, not eradication, was the usual fate of those who lost factional battles. So it was in 1540 in the wake of Charles V's decision to invest his own son with the duchy of Milan. Anne de Montmorency's policy of Franco-Imperial peace was seen to have failed. Attacked by his enemies, he lost the king's favour, retired from court and lived quietly on his estates. He retained his offices although he was forbidden to exercise them. His successor as the king's principal advisor was his rival Philippe de Chabot, who was in turn succeeded by Claude d'Annebault and Cardinal François de Tournon. Although influential, none enjoyed quite the same favour with the king or freedom of political movement as had Montmorency. Francis remained master of his own house at least until his last years, when by his own admission according to one source, he allowed Madame d'Etampes too great an influence over him. Her undue sway, together with Francis's poor relationship with Henry (whose brothers had both died young) created the fault lines along which the court fractured at the king's death. Henry particularly resented Madame d'Etampes both as rival for influence with his father and as threat to the pre-eminence at court of his own mistress, Diane de Poitiers. At Francis's death he was somewhat reconciled to his father but this did not prevent 'a palace revolution' and the complete overthrow of his father's regime at his accession in March 1547. Henry II's first act was to recall Anne de Montmorency. He restored him to the exercise of all his offices, reimbursed him for all his unpaid salary, made him chief counsellor and created him a duke and peer of France.[25]

ROYAL PATRONAGE IN SPAIN

Like his contemporaries in England and France, Charles V as ruler of Spain owed much to his predecessors. Royal authority in the kingdoms of Aragon and Castile had finally been established after long periods of unrest among the nobility during fourteenth and fifteenth centuries. The nobles still dominated the political, economic and social life of the two kingdoms whose joint a population has been estimated at around 5.5 million in 1516. These individuals were mostly all 'new' nobles, having had been created by Henry II of Trastamára in the 1360s and 1370s and by his successors up to 1474. The royal dynasty had also alienated a large amount of crown land to a group of 15 families. Historians of Spain speak of this process as the 'seigneurialisation' of Spanish, and specifically Castilian, society during the fifteenth century. Noble families also used force to usurp the liberty of towns and to absorb smaller territories on the fringes of their lands. The definition of noble status and its attributes was much debated in sixteenth century Spain and those claiming such status constituted approximately 10 per cent of the population, one of the highest proportions in Europe.

The nobles were divided into four broad categories. At the top were approximately 5000 magnates or *ricos hombres*. The highest ranked families were known as the *títulos* or 'lineages'. They possessed the right of access to the sovereign and occupied the principal posts at court. They controlled vast tracts of land over which they exercised near-complete señorial jurisdiction and usually the right to levy the *alcabala* on their estates and often beyond them. This group included the Enríquez, Mendoza, and Guzmán families. Below the high nobles were the *caballeros* or knights who traditionally served the king in warfare. In contrast to the English gentry who served a similar function and who lived in rural areas, most *caballeros* were urban property owners living in the major towns and who dominated the membership of town councils. Below them were about 60,000 *hidalgos*, who had noble status without specific titles because they lived 'gently' off the land. Like their French counterparts, all Spanish nobles were exempt from direct taxation. They shared this privilege with the university-educated lawyers, the *letrados*, who increasingly joined the ranks of the royal administration from the late fifteenth century and who had acquired noble status. The remainder of the Spanish population was divided between the 12–15 per cent who worked and traded in urban centres or were ecclesiastics and more than 80 per cent who were peasants. It was this vast majority who paid the taxes upon which the monarchy lived.

It remains difficult to assess in detail how Charles V's patronage of his nobility worked because historians have done very little work on Spain's internal history under him. Broadly, it seems that after a poor start Charles followed the example of his predecessors, managing the aristocracy by respecting its rights and jurisdictions. By their personal energy and careful patronage of the nobility, Ferdinand and Isabella established their joint monarchy as, in the words of Glyn Redworth, 'the undisputed senior partner in Spanish government.' In 1520 Charles named 35 families as the grandees, the most senior nobles of the realm who held titles of duke, marquis and earl. They included the Medina-Sidonia and Ponce de León families in Andalusia, the La Cerda and Manrique families in Old Castile and the Dukes of Medinaceli. Charles extended to the grandees the privilege of calling him 'cousin' and being so addressed by him. They were entitled to be seated in the royal chapel and also enjoyed the extremely important privilege of wearing their hats in the king's presence after first doffing them to him. Politically, these privileges reflected the fact that the powerful families had extensive networks of dependent nobles of lower status and hundreds of servants. In recognising these individuals and according them notable privileges, Charles hoped to secure their adherence and that of their armies of clients.

The importance of Charles's doing so was shown in 1521 when these great nobles defeated the revolt of the *Comuneros* and saved his fledgling regime. They clearly decided that there was nothing to be gained from rupturing an alliance with the crown which had served their own interests so well to date. Nevertheless the revolt still shocked Charles out of his complacency in dealing with the rest of Spanish society. He formally conceded nothing to the Castilian *Cortes* in the aftermath of the revolt, but he stayed in Spain for the next seven years. He learnt Spanish and his entourage slowly became more Hispanic. He travelled around his dominions as his predecessors had done. In April 1526 he married Isabella of Portugal and in May the following year the succession was secured with the birth of his son Philip. These events created dynastic security and increased Charles's popularity with his Spanish subjects.[26]

The emperor did use high nobles in his councils but did not particularly invite their participation in his administration. Nevertheless, for those prepared to work with the monarchy he offered prominent places at court with lucrative salaries, together with senior military commands, governorships in his empire and appointment as knights of the Golden Fleece. One of those who did well out of such co-operation with the new Habsburg dynasty was

Luis Hurtado de Mendoza, second Marquis of Mondéjar. He was a member of a cadet branch of the Mendoza family, one of the most prestigious in Castile. Its members were wealthy but had a modest estate compared to that of the main branch of the family, the Dukes of Infantado. The first marquis had supported the Trastámara dynasty and to a single señorial estate, that of Tendilla in Guadalajara, he added four others together with non-señorial lands in Granada. He also bought mills, olive presses and commercial property in the city of Granada. Having built a reasonable fortune and considerable political capital, the first marquis then accepted the post of captain-general of Granada. Although prestigious, the rewards he received from Ferdinand were nothing like he expected and he found himself sinking enormous sums of family money into the maintenance of fortifications and other works. This poorly rewarded and lengthy royal service left him seriously in debt at his death in 1515.

The second marquis inherited the office of captain-general and held it for 28 years during which time the income from it remained as inadequate as it had been under his father. However, rather than rejecting royal service as unprofitable, Luis Hurtado varied the range of services he provided to the monarchy. He accepted short-term commissions alongside the captaincy-general. He supported Charles in the revolt of the *Comuneros* and then was host to the emperor and his bride Isabella during their honeymoon in the Alhamabra in 1526. He also oversaw much of the work on a new palace Charles built there. He contributed troops and money to the Tunis campaign of 1535. Crucially, and unlike his father, he was also prepared to move to court and was therefore able to secure yet more lucrative royal offices. He became viceroy of Navarre in 1543 and president of the Council of the Indies in 1546. A portion of his salary for this post was paid in gold or silver bullion directly from Mexico. He became president of the Council of Castile in 1559, receiving an annual salary of 650,000 maravedís together with a lifetime pension of 6000 ducats and a special lump sum of 20,000 ducats. With this level of income he was able substantially to reduce the debt incurred by his father. His sons in turn held similar offices and rebuilt the family's fortunes, creating at least four new estates by 1580. By the mid-sixteenth century the marquises of Mondéjar were among the most prominent nobles in royal service. As such they were exceptional but insofar as they restored and then maintained their fortunes by a combination of land acquisition, commercial activity and some sort of royal service, they were typical of most Spanish noble families.[27]

ROYAL PATRONAGE IN THE NETHERLANDS

In contrast to his Iberian kingdoms, Charles spent hardly any time at all in his Flemish and Dutch dominions after 1516. Nevertheless, he depended upon the co-operation of his nobles in the Netherlands to enforce his authority and to represent him to the cities and towns whose wealth was so crucial to his ability to sustain his monarchy and empire. The social structure of the early Habsburg Netherlands closely paralleled that of Valois France. Many senior noble families had branches in both realms, especially those based in Picardy and Flanders. Charles was conscious of the role in government traditionally played by the Burgundian high nobility. He encouraged active participation by the great families and instructed the two regents of the Netherlands, Margaret of Austria and Mary of Hungary to consult the most important nobles on all matters of policy and not to transact business without their knowledge.

Margaret of Austria often consulted individual nobleman on policy questions but was also accused by the high nobles of ignoring the membership of her Regency council as a whole. They maintained that she relied too heavily on the advice of lawyers and administrators. The Council of State set up for her successor in 1531 was constituted so as to allow the high nobility to advise her on major issues of political organisation and defence. Mary was as, if not more, authoritarian than Margaret. She too consulted informally but among the high nobles such as Philippe de Croy, the Duke of Aerschot. Mary was principally concerned to secure the advice and co-operation of the s*tadholders*, the provincial governors. As in France, these high officers used their own patronage networks to constitute a royal affinity. They had a number of jealously guarded prerogatives such as the right to be consulted about appointments to regional councils and to appoint town magistrates within their governorships. They sought the greatest freedom of action for themselves as Charles's representatives in their individual provinces.

Mary was keenly aware of their potential to become 'overmighty' subjects. She clashed with a number of *stadholders* over subsidiary appointments they made and was eventually vindicated by Charles's confirming her own appointees. The regent was careful to keep the *stadholders* under her authority and to prevent them gaining a dynastic hold on their offices. As part of the effort to enforce her authority, the *stadholderate* of Flanders was kept vacant for most of the 1530s. Adrien de Croy succeeded to it in 1541. Members of the Croy and Lannoy families held successive governorships but in different provinces. In the mid 1530s Mary shuffled appointments around between a number of the region's principal clans, respecting their status while limiting their capacity to dominate the politics of any one province. The powers of *stadholders* were restrictively defined and they were required to act in co-operation with the regent's officials. Nevertheless, her relations with the *stadholders* were good, at least until the last years of her regency. The high nobles felt sufficiently respected that, in contrast to what later happened under Philip II, they did not fundamentally question their collaborative relationship with their sovereign and his representatives.[28]

THE COURTS OF CHARLES V

Henry VIII and Francis I each had a recognisably national court centred on a royal household that was staffed by predominantly English and French courtiers respectively. Both courts functioned according to long established, if constantly evolving, national traditions. The court of Charles V was rather more complex because the higher echelons of its courtiers were drawn from a number of different kingdoms under Charles's rule. The core of his household staff remained reasonably constant over time but, as he also travelled widely, the imperial entourage was routinely augmented by local gentlemen and nobles who wanted the honour of serving their prince in his household and of course the fees due for such service.

To a greater extent than was the case in England or France, a formal separation was maintained between the emperor's private service and his political decision-making, which was centred in his councils. Nevertheless, places at court were still worth having because they gave access to the emperor. Influence with him was as important an indicator of status in his court as it was anywhere else. Charles was raised in the Netherlands under the highly ritualised and self-consciously ceremonial traditions of the Valois dukes of Burgundy. The Burgundian court strictly separated the prince's private space from that of the rest of the court through a series of antechambers and receptions rooms. Its numerous offices and its complex daily rituals were intended to preserve a carefully measured, awe-inducing, distance between him and most of his courtiers. However, from 1516, Charles was also king of Spain. Between 1522 and 1543 he spent more time in Spain than anywhere else and here the courtly traditions were rather different. The Castilian court in particular did not lack formality on important occasions but under Ferdinand and Isabella its daily routines were not overly elaborate. Their private apartments were not as strictly separated from the rest of the household in the way characteristic of Burgundy and England. There was greater freedom of interaction between the rulers and at least their high-born subjects. The number of household officers was also fewer than in Burgundy.

When he returned to Spain in 1522 Charles showed greater sensitivity to the expectations of his subjects than he had in 1517. Although hard evidence is limited, it seems that Charles decided to adopt a modified, somewhat less formal, type of Burgundian court etiquette when in Spain. The author of a memoir on Charles's court, written later in the century for Philip II, expressed the view that it was not very 'Burgundian' at all. He also revealed that when he had once raised this point with the emperor, Charles had defended his freedom to adopt household arrangements which suited him. What the precise adaptations of Burgundian etiquette were no one is certain, but they were evidently successful because when, in 1548, Charles ordered a more rigorous Burgundian style to be introduced into

Prince Philip's household it caused considerable resentment. In 1555 Philip was asked, as king, to restore the more open style so that the sons of the great nobles could serve him 'and that his highness would get to know them, and coming to like them, show them signs of favour as this would be of great benefit to these your kingdoms.' In fact access to the king became restricted in a way that it evidently had not been under Charles. In 1561 Philip established a permanent court in Madrid and before the completion of the monastery-palace of the Escorial in 1584, he lived at the Alcázar, or castle, of Madrid. It was enlarged and restructured to create a new suite of private rooms for the royal family and separated all but the most intimate servants from the royal living quarters. These innovations strongly suggest that his father did not have the usual 'Burgundian' arrangement of rooms in that palace during his reign.[29]

One influential factor in Charles's earlier decision to opt for a more relaxed form of court etiquette while in Spain was that, like his illustrious predecessors, he travelled around his Iberian dominions frequently. For example, between March and December 1524 he moved from Pamplona in Navarre south-west across northern Castile reaching Valladolid at the end of July before making his way south-east to Madrid where he arrived at the end of November. He remained there for the winter before setting out on another long journey the following spring. In 1524 he stayed at no fewer than 20 different locations en route and was never more than two weeks at any one of them. On this and all his other journeys, Charles spent significant amounts of time as the guest of the realm's prominent ecclesiastical establishments and of his chief nobles. In these circumstances, a less rigid royal protocol assisted both the emperor's comfort and the ability of his many hosts to provide properly for him during his visits. On these occasions, and even when at home in one of the royal palaces, the emperor's private space was relatively limited. Its dimensions and arrangements were more akin to those for the French king than to the acres of rooms Henry VIII built for himself.[30]

The emperor's household was presided over by the *mayordomo mayor* or lord high steward, the equivalent of the *grand maître* in France. He was responsible for the running of the household and was ranked as one of the great officers of state. For much of the reign, this position was occupied by Fernando d'Alvarez, the Duke of Alba. When the emperor ate he was always served by table servants of noble rank. These were the *gentileshombres de la boca* who, like their French counterparts, were divided into groups serving the emperor's food and drink. The emperor's service in his private chambers was overseen by the *camarero mayor* or great chamberlain. He attended the king as he rose each morning, when he ate and when he retired in the evenings. He also attended the king on his close-stool. Although officially outranked by the *mayordomo mayor*, the *camarero mayor* was, like the Groom of the Stool in England and the *premier gentilhomme de la chambre* in France, a royal servant of considerable status and influence. He was supposed to sleep in the king's room with him and be the first to attend him when he rose in the morning. He dressed the king and supervised the running of the king's private apartments, the preparation of his meals and personal service. The *cavallerizo mayor* was the equivalent of the *grand écuyer* in France or the Master of the Horse in England. He was formally responsible for the king's security and controlled access to the more private areas of the palace. He accompanied the king on all outings from the palace, looked after the king's stables and provided for all his other transport needs. The *cazador* was the officer responsible for arranging the royal hunting expeditions and caring for the king's hunting dogs, falcons and equipment. Charles's spiritual needs were attended to by his confessor, two preachers, by some 40 chaplains and several choirs of the imperial chapel. As emperor, his official guard consisted of approximately 340 troops, including German halberdiers, a corps of 100 Spanish guards, together with 100 mounted Burgundian and Spanish archers.[31]

When Charles was resident outside Spain, and particularly as grew older and was more conscious of asserting his personal dignity, he reverted to the court etiquette familiar to him from his youth. In 1551 the Venetian ambassador Marino Cavalli, reported to the Senate after an embassy spent in the Netherlands, that 'the emperor's court is organised according to the use of the court of Burgundy.' Charles's *camarero mayor* was now usually called his *sumiller de corps*. Among other things, Cavalli noted a group of nearly 40 servants whom he called *gentiluomini de la camera*. This title is the equivalent of *gentilhomme de la chambre* or gentleman of the privy chamber but in contrast to the position in England and France, although these men kept the sovereign company, they did not physically serve him. Instead, Cavalli specified that seven or eight 'minor servants' of the chamber attended to the emperor's immediate needs when in private. This was in keeping with Burgundian traditions dating back to the fifteenth century and the time of the last duke, Charles the Bold.[32]

CONCLUSION

The successful assertion of royal authority over the great magnates in Spain, England and France in the early sixteenth century was once seen as the result of an alliance between the crown and the newly emerging groups of lay lawyers and financial specialists to destroy the power of the traditional nobility. More recent research has established that this is at best a distorted picture of Renaissance monarchy. As previous chapters have indicated, monarchs did indeed draw increasingly on lawyers and trained financial specialists for much of the routine work of their governments. They did use them to strengthen the administration of the realm but monarchs also still relied upon the co-operation of the magnates in the localities, without which royal officials could not do their work properly. Moreover, a large proportion of royal office holders were themselves drawn from families within the retinues of great magnates. Monarchs aimed not to destroy noble power but to control it and harness it to crown's interests. Renaissance monarchs were generally more secure, better informed and better obeyed than kings of a century earlier. They also concentrated greater patronage in their hands than their medieval predecessors but they were still not beyond further challenge from territorial magnates. Their hold on power still substantially depended upon the judicious use of patronage in securing support of a sufficient proportion of the nobles in their realms.

In the early sixteenth century monarchs may have needed nobles, but nobles also needed monarchs more than ever. Politics was the serious game of profiting from the king's favour and wielding personal influence in the elaborate patronage network which sustained monarchical authority. Competition for royal favour was fierce and unrelenting. It was focused increasingly, but never exclusively, on the royal household and personal attendance on the sovereign. For higher ranked nobles it was important to garner a sufficient share of money, titles, lands and profitable offices from the king with which to satisfy the members of their own affinities. For men of lower social status, a post in royal service might be secured through the influence of magnates but it could also be a means to keep themselves independent of the territorial heavyweights.

Royal personality was a vital ingredient in the politics of patronage and those who sought the sovereign's favour had to appeal to his prejudices and ambitions. As the fortunes of the members of the La Trémoille, the Noailles, and Selve families in France show, under a strong and well-respected king like Francis I, there were many ways to do this but being connected directly to the king's affinity was essential for rapid advancement in status and influence. The loss of royal favour could have equally quick and adverse consequences.

As Jean du Tillet's comments quoted at the outset show, Francis I enjoyed a high reputation among his nobles during his life and in the decades immediately after his death. Du Tillet also noted that Francis showed considerable knowledge about the histories of many noble families. He knew how to appeal to their instincts and more than once said that of all his titles, that of 'gentilhomme' was the one he valued most. His wars against Charles V and Henry VIII gave many men, such as Antoine de Noailles, the opportunities to fight which their honour code demanded. Military and political service were closely linked and Francis was very conscious of his patronal responsibilities towards those who aspired to serve the monarchy.

His legal chicanery over Suzanne de Bourbon's lands does not do him credit but the king's anxiety about the Duke of Bourbon's potential in concentrating so much prime territory in central France in his own hands is at least understandable given the prior history of rivalry between the houses of Valois and Bourbon. Potentially powerful the duke may have been but the extended royal affinity proved more powerful. In the absence of widespread support, even a magnate of Bourbon's status was vulnerable. At a more mundane level, factional politics was limited during the early years of Francis's reign, but as the size of the court increased competition between groups of courtiers intensified. Montmorency was not the only close friend of the king to lose favour with him, especially as Madame d'Etampes established a dominance over the court in the mid 1540s.

Charles could be generous to his courtiers and his financial officials despaired of him ever reducing the costs of his household, its entertainments and the jewels he often gave as token of trust and affection to his family and courtiers. His large armies and frequent wars provided many opportunities for young noblemen of Flemish, Spanish and Italian origin to distinguish themselves on the field and to secure profitable posts as town or city governors and military officials. However, in the Netherlands where the regents governed and especially in Spain where great aristocrats controlled so much land and the economic political life lived on it, a career in a great ducal household could still rival the prospect of service to an often-absent sovereign. As the career of Luis Hurtado shows, flexibility and patience were often necessary in attracting Charles's patronage but the rewards for displaying these qualities could be significant. Charles's court had its fair share of intrigue, gossip and competition for favoured posts between prominent nobles but the direct political consequences of much of this were limited while executive power was so concentrated in the royal councils.

In England, the personality of Henry VIII was such that the stakes in the political game were much higher and the consequences of failure more routinely lethal. His anger could blaze as suddenly and as fiercely as his joy and the charming spontaneity of his early manhood turned to malicious unpredictability in older age. He gave an early indication of his readiness to destroy potentially powerful rivals when the Duke of Buckingham was executed for treason in 1521 for some ill-judged boasts and unsubtle threats to Tudor regime. Yet Henry too readily saw himself as the victim of scheming wives or of unfaithful servants and this tendency allowed courtiers to manipulate him. He expressed his regret at losing Cromwell but found the blame to lie outside himself. Perhaps only Wolsey's natural death spared him any onerous remorse over the loss of his first, and greatest, servant. While there is little positive evidence of Henry as a puppet-master lifting his courtiers into and out of the scenery at will and setting them against each other, it is hard to avoid the conclusion that rivalry between them often served Henry's purposes well. It sharpened his servants' instincts for survival through loyalty to him. In the wider realm it instilled enough fear to encourage obedience and loyalty to the regime without being so great as to alienate support among nobles as a whole. His popularity among the majority seems rarely, if ever, to have diminished and he, too, gave ample opportunities in war and in royal service for ambitious noblemen to make their mark in the world.

In England, as in the Continental monarchies, royal government was maintained by a society whose mentality and organisation were thoroughly hierarchical. It was mediated primarily through a network of personal relationships which linked the political nation's lowest echelons to the highest. These relationships provided individuals with opportunities for advancement and had at all times to be honoured and maintained effectively. At the top of the hierarchy was the king and any individual with expectations of playing a role in society had always to bear in mind the nature and extent of his responsibilities to those around him and ultimately his duty to the sovereign. A failure in judgement on these considerations could prove disastrous. During the politically exciting but anxious decade of 1540s, Sir John Gostwick, one of the fast-rising gentlemen of the mid-Tudor period, earnestly advised his son on how to behave in the world. He wrote in terms which neatly encapsulate the dilemmas faced by ambitious men and women in the 'personal politics' of European Renaissance monarchies:

> And be true to God, the king and your friend. And if your friend do open his mind and secret counsel to you, I charge you if it be to keep counsel, I charge you open it not, for if you do, you are not to be trusted by no man, unless your friend should open to you felony or treason, then I charge you not to keep his counsel, but open it to two or three of the next Justices of the Peace which dwelleth next unto you, or else to one or two of the King's most honourable Council, if you may get to them. But in any wise, utter it as soon as possible, for the longer you keep it the worse it is for you, and the more danger toward God and the King's Majesty.[33]

7

Patrons: Royal artistic patronage

> 'And Hampton court' he said, 'is it on the same river also'? I said 'yes', that they [with Windsor] both stood upon the same river with various other goodly houses, naming Richmond for one, declaring to him at length the magnificence of all three of them and especially of Hampton Court; of which he was very desirous to hear and took great pleasure to converse with me about ...
>
> Sir John Wallop reporting a conversation with Francis I.[1]

Charles V, Francis I and Henry VIII all knew the importance of royal magnificence. They strove to demonstrate it at all times in the splendour of their palaces, their personal adornment, the many luxurious objects they owned and the literary talents at their command. Monarchs were mainly interested in artists and writers for what they could do to enhance the royal claims to personal *virtus*, to scholarship and discerning taste. Artistic patronage also advertised the monarch's wealth and was intended to demonstrate 'largesse', or liberality, one of the tokens of sovereignty. It was therefore an essential aspect of sixteenth century monarchy and cannot be divorced from political patronage.

Royal patronage of artists was often initiated through intermediaries who were anxious to improve their own standing with the prince by introducing to him an artist of exceptional talent. An artist or writer who had been 'talent spotted' and who did well, not only augmented the king's reputation but improved his own standing and that of his original patron. Favoured artists and writers were usually given a place at court with a salary, enabling them to concentrate on serving the king. One such was the French humanist poet Clement Marot, who first served one of Francis I's secretaries, Nicolas de Neufville, Lord of Villeroy, before working for the king's sister Marguerite and eventually becoming court poet and a *valet de chambre* to Francis I. Royal patronage encompassed a wide spectrum of creativity, from the relatively mundane expertise of the tailors and jewellers who dressed and adorned kings to the genius of artists like Cellini or Titian and poets such as Marot and Sir Thomas Wyatt.

All three kings competed for talent on the international artistic market and were informed of the endeavours of their fellow sovereigns in this important aspect of monarchy. Sir John Wallop's conversation with Francis I, quoted above, took place after he had seen the king's new gallery at Fontainebleau on which he also reported to Henry VIII. His report raises the question of how much each of the kings in this study influenced the artistic patronage of the others. There is ample evidence of more specific interchange of ideas between Francis and Henry VIII during the frequent periods of peace between them, of which Wallop's report is perhaps the best known. The much more hostile relations between Charles and Francis made such direct exchanges less likely. Nevertheless, there is some evidence that Francis's architectural patronage impressed Charles and influential members of his entourage and that they found it a useful comparison for their own plans. Flemish artists of various kinds worked for Francis I as well as Charles. Several French artists were employed by Henry VIII to work on his palaces and all three monarchs employed Italians artists of distinction.

When making comparisons with each other, these monarchs had two principal thoughts in mind. The first was what informed opinion held was the value, economic and aesthetic, of their rivals' property and the second was whether any advantage might be gained from acquiring similar, or better, things for themselves. Of the three, it was Francis I who had the most sophisticated aesthetic sense. His interest in Italian art was evident by the age of ten. In 1504 Niccolò Alamanni, the Gonzagan envoy in France, wrote to his master suggesting that Mantegna be asked to produce 'something exceptional' for Francis who had asked the envoy to 'obtain for him some pictures by those excellent Italian masters as they give him so much pleasure'. This sort of precociousness had earned him flattering references in Castiglione's *Book of the Courtier* as the foremost of educated French gentlemen. Francis undoubtedly owed much of his love of art and literature to the influence of his mother who was a significant patron of writers and intellectuals in her own right. Louis XII's court where Francis lived from the age of eight, was also responsive to the Italian Renaissance. Louis rebuilt the royal château at Blois in a distinctly French style but its decoration was fashionably Italian in design.

Francis was also deeply interested in poetry and in building up his personal collection of manuscripts and books. From 1522 the king's librarian was Guillaume Budé. He built up the king's collection of several hundred ancient Greek manuscripts, both originals and copies. Many were acquired through Janus Lascaris who acted as Francis's agents at the library of St Mark's in Venice in the early 1520s. In 1530 Francis appointed four royal lectureships in Greek and Hebrew which became the foundation positions for the Collège de France. In the 1530s the first law of legal deposit was introduced to increase the king's holdings of printed books and in the 1540s the royal library at Blois was moved to Fontainebleau. It was included in tours of the château that Francis usually gave to his important guests.[2]

It is difficult to prove conclusively but it is likely that Charles, too, had a reasonably well-developed aesthetic sense although as a young man he perhaps lacked Francis's confidence and passionate interest in all things Italian. His grandfather Maximilian was deeply interested in the patronage of artists and architects but had relatively little money to spend on his palaces. Nevertheless, in the 1490s he remodelled the Hofburg in Innsbruck and built a new suite of rooms there for his second wife, Bianca Maria Sforza. He commissioned portraits of himself and his family, including Charles, from Albrecht Dürer and Bernard Strigel among others. He also wrote at least one thinly disguised autobiography, *Der Weisskunig* 'the white king,' in which he discussed the importance of artistic patronage in glorifying the deeds of one's ancestors.

Several individual portraits were made in oil or chalk of Charles as a boy and a youth. One of the earliest was made in 1507 by the painter known as the Master of the Legend of Magdalene, showing Charles holding a falcon. Charles's aunt Margaret of Austria, in whose household at Mechelen he grew up, was an important patron of Flemish architects and artists. Her favourite was Conrad Meit who, with Albrecht Dürer, was northern Europe's principal sculptor, draughtsman and painter. Barend van Orley painted Charles as a youthful Archduke of Austria in 1516.[3] During the 1520s Charles's own artistic patronage was comparatively modest and focused predominantly on artists from his native Flanders. As he matured however, and as Italy came more under his sway, Charles's interest in Italian designers and artists increased. During the 1530s he patronised a wide range of Italian, German and Spanish artists and assembled a vast array of pictures and objects which testify to a fairly sophisticated taste.

Henry VIII also grew up in a court where literary and artistic patronage were important aspects of government. His father had used much of the money that he might have spent on foreign wars to increase the visible dignity of his royal person and household. The king re-built the palace of Richmond, formerly Sheen, after a fire there in 1497. Franco-Flemish artists and glaziers decorated the palace, painted royal portraits, illuminated and printed books for the royal library. Poets like Bernard André worked alongside Polydore Vergil composing histories which, although based upon classical models, drew upon English and Welsh chronicles and mythology to praise Henry VII's dynasty as the apogee of British kingship.

Henry VIII's taste was for the colourful and showy but he also demonstrated an appreciation of Italian classicism with the patronage of the sculptor Pietro Torrigiano. He may have been in England as early as 1506 but was certainly receiving commissions from the king by 1512. Then came the war with France and in its aftermath, Henry was relatively poor. During the early 1520s it was Wolsey more than the king who lead the way in acquiring objects made in the fashionable antique style and through innovations such as the long gallery at Hampton Court. By the later 1530s when Henry had enough money to commission the sort of work which might have interested Cellini or Michelangelo, he was isolated politically and religiously due to the break with Rome. Many of the direct avenues through which he might have attracted such talent to his court were closed due to strained relations with the emperor and the papacy. Considering the limits he imposed upon himself by his isolation from southern Europe, the quality of the work he patronised was impressive.

ARCHITECTURE

Second only to warfare in levels of expenditure, architecture was the principal area of royal artistic patronage in the early sixteenth century. From the outset Henry, Francis and Charles were all interested in the building and decoration of their many residences. Initially this meant refurbishing or renovating sections of existing palaces. At Greenwich, at Blois in the Loire valley and at Brussels, changes were made to pre-existing royal palaces the better to accommodate the needs of these rulers and their growing courts. These renovations incorporated greater or lesser degrees of classical and Italian influences in accordance with prevailing architectural theory and tastes. As they matured over the following 20 years, all three monarchs also built new palaces as deliberate demonstrations of their wealth and the cultural sophistication of their respective realms.

It was Francis who made the most dramatic debut as architectural patron. Between 1515 and 1524 one wing of the royal château at Blois was completely re-fashioned. The restructuring incorporated two sets of loggias, one on top of the other, along the length of the facade which overlooked new royal gardens. This was the first example on such a scale, of Italian classicism influencing not simply the decoration but the structure of a French château. The wing also featured a monumental external staircase giving access to all three floors from the central courtyard of the palace. This staircase, the wall spaces and windows frames were heavily decorated with the royal symbols of the letter 'F' and the salamander alongside classical elements of *putti*, shell niches and the like. The gardens laid out in front of the royal apartments pleased Francis greatly. In August 1516 the court was at Blois. One evening after dinner and closer to midnight, Francis personally guided the young Federico Gonzaga, the son of the Marquis of Mantua, around them. As Federico reported to his father, the king showed great enthusiasm, pointing out to his guest 'each thing in great detail and with as much love as one would show to a long-absent son or brother.' The following day Francis also showed Federico the library at the château.[4]

Francis's impressive start at Blois was followed in the later 1520s and 1530s by a programme of renovation and building in a number of locations.

There were nine principal royal châteaux, among the most important of which were Chambord in the Loire valley, the Louvre in the centre of Paris and Saint-Germain-en-Laye north-west of the capital. Chambord was built as a grand hunting palace. It was begun in 1519 but not completed before 1539 when Charles V saw it during his tour through France. The Louvre and Saint-Germain-en-Laye underwent extensive alteration and renovation from the late 1520s onwards. However it was the château of Fontainebleau, south-west of Paris, which Francis increasingly regarded as home and upon which he lavished the most personal care and attention. After 1528 he spent more continuous time here than anywhere else except Paris. The king oversaw extensive reconstruction in a number of phases beginning in 1528 with the acquisition of monastic buildings close to the original oval shaped château. New buildings were erected on this site and linked to the old château by a gallery. Much of Francis's work at Fontainebleau has not survived and that which has is much altered.[5]

The most important survival is the *Galerie François Ier* which, as its name implies, was built for Francis as an adjunct to his private space. It was reached originally at one end through his apartments and from the other by a striking double staircase, still in existence today. Unlike today however, the gallery was originally lit by windows on both sides. The wall space between the windows of the gallery is divided; the lower half has carved wood panels decorated with the king's 'F' badges and his salamander. The upper half features frescoed panels, each framed with stucco decorations, by the Italian artist Giovanni Battista Rosso. These show the king in various classical and mythological guises, referring to great warrior kings of the past, chiefly Alexander the Great. The meaning of the whole programme of decoration has been much debated, but in general terms it may be interpreted as a declaration of Francis's *virtus* as ruler. He is shown in the company of allegorical figures representing wisdom and courage and in scenes which allude in a variety of ways to his mastery of the demanding task of kingship. In the 1540s copies of antique statues acquired by Francis I were placed in gallery to assert not only the king's classical learning and artistic sophistication but to remind visitors of the glory of ancient Rome and to invite them to make comparisons between Roman emperors and the king of France. Francis kept the key to this private gallery on his person and enjoyed showing it to his special guests. The English ambassador Sir John Wallop was shown the gallery in 1540 and recommended that Henry should do something similar in Whitehall or St James's palace.[6]

In 1528 construction began on a completely new château just outside Paris called 'Madrid' This was small and built, not around a central courtyard as was conventional in France, but on an adapted Spanish model based on five rectangular blocks. At either end of a large central block incorporating four great halls were square accommodation pavilions each of four floors. These rooms were reached by spiral staircases and this allowed for greater informality and ease of living in the palace which was the intention in its construction. All this work was supervised by a new administrative department called the 'bâtiments du roi.' Between 1532 and 1537 Francis spent 43,233 *livres* per annum on his Paris residences. By 1546 this had risen to 85,800 *livres* or about 1.5 per cent of a total income of 9 million *livres*.[7]

In 1522 Charles V began the renovation of the ducal palace at Brussels first constructed over 80 years earlier under Duke Philip the Good of Burgundy. The chief feature of this palace was an impressive hall or *Grande Salle* completed in 1461 measuring approximately 40 × 16 meters. In 1522 work began on a new chapel of St Philip and St John the Baptist, dedicated to Charles's parents Philip of Burgundy and Juana of Castile. The chapel was Gothic in style but incorporated classical style balustrades on the lateral facade. In 1533, Charles V began a second stage of renovations to the ducal palace at Brussels. From the main courtyard, access to the principal public room, the *Salle de Philippe le Bon*, was now afforded by a monumental staircase at the top of which was a triumphal arch featuring a statue of the emperor with his imperial eagle, bearing a sword in his right hand. The sides of the arch featured statues of Hercules fighting the giant Antaeus (perhaps a reference to Francis) together with the imperial device of the pillars of Hercules and the emperor's *Plus Oultre* motto.

New apartments for Charles were also built and these included a gallery on the first floor which was about two-thirds the length of that at Fontainebleau and resembled the latter in its basic configuration. Below it on the ground floor was an open colonnade. Between the windows of the gallery were statues of Habsburg emperors, rather than Roman figures as at Fontainebleau. The emperor's gallery looked out over the tiltyard of the palace, over the royal park and the adjacent forest of Soignes where he had liked to hunt since his childhood. After Charles's visit to Fontainebleau, Francis had commissioned a set of tapestries depicting the *Galerie François Ier* as a gift for him. The emperor planned to reciprocate with a set of tapestries, now known as the *Hunting Parties of Maximilian*, portraying, not the decoration of the Brussels gallery itself, but scenes which might be seen from it. Several tapestries showed towns, churches and other recognizable features of the duchy of Brabant. Thus the tapestries were intended to show off to the French king the splendours of the territories governed by his Habsburg rival. In the event only six of the French tapestries and none of the Brussels ones were actually delivered to their intended recipients because relations between Francis and Charles quickly soured after their rapprochement of 1538–40.[8]

In 1533 work also began on a new royal palace in the Alhambra fortress at Granada. Much of the work was overseen by the governor of the Alhambra, Luis Hurtado de Mendoza. Charles's pre-eminent Spanish secretary Francisco de los Cobos was also involved through the establishment of a special administrative department, the 'Obras Reales', which coordinated payments for work on the emperor's Spanish palaces, in much the same way the 'bâtiments du roi' did in France. The palace at Granada was designed by the Toledan architect Pedro Machuca who had trained in Italy and who, by the late 1520s, was known to Luis Hurtado. Its design and decoration owed much to contemporary Roman palaces designed by Raphael and Bramante. It consisted of a square block in four ranges with apartments for the royal family and its entourage. In the centre of this square was a very large, and unusual, circular peristyle courtyard with a Doric double colonnade. The palace also featured a large reception hall and a new chapel. It was not finally completed until after Charles's death but the four ranges were substantially complete and a start had been made on the courtyard by 1558.

The iconography of the palace was planned by Luis Hurtado. The Mendoza family saw itself as the spiritual heir of the Romans in Spain and the architectural features of the palace emphasize Charles's position as the modern Caesar. Each of the facades was executed in the Roman Renaissance style which was quite formal and restrained compared with the lively 'Plateresque' favoured in Spain in the late fifteenth century. The Doric order used on the ground level throughout the palace was seen as appropriately austere and strong, reflecting the emperor's authority. The three-door entry in the west range specifically recalled a Roman triumphal arch, the central door being twice as large as the two flanking ones. This entrance was itself surmounted by a large triple-bayed window, recalling the open loggias above entrance ways where Roman emperors, and their Renaissance princely imitators, showed themselves to their people. It has also been suggested that the circular courtyard was a reference to Charles's *imperium* over the globe, particularly as its proportions were reminiscent of the circular portico at Hadrian's villa at Tivoli – the only circular courtyard known to have survived from antiquity.

Much of the decoration and ornamentation of the palace was done by two foreign sculptors, Niccolò da Corte and Antonio de Leval. It includes carved panels and relief sculptures of the Habsburg eagle clutching a variety of globes, together with symbols of the Order of the Golden Fleece and representations of the columnar device used by Charles V with his *Plus Oultre* motto. A number of the crosses of St Andrew, the patron of the Golden Fleece, are depicted in the palace with pomegranates growing at their tops and sides. This heraldic reference to Granada elides the re-conquest of southern Spain from the Moors by Charles's grandparents, with Charles victories against the Turks in North Africa and his hopes for the Burgundian crusading order. Other decorations on exterior and interior palaces surfaces included winged victories, crouching lions and the emperor's name in Latin on a frieze over the southern entrance way. In 1548–49 a reference to Charles's victory at Mühlberg and the hoped-for peace under the Interim of Augsburg was carved on the west facade.[9]

During the 1540s it was not the new Alhambra palace, still largely a building site, but the ducal palace at Brussels which became as near as anything Charles ever had to a permanent residence. By then it had not only become rather old-fashioned but could not properly accommodate the court. Plans were therefore put in hand for significant extensions under the supervision of Antoine Perrenot de Granvelle. He was evidently impressed with what he had seen in France as he accompanied the emperor there in 1539–40. He commissioned a set of duplicates of the casts of antique sculptures which Primaticcio had obtained for Francis I. He also had a model of Francis' château of Chambord in the Loire valley. This model seems to have been uppermost in Granvelle's mind when planning the new ducal palace for Charles but the end result bears little resemblance to Chambord. The emperor had himself praised that château when he visited it in 1539 describing it as 'embodiment of what human artistry was capable of bringing forth.' While these grand plans were being formulated, Charles actually lived in a small house in the park of Brussels, formerly belonging to the Count of Sassegnies. It consisted of one floor with only two rooms for the emperor's use.

During this decade new palaces were constructed at Binche and Mariemont for Mary of Hungary and for the emperor. Both were destroyed by the French in 1554 and although subsequently rebuilt have not survived to the present day. Both these palaces incorporated Italianate features and set the tone for royal domestic architecture in the Netherlands well into the latter part of the century. Plans were also discussed for a new fortified palace at Ghent following the suppression of a revolt in that city. Jacques de Broeucq, sculptor and architect to the emperor made several models for an imperial residence. In the event after Charles's abdication in 1555 and his departure to Spain the following year these projects were abandoned as Philip II preferred to concentrate his architectural patronage in Madrid.[10]

In England during the 1520s Henry VIII's building programme focused mainly on renovations and additions to the principal palaces of Richmond, built under his father, and to the riverside palace at Greenwich. The coming of Imperial and French embassies of 1517 and 1518 prompted the building of new tiltyards and tennis plays at Greenwich and repairs to the London palace of Bridewell where ambassadors were often accommodated. While the king's architectural projects were initially comparatively modest, Cardinal Wolsey maintained a steady programme of works at his manor house of Hampton Court. This palace featured the earliest English example of a long gallery in the Italian style, as well as tennis plays and gardens. In 1527 the cardinal made over the palace to the king in a desperate attempt to remain in favour. Thereafter, Hampton Court was the principal royal residence outside the immediate London area. Henry enlarged the Great Hall and made extensive renovations to the Chapel. In common with his other palaces, the king also added a series of private apartments, galleries and outdoor sports facilities.

In a move partly forced on him by his advancing age and increasing girth, during the 1540s the king became more or less permanently established in his capital. Accordingly, a large proportion of Henry's profits from the seizure and sale of monastic lands was spent on the expansion and renovation of his principal palaces at Greenwich, Hampton Court and particularly Whitehall which became his main residence in the last decade of his life. To these were added the new palace of Nonsuch begun in 1538. Like Francis's palace of Madrid, that of Nonsuch functioned as 'pleasure palace', what the French called a 'palais de retrait', from where the king could hunt with favourites and avoid the relatively formal style of life in the great metropolitan palaces. Both buildings were also intended to be propaganda for their owners, incorporating the latest decorative ideas. Given their similarity of purpose and the proximity in the dates of the construction, it might be expected that Madrid offered a ready model for Nonsuch. In fact there are close parallels, but little direct borrowing. If anything, Nonsuch superficially resembled the older style château at Chambord.

The ground plan of Nonsuch was thoroughly conventional. It was arranged around an outer and inner court with a narrow kitchen wing on the north-east side. A gallery overlooked a privy garden at the south-east corner of the building. Here the main access to the royal apartments was via two sets of 'generous winding steps magnificently built' with entrances at either side of the inner court. Nonsuch was decorated in classical style. The walls facing the courtyard featured paintings of Roman emperors, rather than busts or statues as at Madrid, together with scenes from the life of Hercules and figures of the Arts and Virtues. This iconographical programme as a whole is unique to Nonsuch though its separate elements were common throughout Europe. Like that of the gallery at Fontainebleau, the decoration at Nonsuch was intended to remind visitors primarily of the owner's wealth, intellectual sophistication and artistic discernment, all part of his princely *virtus*.[11]

PAINTING, SCULPTURE AND TAPESTRIES

Royal patrons of the sixteenth century valued talented artists who were often skilled in more than one medium. In his influential book, *The Lives of the Artists*, Giorgio Vasari, himself a noted artist, described his subjects as 'artefice' or 'artificers.' This word better describes the range of talents which those who sought royal patronage ideally possessed and the type of work to which they turned those talents. Thus, 'painters' like Rosso were often also draughtsmen, cartographers, and architects of churches, palaces and defensive fortifications. They also produced temporary decorations for royal entries, festivals and banquets.

For whatever purpose it was intended, good painting was highly prized. Sculpture was valued for its potential to render three-dimensional reality and for the expense of the stone or precious metals used in statues. Roman and Greek civilisations were of course known about mainly through their architectural and sculptural remains. Ancient rulers were represented in sculptures and on coins. A desire to equate their own realms with the greatness of these cultures and to ensure for themselves the same recognition and longevity of fame as the Roman emperors drove Charles, Francis and Henry to collect such items and also to commission paintings, sculptures and medals of themselves in the antique style.

The most expensive decorative items possessed by monarchs in the sixteenth century were undoubtedly tapestries. Made with large quantities of gold and silver thread, tapestries were valued principally as a means of declaring the wealth of the owner. Practically, they were used as adaptable decoration and as insulation in draughty palaces. Unlike frescos and many paintings, tapestries were also portable and could therefore accompany the owner when he moved from palace to palace or be brought out to augment the splendour of his person on special occasions such as the reception of important subjects and foreign ambassadors. They were also ideal for ostentatious gift-giving between rulers. Reference has already been made to the planned exchange of tapestries between Charles V and Francis I in the late 1530s.[12]

Charles V patronised many sculptors and painters. As a child he had seen the works of a number of Flemish artists in the service of his grandfather Maximilian and his aunt and guardian Margaret of Austria. Apart from Conrad Meit, mentioned earlier, the court at Mechelen patronised Barend van Orley, Lucas Cranach, Albrecht Dürer and Bernhard Strigel. Strigel's best known work is probably the composite portrait of Maximilian and his family, including Charles and his brother Ferdinand, painted in 1515. One of the first painters whom Charles V patronised directly was Jan Cornelisz Vermeyen who enjoyed a royal pension from 1522. He produced a number of portraits of court figures as well as maps and plans of the Mediterranean for Charles's use. In 1535 he accompanied the emperor on his Tunis campaign in order to make drawings of the action. These, together with a map of the Mediterranean, were then used as cartoons for a series of twelve tapestries, known as the *Conquest of Tunis* cycle, commemorating the emperor's victory over Barbarossa. These were woven in Brussels by Willem de Pannemaker and later sent to Madrid. Another set of the same cycle was made for Mary of Hungary and hung in her palace at Binche.

The first sculptor Charles retained was Jean Monet. He was born in Metz but initially worked in Barcelona from 1517–19 collaborating with Bartolomé Ordóñez, on the choir stalls and altar screen of the cathedral there. With Ordóñez, Monet acquired the repertory of the Renaissance classicism which he did much to introduce to the Netherlands. In 1524 he was made 'emperor's artist' and a *valet de chambre* of his household. The emperor also later intervened in a legal case to ensure that Monet was able to purchase the manor of Luttingen. His best known work is an alabaster altar piece for the ducal chapel at Brussels, carved by 1541. In Spain the emperor's principal sculptor was Niccolò da Corte who was responsible for much of the decoration at the royal palace at Granada.

Monet was succeeded as imperial sculptor and artist by Jacques du Broeucq whose masterpiece is the choir screen of the church of Saint-Waudru in Mons. Du Broeucq was also an architect who designed the palaces of Binche and Mariemont for use by Mary of Hungary and that at Bossu built for Jean d'Alsace de Hennin Liétard, Count of Bossu. During his stay in Paris in December 1540, Charles was presented with a seven-foot high silver statue of Hercules carrying the two columns as chandeliers, decorated with the emperor's motto designed by Rosso. Although Francis I was privately scathing about the ugliness of the object, Charles received it politely and subsequently presented it to Jean de Henin, who made it the principal decoration in the *Salle d'Apollon* at the château of Bossu.[13]

The most prolific sculptor patronised by Charles and by his son Philip was Leone Leoni. He had worked in Padua and Rome before entering the emperor's service in the 1540s. He carved busts of Charles, Empress Isabella, Philip and Mary of Hungary. Like Titian and Cellini, with whom he has been compared, Leoni's appeal for patrons was his capacity to produce images in fine detail which were at once naturalistic and heroic. His allegorical statue *Charles V restraining Fury* was begun in 1549 although not finished until the 1560s. It is probably the sculpture which most closely accords with the emperor's self-image. It shows him dressed in contemporary, but highly classicised, armour with a lance in his right hand standing over the chained and crouching form of vanquished Fury or War, itself an allegory of all Charles's enemies.[14]

By 1535 Charles had also begun receiving or commissioning work from a number of important Italians artists. Much of this patronage dates from his two visits to northern Italy in 1529–30 and 1532–33. During his 1530 visit to Bologna, an allegorical portrait of Charles, now lost, was painted by Parmigianino. This featured a small boy, the infant Hercules, dressed with a lion's pelt presenting a globe to the emperor. Together with the depiction on the scabbard of Charles's sword of his motto and the columns of Hercules, this imagery flattered Charles as the inheritor of the tasks and glory of the classical hero at the moment of his coronation in Bologna as Holy Roman Emperor. In 1532, shortly after Charles had raised him from Marquis to Duke of Mantua, Federico Gonzaga commissioned four paintings from Correggio. This was the 'Loves of Jupiter' series – the *Leda*, the *Danae*, the *Io* and the *Ganymede*. The subjects of these paintings were taken from Ovid's *Metamorphoses* and current scholarly opinion is divided as to whether they were intended as a gift for the emperor or were part of a set of eight paintings designed for the *Sala di Ovidio* in the Palazzo Te at Mantua. This pleasure palace was designed and decorated principally by Giulio Romano and much of its decoration has been interpreted as praise of Charles V who was entertained there on at least one occasion. The association between the emperor and Jupiter was a common one, the sensual content of the paintings, like that of *Sala di Amore e Psiche*, alluded in flattering ways to the emperor's personal sophistication, and that of his host. The expense and high quality of the Correggio paintings, together with gifts given to the emperor, expressed the value of Gonzaga's allegiance to him. This was the same Federico Gonzaga whose development as a patron had been helped in part by his time at Francis I's court in 1516–17.[15]

Perhaps the most convincing proof Gonzaga offered of his own cultivated taste and of his influence upon Charles was to introduce Titian to the emperor in 1529–30. According to Vasari, he subsequently became Charles's favourite painter. Among the first works Titian did for Charles was a copy of a painting by the German artist Jakob Seisenegger, entitled *Charles V with Dog*. One has only to compare Titian's version, now in the Prado in Madrid, with Seisenegger's to see why Charles patronised the Venetian master. The luminosity and warmth of Titian's portrait almost literally outshines Seisenegger's. His depiction of the emperor's face in particular gives the subject a lively quality entirely lacking in Seisenegger's perfectly competent portrait. Titian painted at least five original portraits of the emperor, only three of which now survive. The first was of the emperor in armour, thought to be *Charles V with Drawn Sword*, unfortunately now lost and known only through copies by Rubens. In Augsburg in 1548 he painted *Charles V with Baton* and what is probably the most famous image of the emperor, the equestrian portrait, *Charles V at the Battle of Mühlberg*. From this period came another portrait of the emperor, shown seated at a table. Titian also made portraits of Empress Isabella and Prince Philip. It was to Titian that Charles entrusted the commission of an altarpiece featuring the imperial family adoring the Trinity for the high altar of the monastery at Yuste where Charles spent his retirement.[16]

In 1533 Charles commissioned a portrait medallion of himself by the sculptor Alfonso Lombardi who was also involved in preparing the triumphal arches which greeted the emperor at his entry to Bologna in November 1529. While there in 1529–30 Charles invited the crystal engraver Giovanni Bernadi de Castelbolognese to join his entourage. The artist declined the invitation but six years later Bernadio Clesio, the Bishop of Trent, presented the emperor with a crystal medallion depicting the capture of Francis I at Pavia which is now attributed to Bernadi. The medallion was kept in the royal apartments as Brussels suggesting it was valued by the emperor. The emotional significance of such an object for the ageing Charles, representing the moment of triumph over his life-long rival, can be easily imagined.[17]

Francis I's official court artists for the entire reign were the Flemish born Jean Clouet and his son François. Together they produced some of the best portraits of the king and his court, on paper, canvas, and in the form of miniatures both enamelled and on velum. Perhaps the most famous portrait of Francis, now in the Louvre, dates from 1526 and is attributed to Jean and François Clouet. It quickly became the standard contemporary image of the king and an illuminated miniature of Francis closely resembling it appears on the Treaty of Westminster which Francis signed with Henry VIII in 1527.

Jean Clouet also produced a number of portrait miniatures of members of the royal family used in diplomatic gifts, especially in relations with England. François Clouet also produced the only known equestrian portrait of the king and he may also be responsible for one extraordinary image of Francis as King David with sceptre and harp which probably dates from around 1539–40.[18]

From the start of his reign, Italian Renaissance classicism appealed very much to Francis both personally and as a means of projecting an image of imperial monarchy. The first significant Italian paintings in his collection were gifts from Leo X and Francesco Gonzaga. These include a *St Michael* by Raphael, the portrait of *Joanna of Aragon* by Giulio Romano and a *Visitation of Elizabeth* by Sebastiano del Piombo. Francis attempted unsuccessfully to retain the services of Michelangelo but a giant statue of *Hercules* by him stood in the grounds of Fontainebleau. Francis did attract Leonardo da Vinci to France in 1516. He already owned a number of works by the great Florentine but Leonardo was by then too elderly to do much work for the king. Francis gave him a small villa near the royal château at Amboise in the Loire valley and it was here that Leonardo died in 1519.

The first prominent Italian artist to work for Francis was the Florentine sculptor Girolamo della Robbia who came to France early in Francis's reign. He worked on the Angoulême family château at Cognac before, from 1531, overseeing much of the external decoration of the château of Madrid. This included multi-coloured glazed terracotta facings on the columns of the lower floors and medallions with busts of Roman emperors over the loggias which flanked the central pavilion. Internal decoration seems to have included stucco work but no detail of it is known. Della Robbia was followed by Giovanni Battista Rosso and Francesco Primaticcio whom Francis employed at Fontainebleau. Primaticcio decorated a number of the royal apartments with stucco figures of gods, goddesses, herms and nymphs whose alluringly elongated lines became the basis of a style known as Fontainebleau mannerism.[19]

Francis also established a tapestry workshop at Fontainebleau in 1540. Its most notable products were six hangings reproducing the Rosso frescoes on the south side wall of the *Galerie François Ier*. The king's collection, variously estimated at between 213 and 480 pieces, included several remarkably expensive sets, most made in Brussels and Antwerp. Francis owned a set depicting the life of King David and one of the Acts of the Apostles. Among the most expensive tapestries was a set of 23, depicting the deeds of Scipio Africanus. Designed by Giulio Romano, they were woven in Brussels in 1532 under the supervision of Primaticcio at a cost of 50,000 *livres*. The first four of them arrived in time to decorate Francis's apartments at Boulogne during his meeting that autumn with Henry VIII. Twenty years earlier, tapestries had been used in great numbers at the Field of Cloth of Gold. Many of the king's tapestries were stored at the Louvre in the charge of the chief tapestry expert, Guillaume Moynier. He was assisted by two other *tapissiers du roi*, based at Blois and Amboise. From these sites, the king's tapestries and other items of furniture could be moved relatively easily, usually by river, to wherever they were needed.[20]

Francis was a thoughtful patron who was also interested in acquiring high quality art through agents in Italy. In the 1530s he engaged the Florentine Battista della Palla in this capacity. Della Palla once wrote to his Florentine patron Fillippo Strozzi seeking antique statues for the king of France. He explained that:

> ... there are indeed excellent things to fill our need – which is not so much for quantity (mediocre pieces, just because they are antique) as for quality, (the most excellent).[21]

It is not known whether Francis gave della Palla specific instructions to collect works by particular artists but the agent seems to have had a good understanding of his master's requirements and searched his native Florence and beyond quite systematically. Alongside della Palla, the antiquarian and humanist Pietro Aretino worked as an agent for Francis and Charles V. It was he who, in 1538, sent Francis the famous portrait of the king by Titian.

Benvenuto Cellini came to France for five years after 1540. At their first meeting, Cellini presented the king with a vase and basin he had created. Francis was impressed with the offering, telling Cellini's erstwhile patron, the Cardinal of Ferrara that:

> Of a truth, I hardly think the ancients can have seen a piece so beautiful as this. I well remember to have inspected all the best works, and by the greatest masters of all Italy, but I never set my eyes on anything which stirred me to such admiration.[22]

Francis certainly exaggerated his familiarity with antique statues at this point but always remained receptive to what artists could teach him. Among many works Cellini did for the king, was the bonze medallion of him as a Roman emperor which is now in the Fitzwilliam Museum in Cambridge. He also designed a fountain for the palace of Fontainebleau, the centre piece of which was to be a colossus representing Francis in the guise of Mars and as patron of the arts. Although Cellini showed Francis a maquette, the project was not completed.

In 1540 Francesco Primaticcio was sent to Italy to collect casts of the most important Roman antique statues still available. This expedition followed a conversation in which, according to Cellini, Primaticcio had told the king:

> that when his Majesty had once set eyes upon those marvellous works, he would then, and not till then, be able to criticise the arts of design, since everything which he had seen by us moderns was far removed from the perfection of the ancients.[23]

Francis duly received casts of these ancient statues, copies of which he promised to send to Henry VIII. They included the *Apollo Belvedere*, the *Laocoön* and the *Sleeping Ariadne*, all of which were placed initially in the *Galerie François Ier*. A plaster cast of the horse from the equestrian statue of Marcus Aurelius was also brought back by Primaticcio. However it was never used in manufacturing a statue in France and was later placed prominently in the base court at Fontainebleau which was thereafter known as the Cour de Cheval Blanc.

Perhaps the most famous of Cellini's works for Francis was an exquisite gold salt cellar inlaid with jewels featuring figures of Venus and Neptune on the sea. When he received the object in 1543, the king cried aloud in astonishment and gazed at the object with rapt attention. He also revealed a self-assured approach to collecting and judging what he was offered. Francis presumably felt he had learnt a good deal from these acquisitions because when, a short time later, Cellini presented him with a candelabra in form of a life-size statue of Jupiter, the king responded:

> This is by far the finest thing that has ever been seen; and I, although I am an amateur and judge of art, could never have conceived the hundreth part of its beauty.[24]

Francis obviously used the term amateur in its strict sense, where we might say connoisseur and saw himself as a discerning and deserving patron. His extensive use of agents and his direct patronage of leading Italian artists advertised his monarchy in a very sophisticated way. In return he paid artists well, Primaticcio received 600 *livres* and livery annually, as much as many of Francis's table servants of noble rank received.

Henry VIII was keenly aware of the standards in artistic patronage set by his French rival. A great deal of his effort in this area was designed to match, and if possible to outdo, the splendours assembled by Francis I. His ambassadors kept him well informed of what Francis was up to and some of the most important works he commissioned were made in the context of his personal relations with Francis. Most of the significant artists who worked for Henry VIII were of European origin.

Henry commissioned comparatively little sculpture but in Pietro Torrigiano, he patronised the first Italian to bring the Renaissance style to England. In addition to designing and executing tombs for Margaret Beaufort, Henry VII and Elizabeth of York at Westminster Abbey, he also designed tombs for Dean Colet and Dr John Younge, the Master of the Rolls. He also made a bust of John Colet. Henry owned a large number of statues and busts bought on the Continent, some of which he kept in his study at Whitehall and which were recorded in the inventory made after the king's death. When he acquired Hampton Court from Wolsey he also obtained the six pairs of busts of Roman emperors by Giovanni da Maiano, set in round niches in several of the gateways in the palace.

In 1540 Francis I promised to send Henry copies of the moulds of antique statues which Primaticcio had brought back from Italy but there is no evidence that any actually arrived. Francis did however indirectly provide

Henry with a talented sculptor. This was Nicolas Bellin of Modena, who worked for Henry at Nonsuch. He had previously worked with Francesco Primaticcio at Fontainebleau. He left France and went to England after being charged with embezzling the king's money. His sculptured stucco panels at Nonsuch showed classical scenes and owed much to the work he had earlier done in France. These panels covered the walls of the inner courtyard at Nonsuch and Bellin's carved slate tiles covered the exposed structural timbers of the walls. Other external and internal decorations of 'antique work' exhibited a wide range of complicated designs and it was at least partly through Bellin that Henry was kept in touch with the latest decorative ideas in European architecture.[25]

In the fine arts, too, Henry turned early to Continental talent. The Flemish miniaturists, Gerard and Lucas Horenbout, were working for the king by the mid 1520s. Their most famous work for him was a set of miniatures of Henry, Katherine of Aragon and Princess Mary dating from 1525–27. These are most likely to have been made as gifts for Francis I, sent in response to a set of miniatures which Henry received from France in late 1526 of Francis I and his two sons, probably by Jean Clouet.[26]

The greatest artist whom Henry VIII patronised was the German, Hans Holbein the Younger. During the 1520s and 1530s he produced dozens of portraits in oils and in chalk of the royal family and prominent members of the Tudor regime. He also painted lesser members of English court, German merchants and ambassadors in London. In fact the vast majority of English portraits of any distinction at all which survive from this period are by Holbein or his studio. This work parallels directly that done at the French court by the Clouets and their followers. Just as Francis I used his gallery at Fontainebleau, Henry used his private apartments to make statements about the nature of his monarchy. The emphasis in the composition of all Holbein's portraits of the king is on his strength and independent character but in the famous Whitehall portrait of Henry, his parents and third wife, Jane Seymour, there is an equal stress placed on the security of his dynasty and thus stability and continuity for his kingdom. Holbein also collaborated with other 'artificers' such as Niklaus Kratzer, the German-born astronomer royal, on decorations for important occasions at the Tudor court. The most famous example of such collaboration was the temporary banqueting house constructed to receive a French embassy to England in May 1527. Among the many decoration he provided was a scene of the 1513 siege of Thèrouanne designed to remind Henry VIII's guests of his military capability should the peace treaty agreed that year be broken by Francis I.

There was one area of artistic patronage in which Henry outshone Francis, and probably Charles V as well, namely the collection of tapestries. At his death Henry had over 2000 individual pieces in an extensive range of styles, many dating from the mid fifteenth century. Many more were bought in Brussels during the last decade of the reign and show strong Italian influences in subjects and style. Among the most important sets Henry possessed was one of the *Story of King David and Bathsheba*, attributed to Jan van Roome and made in Brussels between 1510 and 1525. This set now hangs in the Musée de la Renaissance at Écouen.[27]

SCIENTIFIC INSTRUMENTS AND *OBJETS D'ART*

In addition to patronising the military expertise of armourers, artillery-makers and the like, all three monarchs in this study were fascinated with scientific instruments. Cartography, geometry, chronometry and astronomy were very fashionable sciences in the sixteenth century and the skills and instruments used in them were in great demand. The inventories of the kings all show significant numbers of maps, charts and globes together with clocks, dials and other time-pieces of various kinds as well as quadrants and astrolabes. Holbein's painting *The Ambassadors* assembles a number of these types of instrument on the table between its subjects, alluding to the knowledge and intellectual interests which Renaissance gentlemen, especially kings, were expected to have. Such items were usually kept in special cupboards or rooms in the private royal apartments, a *Kunstkammer*, where they were available for the king's use or to be shown to important guests.

Charles V patronised a number of scientists directly and numerous mathematical and geometrical treatises were dedicated to him. A number of contemporary chronicles of his reign refer to his love of maps and his enjoyment of scientific instruments:

> ... he wished to know all the particularities of the philosophy of nature and of the stars. He grasped things much more quickly than most men. He wanted to understand every kind of mechanical device and clock, both Arabic and Western, and how they were made.[28]

Probably the most famous scientist whom he patronised was the astronomer Peter Apianus who dedicated to the emperor his *Astronomicum Caesareum*, printed in Ingolstadt in 1541. This book explained a number of astronomical problems and the significance of heavenly events, including a lunar eclipse at the time of Charles's coronation as emperor in 1530. Apianus also presented some of his own instruments to the emperor. Another scientist who worked for Charles was Gemma Frisius. In 1536 he and his student Gérard Mercator produced, under imperial privilege, terrestrial and celestial globes incorporating what were described as 'countries and islands recently discovered.' In 1541 at Leuven, Mercator made a large terrestrial globe for the Cardinal de Granvelle and is known to have made a celestial globe in crystal for the emperor, together with a number of other scientific instruments, all now lost.[29]

Charles also possessed a large number of clocks, including one extraordinary piece in the form of a classical temple 42 centimetres high made of ebony, gilt copper, precious stones and enamel. A figure of the emperor enthroned, flanked by two eagles and under a canopy or *baldacchino* is set above the temple. The craftsman responsible for the object has not been established definitively but the most likely candidate is the Cremonese master Gianello Torriano. Another clock owned by the emperor is the famous *Ship of Charles V* now in the Musée de la Renaissance at Écouen. This remarkable object, one metre high, is a scale model of a carrack, a Mediterranean warship from Charles's reign. It is now attributed to the Augsburg horologist Hans Schlottheim. Its design is a deliberate variation on medieval tradition of the decorative salt holder in the shape of a vessel or *nef*. This model features on its decks a figure of the emperor himself, seated on a throne holding a sceptre and globe. Ten figures of imperial dignitaries surround the throne. There are also minstrels and sailors in the rigging. The emperor's head nods and he raises his sceptre to acknowledge them as the clock strikes the hours.[30]

Francis I's most precious and favourite possessions were kept in a *cabinet des curiosités* in or above the king's private apartments either at Fontainebleau or the Louvre. Its exact location and contents cannot now be identified definitely but his collection evidently included silverware, vases, figurines, clothing, porcelain, carved and engraved crystal and a one and a half foot long sculpture of a seven-headed hydra, presented to Francis in 1530 by Süleyman the Magnificent. The king also patronised a select group of Parisian goldsmiths, particularly Pierre Mangot and Jean Hotman who made clock-salts, reliquaries, candelabras, chains and collars for him and for use as gifts for friends and visiting ambassadors. Francis also regularly bought large quantities of precious stones, gems and jewellery from merchants, most based in Paris, who had trading connections in Italy and the Orient. One such was Alart Plymaître or Ploumier who, on one occasion, sold the king items to the value of 14,625 *livres*. In 1533, a list was made of the king's jewellery then in the care of Jean de la Barre, the *premier gentilhomme de la chambre*. It comprised 26 items with a total value 95,710 *écus*. What proportion of the king's entire jewellery collection this represents it is impossible to say. La Barre also accounted for a further 20 items given away by the king as gifts. These included a reliquary and diamond given to Henry VIII and a diamond given to Anne Boleyn at Calais in October 1532.[31]

Despite his public belligerence towards the French, Henry VIII in fact employed a significant number of French artisans and merchants in acquiring his personal possessions. His accounts are scattered with references to French traders visiting the English court. Two Frenchmen in particular, Ploumier called 'jueller of Parys' in the English accounts and Jean Crespin or Cryspyn 'jeweler of France' sold items to the king regularly. In 1532 Henry bought from Ploumier unspecified items worth £1052 11s 8d. In Paris in June 1546 Alart Ploumier repaired a gold salt cellar which was 'broken in diverse thinges' as it was being taken by Sir Thomas Cheyne to Fontainebleau. It was there presented as a baptismal gift from the English king to Elizabeth, the grand-daughter of Francis I.

Henry also bought clocks and instruments from Frenchmen. Vincent Quenay and one Drulardy supplied the king with over a dozen instruments variously described as clocks and dials. In April 1531 the departing French ambassador, Gabriel de La Guiche presented Henry with 'a very fine and artistic clock, on the dial of which the movement of several celestial spheres and planetary systems can be distinctly observed.' Perhaps Henry's best known horologist after Nicholas Kratzer was the Frenchman, Nicholas Oursain or 'Wourston' as he is often called in English sources. He first appears officially in royal accounts in 1538, but given the wide variations in the spelling of his name, he may plausibly be identified with the 'nycolas Curcean clockemaker' to whom Henry paid £5 3s in May 1532 for 'stuf made for the kinges grace.' In 1540 Oursain made the large astronomical clock which can still be seen on the inner gatehouse at Hampton Court. It features three moving copper dials, planets and the sun, which in accordance with contemporary scientific theory, is shown orbiting the earth. From April 1541 Oursain was paid 10s 4d per month as clock-keeper at Hampton Court. In 1537, another French clockmaker, Sebastian Leseney also entered Henry's service for a monthly fee of 20s. An astrolabe by Leseney is now in the British Museum.[32]

PATRONAGE, PROPAGANDA AND THE ROYAL IMAGE

The subject which bulked largest in the artistic patronage of all three monarchs was themselves. They were depicted in naturalistic or allegorical portraits, on wood, canvas and in fresco. They were featured on jewels and cameos, on coins, in stained glass and as statues. They were also praised in literature. Panegyrics, epigrams, sermons and scripts for street pageants were produced to mark milestones in their reigns. Between them they received hundreds of works of sacred and secular literature as well as scientific, philosophical and political treatises. All these forms of representation helped to 'popularise' their image both with the comparatively small numbers of people who belonged to national elites and who actually saw the king as well as larger public audiences at home and abroad.

There are at present well in excess of 100 contemporary images of Charles V still extant or known from engravings and other evidence. Numerous medals were struck of him including one showing him as the victor over Süleyman the Magnificent. Another, commissioned by the Cardinal de Granvelle, shows him in armour, also wearing a laurel wreath of victory, at the time of his abdication in 1555. Titian's magnificent portrait of Charles V in full armour at the Battle of Mühlberg in 1547 would have been seen by relatively few people during the remainder of the emperor's life. Nevertheless, it functions as a definitive and self-conscious statement of the power of Habsburg emperor at the moment of his greatest triumph, designed to impress those whom the subject most needed to impress, his own noble friends and representatives of other princes.[33]

Janet Cox-Rearick has identified over 40 different extant images of Francis in a wide variety of media. He was first pictured in illuminated manuscripts presented to his mother. The first medal of Francis I was struck even before he was king, when in 1512 he was Duke of Valois and titular commander of Louis XII's forces which defeated a joint Anglo-Spanish attack on south western France. He was portrayed in profile in classical garb, with the victor's laurel wreath around his head. Another was struck in 1515 after his victory at Marignano, commemorating him as 'first conqueror of the Swiss.' That event also prompted the production of the *Commentaires de la guerre gallique* written by François Demoulins with illuminations by Godefroy le Batave and Jean Clouet. This three volume work effectively equates in importance Francis's conquest of Milan with Julius Caesar's conquest of Gaul. Its illustrations amplify this theme in a variety of ways. In volume two for example the king is depicted in conversation with Julius Caesar while on a hunting trip in the forest near his ancestral home at Cognac.[34] This imperial imagery set the tone for the remainder of the king's reign and reached its high point in the decoration of the *Galerie François Ier* at Fontainebleau. The king was also painted in naturalistic portrait, in illuminations on treaties, in devotional literature. Finally, he was sculpted on his tomb in the abbey church of Saint-Denis. Either as classical emperor or in naturalistic portrait, Francis is probably, with Louis XIV, the most easily recognized king in the whole history of the French monarchy.

There are several surviving anonymous portraits of Henry VIII in the first decade of his reign. During the 1520s and especially in the context of Anglo-French relations, miniatures of him were painted as gifts for Francis I. Henry also appears in highly coloured frames in the margins of treaty documents and on medals. These images are all naturalistic, and whether three-quarter, face-on or in profile, they conform to types of royal portraiture common throughout Europe in the early 1500s. They emphasise Henry's noble bearing, his wealth and his dynastic connections. During the 1530s Henry became less concerned with himself as a new Henry V and more interested in being seen as the religious leader of his people. He was most famously presented in this guise on the frontispiece of the *Great Bible* of 1539 where he is depicted handing the book to his servants, including Cranmer and Cromwell. In or around the same year he was presented as King David in a psalter which contains illuminations by the French artist Jean Mallard. He had previously worked for Francis before serving Henry between 1539 and 1541. The most famous of seven illuminations shows

Henry reading his bible in an idealised and ornately classical privy chamber at Whitehall.[35]

It was Holbein's privy chamber portrait of the king and his family, of which only the cartoon now survives, that made him the most recognizable sovereign in English history. The portrait demonstrates how the German artist's exceptional talent really held its own against that of Lucas Cranach, Barend van Orley, Jean Clouet and perhaps even Titian. Like the images in the *Galerie François Ier*, the Whitehall image was intended to be seen by the elite and the most important foreign visitors invited to the king's private apartments. Set before an elaborate neo-classical, architectural background, Henry appears tall and imposing but not yet grossly overweight. He stands with legs astride and hands set imperiously at the hips. An inscription set within the painting declares that although his father was great, Henry VIII is greater for having recovered true religion in England and defended his island realm from its enemies. The king is portrayed as everything he, and others, believed him to be; the epitome of powerful Tudor monarchy. The image has virtually become Henry VIII's trademark.

CONCLUSION

Despite prominent military and political successes at times, neither Francis, Charles nor Henry carved out the hegemony over Europe, or part of it, that he desired. In this context, the fame and reputation which generous artistic patronage could bring was important to all of them. Beyond a reputation for discerning generosity, patronising artists was itself part of the art of magnificent monarchy.

Henry VIII's artistic patronage should be seen in the context of the history of English royal traditions and the comparatively meagre resources at his disposal. During the first one to two decades of the reign, the king himself was the English's court's great masterpiece. Henry lavished money and energy on his own spectacular participation in tournaments, masques and pageants of all kinds. His aesthetic sense was quite conservative, medieval in conception and informed by the courtly world in which he grew up. In his conversation with Wallop in November 1540 quoted at the outset, Francis I contrasted his own preference for unadorned natural woods with Henry's use of 'much gilding' in his palaces. As the ceiling of the Chapel Royal at Hampton Court attests, Henry's personal taste was for the brighter sheen of royal purple, for the vibrant reds of Tudor roses and the sky-blues of Garter mantles or ceilings powdered with gold stars.

Although he undoubtedly went in for colourful, even glitzy, decoration at times Henry was also deeply fashion conscious. He was as aware as anyone of the growing preference in Europe for classical elements in architecture and design. In the 1530s he learned a great deal from reports of Francis I's artistic patronage and this helped keep him abreast of European developments but, although his artists borrowed ideas from France, there is little evidence of slavish imitation of all things French. As the work of Bellin and Mallard in particular shows, Henry's client artists adapted the expertise they had gained in Europe to an English setting and produced work at Nonsuch and elsewhere which persuaded observers of Henry's claims to possess some artistic discrimination. Nevertheless, with the important exceptions of the Horenbouts and Holbein, Henry only had available to him second-division artists, however competent, who were themselves just keeping up with the techniques and ideas produced by the exceptional talent available to Francis I and Charles V. Ultimately it is with Holbein that Henry's image and his reputation as a patron of the arts is forever inextricably linked.

The considerable talents of prominent Italian, German and Flemish artists reinforced, indeed gave exceptional shape, form and colour to Charles V's 'monarchia'. They helped to determine not only the style of artistic patronage he practised but also its grand, not to say sometimes grandiose scale. As a patron of architecture he comes a distant third behind his two contemporaries. He seems not to have shared to the same extent their personal interest in acquiring new palaces, being far more prepared than they were to make do with what he had inherited. As he famously remarked to his son at the time of his abdication, 'monarchs do not need residences.' However he was personally interested in architecture and engineering, especially military engineering. The palace at the Alhambra remains an impressive monument to architectural talent Charles could marshal when he chose to. It relied heavily on Bramantesque models and would not have seemed particularly noteworthy in Italy, but in Spain, and especially when surrounded by the Islamic architecture of the Alhambra complex, it made a remarkable statement about Charles's power as patron, not just as king of Spain but as emperor in Europe.

His aesthetic instincts were more conservative than those of Francis and less florid than Henry VIII's but he knew the importance of projecting an appropriately regal image to his many different subjects. There are more paintings, sketches and busts of Charles V in his youth and early manhood than all those of Henry and Francis at equivalent ages put together. During the 1530s the dominance of Flemish conventions in his artistic patronage was replaced by a more classical style. He readily appreciated the talents of artists such as Titian and Leoni and gave them a high profile, international, forum in which their work would be appreciated. They repaid him with some of the most memorable images of sixteenth century monarchy ever created.

Francis I's claims to connoisseurship were genuine and plausible. From an early age he developed his knowledge of literature and a wide range of arts. He employed that knowledge effectively to enhance his reputation in the world. He seems always to have been more at home with the ideals and examples of Italian Renaissance classicism than either Henry VIII or Charles V. As king, the model of the victorious and peace-giving Roman emperor was fused in him with the ideals of ancestral chivalry. It inspired him directly in his military and political interventions in Italy from 1515. His wealth and the fierce competitiveness he felt towards Charles V and, to a lesser extent towards Henry VIII, drove him to emulate the Italian style because it evoked so directly the supposed splendours of imperial rule to which he aspired. He sought objects and artists who could produce such work for him and gave them an apparently endless vocabulary on which to draw in presenting his kingship to the rest of Europe. Through his large court and multiple international connections, Flemish and Italian influence spread not just through France, but also to England and to eastern Europe.

Francis was also genuinely impressed with the skills of artists and showed great enthusiasm for work of high quality. This made him an attractive, if demanding, patron for whom to work. The Clouets, Rosso and Primaticcio are known today mainly because of Francis's patronage. Although he left Francis's service under a cloud, Cellini acknowledged his debt to him to Duke Cosimo de' Medici and, in a poem written in 1556, he described himself as 'in part immortal, since the French king set me on the path of sculpture.'

Conclusion

Henry VIII died early on the morning of Friday 28 January 1547. Francis I died two months later in the early afternoon of Thursday 31 March. Charles V lived for another 11 years. In the summer of 1556, having abdicated from all his titles, he retired to a villa attached to the monastery of San Jeronimo at Yuste in Estremadura. After two years of comparatively quiet and simple pleasures, he died shortly before dawn on Wednesday 21 September 1558. The exertions, excesses and anxieties of rule had taken a heavy physical toll on all three kings. All made good Catholic deaths, ministered to in their final hours by their confessors and high prelates. Francis and Charles were worried about some of their deeds as kings, but were assured of God's mercy by those around them. Amateur theologian to the end and head of his own church after all, Henry found words to offer himself the same assurance.

Between them these kings had dominated the international politics of Europe for the best part of 50 years. In the centuries since, historians have taken widely differing views of their significance. Until the eighteenth century they were seen as exemplars of kingship and praised for their heroic qualities. In the nineteenth and earlier twentieth centuries the reviews were not so favourable. Henry and Francis were sharply criticised by Michelet, Stubbs, Pollard, and even Elton for their indecisive wars and their personal extravagance. On the whole, these historians would have preferred the kings to be busy about defensible borders and husbanding royal resources rather than indulging their passions for women, art and horses or engaging in 'wasteful' junkets like the Field of Cloth of Gold. Charles V had rather more favourable treatment, although he, too, was criticised by Ranke and others for clinging to an outmoded medieval vision of a Christian world empire in the face of the rise of modern nation-states.

In more recent decades their reputations have staged something of a recovery. Modern biographers have presented more rounded accounts of them while the context of their reigns has been more fully explored in specialist studies of early-modern government and Renaissance political culture. At the centre of that culture was the concept of *virtus*, characterised chiefly by valour in battle and just rule of subjects. The king was charged by God and trusted by his people to maintain a proper hierarchical order and balance in society. He was also to be an inspirational figure to the political nation; one who treated the nobles munificently and respected the views of these entitled to offer counsel but who also led from the front.

Henry VIII did lead from the front – eventually. As a young king he was endowed with the natural advantages of a born soldier, but it was not until 1513 that he finally threw himself into his first war against France with as much relief as determination. While it did not result in his being crowned king of France, Henry did enough in that war to make his sister Queen of France the following year and to get for himself a seat at Europe's top table. He had sufficient wit and imagination to learn from Wolsey that making peace with the king of France could be advantageous when war against France was not possible. He still spent hugely to build, maintain and advertise his military capability and when, in 1523 and 1544, circumstances for war were propitious, he plunged in with gusto. He was sometimes gulled by Francis I and often played false by Charles V, most obviously in 1525, but both also needed him and he manipulated that need constantly to assert his power in the world beyond England's shores.

Henry's impact within those shores was more impressive. He built much and he destroyed much. He raised talented people to high office and he destroyed them too. The English Parliament had never worked as hard, or to greater effect in extending royal power, as it did between 1529 and 1545. He took England out of Rome's jurisdiction and brought Wales within England's. As his ministers dissolved the monasteries, and with them his people's spiritual ties to Europe, his propagandists taught them anew what it meant to be English. He punished recalcitrant papists and Lutheran converts with equal cruelty. In the minds of his Protestant successors, Henry's reputation as rescuer and defender of 'true religion' in England was thereby safeguarded. In the process, most of England's medieval ecclesiastical heritage was ruined.

Henry spent the money he gained from sale of monastic estates to fortify England's southern coast. He also used it to acquire or renovate most of the 55 palaces that he owned at his death and to furnish them with the vast hoard of tapestries, paintings and plate which is meticulously detailed in the inventories of his possessions taken after his death. Henry took royal material acquisition to new heights and with it England's engagement with Renaissance artists and styles. He was portrayed by Holbein as a rock-solid king, but his spending on himself and on his reputation undermined his kingdom's financial stability.

In the half century after his death Francis I was known as 'le grand roi François' and, amidst the dissension and strife of his grandsons' reigns, his time was looked upon as something of a golden age. He was praised for doing what they evidently could not, namely maintaining the status and authority of the monarchy within the realm and asserting its power beyond it. He did one by doing the other. Francis's used his claim to Milan as an outward focus for the aggressive energies of the French nobility and his wars in Italy generated enthusiastic support for the monarchy among the majority of French nobles. He was never history's greatest strategist and in the early 1520s was as impetuous on the battlefield as anywhere else. This quality helped him win Milan in 1515 and was partly responsible for his losing it a decade later. He never achieved his aim of permanent French control over Milan. He had to concede French feudal claims in Flanders and Artois and he also lost Boulogne. On the other hand, he fought strenuously for 30 years against the most powerful monarch Europe had ever known, withheld Burgundy from him and simultaneously enhanced the French patrimony by the final incorporation of Brittany into the realm.

Francis had a pronounced sense of his own authority and expressed it frequently in dealing with the provincial estates and the Parlements. He underpinned his formal authority by maintaining good personal ties with influential figures in the localities such as his governors and *baillis*. Through them and through such innovations as the *gentilshommes de la chambre du roi*, he created an impressive personal entourage and extended the royal affinity. He also extended at least the theoretical reach of the king's power. Through edicts like Villers-Cotterêts, he worked towards a more uniform application of royal law throughout France. His need for money to finance his wars, his court and his building programme, led him to overhaul the crown's ramshackle finance system but also induced him to sell its judicial offices on an unprecedented scale. Although profitable enough in the short term, in the longer term venality lessened the accountability of officials to the crown and created problems for his successors.

Like the greatest of those successors, Louis XIV, Francis appreciated the importance of artistic patronage in creating an impressive style of monarchy and a good reputation. For all the dazzling brilliance of the 'Sun-King,' and Versailles, to which the tourists flock, Francis's contribution to French artistic and intellectual history is as great, or greater, than Louis'. It was Francis's patronage which laid the foundation for the formal study of classical languages in France and for the development of French vernacular poetry in the classical style. It was due largely to the king's building projects in the Loire Valley and Fontainebleau that the classical style in architecture was introduced on a wider scale in France and under his direct patronage, French portraiture, sculpture and music developed significantly. It was as the great royal patron of the French Renaissance that Francis I's monarchy was at its most magnificent and that his reputation is now most secure.

After his death Charles V was remembered fondly in Spain and particularly in the Netherlands, where, thanks largely to Philip II's harsh religious policies, his reign took on a rosy hue. In fact his rule of the Netherlands was not especially benign and in 1540 he imposed his authority on Ghent with considerable force. Nevertheless he succeeded in the Netherlands where Philip failed because for the most part he respected the nobility's traditional role in government and left his subjects there to get on with making money which is what they wanted. He certainly failed in Germany. Whether he could ever have imposed a Catholic settlement there is doubtful but it was certainly too late to do so in the wake of the Battle of Mühlberg in 1547. He might have done more to assist Ferdinand in the 1520s but, had he spent that decade attempting to settle the religious issue in the Empire, would he have had the effective control over Spain that his presence there in the same years enabled him to achieve? Without firm control of Spain, how would he have sustained the wars against Francis over the following two decades, or consolidated his hold on Italy, or had any success against the Turks in North Africa?

These were the frustrating paradoxes of Charles's reign, with which his many councils and advisors struggled daily. Had it been possible to resolve them tactically or logistically, the immense cost of doing so would surely still have defeated even Charles's massive resources. As a ruler Charles was conscientious and deeply committed to the idea of Christian unity in the face of the apparent threat posed by the Turks. Yet the sheer diversity of his dominions and his decision, sensible in itself, to rule each of them as its individual sovereign, hindered as much as encouraged the great enterprises of which Charles dreamed. He was conscious of his failures, especially his inability to reconcile the German Protestants to his faith. Nevertheless, at his death in 1558 he was able to pass on to his son a peaceful Spain and the Burgundian patrimony, augmented by a surer grip on Flanders and Artois. He had also secured his dynasty's hold on Austria and the Empire; a hold that was to last until the twentieth century. Modest though these achievements are when set alongside his potential, they required forty years of constant effort in the turbulent politics of the age. They were a source of some satisfaction to Charles, who, whatever else he may have been, remained essentially as Titian portrayed him in the portrait, *Charles V at the Battle of Mühlberg*, a determined but deeply conventional Flemish knight and nobleman.

Charles, Henry and Francis all had mixed records as kings and none entirely achieved his initial ambitions. However if a defining characteristic of their 'Renaissance monarchy' is required, then it is probably the intensity with which these kings felt that ambition to be 'great'. Each of them fought, plotted with, charmed and intimidated each other, and their subjects alike, as they strove to demonstrate their supposed exceptionality. They may not have sought to do essentially different things from their predecessors but whether it was commanding armies in war, building fine palaces or acquiring wives, they wanted (or were forced) to do so on a grander scale and over a longer period than most medieval monarchs. For, as Machiavelli also said: 'Above all, in all his doings a prince must endeavour to win the reputation of being a great man of outstanding ability.'

Extended chronology.

Year	Henry VIII	Francis I	Charles V
1490			
	28 June 1491 Born at Greenwich, near London.		
		12 September 1494 Born at Cognac, Loire Valley.	
1495			
1500			**24 February 1500** Born in Ghent, Flanders.
	February 1503 Becomes Prince of Wales and heir following the death of his elder brother Arthur in 1502.		
			September 1506 Death of Charles's father Philip of Burgundy. Charles inherits the ducal title and lands. Maximilian's regency for Charles exercised by Margaret of Austria.
		1508 Aged 14, Francis begins residing at the French court.	
	23 April 1509 Henry becomes **King of England**. In June marries Katherine of Aragon.		
1510			
	June 1513 Henry invades France in alliance with the emperor Maximilian and Ferdinand of Aragon. In August captures Thérouanne and Tournai.	**June 1513** Francis made *lieutenant-général* for the king's army in Picardy.	

Extended chronology (*continued*).

Year	Henry VIII	Francis I	Charles V
	9 September 1513 An English army defeats the Scots at the Battle of Flodden. James IV of Scotland killed in the battle.		
		18 May 1514 Francis marries Claude, daughter of Louis XII and Anne of Brittany.	
	6 August 1514 Henry signs first Treaty of London with Louis XII. In November, Mary Tudor marries Louis.		
1515		**1 January 1515** Becomes **King of France** at the death of Louis XII.	**1 January 1515** Majority as overlord of the Netherlands declared by the States-General.
		14 September 1515 Conquers the duchy of Milan after battle of Marignano.	
		1516 Proclamation of the Concordat signed with Leo X. In November signs the 'Perpetual Peace' of Fribourg with Swiss Cantons.	**January 1516** Becomes **King of Spain** at the death of Ferdinand of Aragon.
			November 1516 Treaty of Noyon signed with Francis.
	3 October 1518 Henry VIII swears to an Anglo-French alliance under the Treaty of London.		
		14 December 1518 Francis swears to the Anglo-French alliance.	

	January 1519 The city of Tournai, captured in 1513, is returned to the French king for 600,000 crowns.		
			June 1519 Charles is elected **Holy Roman Emperor** by the German Electors.
1520	**June 1520** Henry and Francis meet at the **Field of Cloth of Gold** between Guînes and Ardres in northern France.		
			July 1520 Charles meets Henry VIII at Gravelines.
		April 1521 Acting with Francis' covert support, Robert de la Marck attacks Luxemburg.	**April 1521** repulses the attack on Luxemburg. Armies mass to invade France.
			In Castile, the revolt of the *Comuneros* put down at Villalar.
		October 1521 Francis tries to relieve the siege of Tournai.	
		November 1521 French under Odet de Foix, Lord of Lautrec expelled from Milan.	**November 1521** Tournai captured.
			December 1521. Death of Leo X. Succeeded by Adrian VI, Charles's former tutor.
		April 1522 Marshal Lautrec besieges Milan but is forced to withdraw; defeated at the Battle of La Bicocca.	
	May 1522 Declares war on Francis.		
		7 September 1523 Duke of Bourbon rebels against Francis.	**September 1523** Giulio de' Medici succeeds Adrian VI as Clement VII.

Extended chronology (*continued*).

Year	Henry VIII	Francis I	Charles V
	19 September 1523 English army under the Duke of Suffolk invades Picardy and advances to within 50 miles of Paris before halting.		
	May 1524 Agrees a new treaty with Charles V and Bourbon.		
		October 1524 After defeating Bourbon in Provence, Francis invades Milan for the second time.	
1525		**24 February 1525** Francis's army defeated by Imperial army at the Battle of Pavia.	**24 February 1525** Charles's 25th birthday. His Viceroy of Naples accepts Francis I's surrender.
	March 1525 Henry's plans for a 'Great Enterprise' against France frustrated by Charles V's lack of interest and the failure of the Amicable Grant.		
		17 June 1525 Francis arrives in Spain escorted by the Viceroy of Naples. Later taken to Madrid.	
	August 1525 Treaty of the More signed with representatives of the French regent, Louise of Savoy.		
			18 September 1525 Charles meets Francis for the first time while the king is gravely ill at Madrid.
		14 January 1526 Signs the Treaty of Madrid with Charles V.	

		10 March 1526 Charles marries Isabella of Portugal in Seville.
	17 March 1526 Francis returns to France after being exchanged for his sons Francis and Henry who are then held by Charles as hostages.	
	22 May 1526 League of Cognac signed. War against the emperor begins in Italy.	
30 April 1527 Treaty of Westminster signed with Francis.		
		6 May 1527 Imperial troops under Bourbon, sack Rome.
		21 May 1527 Birth of Charles's heir, Philip, at Valladolid.
22 June 1527 Henry tells Katherine that their marriage is illegal and must be annulled.		
	24 July 1527 Francis holds a *lit-de-justice* in the Parlement of Paris to re-establish his authority.	
July-August 1527 Wolsey travels to Amiens to secure an alliance with Francis.		
	18 August 1527 Treaty of Amiens signed with England.	
	22 January 1528 France and England declare war on Charles.	
18 June 1529 Legatine Court at Blackfriars opens to hear the king's case for an annulment of his marriage to Katherine of Aragon. She appeals to Rome.		

Extended chronology (*continued*).

Year	Henry VIII	Francis I	Charles V
		21 June 1529 French army under the Earl of Saint-Pol at Genoa is defeated.	
			29 June 1529 Clement VII signs Treaty of Barcelona with Charles. Moves against Henry VIII.
	16 July 1529 Clement VII revokes the king's matrimonial case to the Curia in Rome.		
		3 August 1529 Treaty of Cambrai signed with Charles V. England all but excluded from settlement.	
	22 September 1529 Wolsey falls from power. Ordered to relinquish the Great Seal.		
1530			**24 February 1530** Charles crowned **Holy Roman Emperor** in Bologna on his 30th birthday.
			June 1530 Diet of Augsburg. Emperor attends but fails to achieve religious consensus. Protestant Confession of Augsburg formulated.
		July 1530 Francis's sons released. He marries Charles's sister Eleanor of Portugal.	

		January 1531 Ferdinand of Habsburg elected King of the Romans.
		February 1531 Protestant League of Schmalkalden formed.
	26 May 1532 Francis signs the anti-Habsburg Treaty of Scheyern with leaders of Saxony, Hesse and Bavaria.	
June 1532 Henry signs mutual assistance agreement with Francis.		
		August 1532 Charles and Ferdinand advance to counter-attack the Turks in Austria.
1 September 1532 Henry ratifies treaty with Francis. Anne Boleyn created Marquess of Pembroke		
		23 September 1532 Charles enters Vienna after Turkish withdrawal.
October 1532 Henry and Francis meet for the second time at Calais and Boulogne.		
March 1533 Act in Restraint of Appeals passed.		
May 1533 Archbishop Cranmer pronounces Henry's first marriage annulled.		
1 June 1533 Anne Boleyn crowned queen.		
7 September 1533 Princess Elizabeth born at Greenwich.		

Extended chronology (*continued*).

Year	Henry VIII	Francis I	Charles V
		28 October 1533 Henry Duke of Orléans is married to Catherine de' Medici during a meeting at Marseilles between Francis and Clement VII.	
			November 1533. After killing the Inca king, Atahulpa, Pizarro reaches Cuzco, ancient capital of Peru.
			January 1534 Lima founded as new capital of Peru.
	November 1534 Act of Supremacy completes Henry's break with Rome.		
1535	**May and June 1535** Execution for treason of Sir Thomas More and Bishop John Fisher.		
			July 1535 Charles conquers Tunis from Barbarossa.
		October 1535 Death of Francesco Sforza renews Francis's interest in Milan.	
		February 1536 Francis invades the duchy of Savoy and the north of Piedmont.	
	May 1536 Fall and execution of Anne Boleyn. Henry marries Jane Seymour.		

			June 1536 Counter-attacking through Savoy, Charles invades Provence but is eventually repulsed. Imperial armies invade Picardy.
	12 October 1537 Birth of Henry's son Edward.		
		June 1538 Francis and Charles agree to a truce. Meeting at Aigues-Mortes on 14–16 July.	
	1539 Franco-Imperial rapprochement provokes fears of invasion. Coastal fortifications begun by Henry VIII.		**1539** Revolt against Charles in Ghent.
		November–December 1539 Francis escorts Charles through France as his guest. Montmorency's peace policy appears to be successful.	
1540	**6 January 1540** Henry VIII marries Anne of Cleves under terms of Anglo-Protestant alliance negotiated by Thomas Cromwell.		**January 1540** Charles reaches Flanders and restores his authority in Ghent.
	June 1540 Cromwell falls from power, is convicted of treason and executed.		
	July 1540 Following annulment of his marriage to Anne of Cleves, Henry marries Catherine Howard.		
			October 1540 Charles invests his son Philip with the duchy of Milan.
		November 1540 Fall Montmorency of following collapse of his pro-Imperial policy.	

Extended chronology (*continued*).

Year	Henry VIII	Francis I	Charles V
	June–September 1541 Henry 'progresses' to York for a meeting with James V of Scotland, who declines to attend.		**1541** Failure of the Colloquy of Regensburg. Süleyman invades Hungary. Failure of Charles's expedition against Algiers.
		July 1542 Francis declares war on Charles. The Duke of Orléans invades Luxemburg. The dauphin Henry attacks Perpignan.	
	23 November 1542 Battle of Solway Moss. James V's army defeated, the king dies a few weeks later.		
	February 1543 Henry agrees to an alliance with Charles V and a joint invasion of France within a year.		
		April–September 1543 Fighting between Francis and Charles continues.	
			Charles defeats the Duke of Gheldres. Annexes the duchy as the province of Gelderland.
	1 July 1543 Treaty of Greenwich signed with Scotland.		
			April 1544 An imperial army under Ferrante Gonzaga besieges Saint-Dizier.

	June 1544 English invasion of northern France. Siege of Boulogne through July and August.		
		August 1544 Francis initiates peace talks in the hope of breaking Anglo-Imperial alliance.	**August 1544** Fall of Saint-Dizier, Charles V pushes further into Champagne.
	18 September 1544 Henry enters Boulogne.		**18 September 1544** Treaty of Crépy signed with Francis I.
1545	**19 July 1545** Henry oversees naval engagement with the French off Southsea. Witnesses the loss of the *Mary Rose*.	**July 1545** French fleet sails against England. Battle in the Solent. Raids on the Isle of Wight.	
	June 1546 Peace of Ardres agreed with Francis I.		Outbreak of the Schmalkaldic War.
1547	**28 January 1547** Dies, aged 56, at Whitehall Palace.		
		31 March 1547 Dies, aged 53, at the château of Rambouillet.	
			24 April 1547 Battle of Mühlberg. Charles defeats the army of the Schmalkaldic League.
			1548 Diet of Augsburg convened. Charles imposes the 'Interim' Catholic settlement on the German states.

Extended chronology (*continued*).

Year	Henry VIII	Francis I	Charles V
1550			**1552** Charles looses the towns of Metz, Toul and Verdun to Henry II of France. Besieges Metz in November but forced to withdraw.
1555			**Peace of Augsburg** agreed in the emperor's absence at the Diet of Augsburg. **1555–56** Charles gradually abdicates from all titles and sovereignty. Leaves the Netherlands for Spain. Retires to the monastery of Saint Jeronimo at Yuste.
1558			**21 September 1558** Dies, aged 58, at the monastery of Saint Jeronimo.

Notes

INTRODUCTION

1 *Four Years at the Court of Henry VIII: Despatches of Sebastian Giustinian*, ed. R. Brown (2 vols, London, 1954), I, p. 79.
2 *The Book of the Courtier* by Baldesare Castiglione, translated by George Bull (London, 1967), p. 299.
3 J.H. Green, *A Short History of the English People* (London, 1893); G. Pagès, *La Monarchie d'ancien regime en France* (Paris, 1946); G.R. Elton, *The Tudor Revolution in Government* (Cambridge, 1953); *England under the Tudors* (2nd edn, London, 1974); J.H. Elliott, *Imperial Spain 1469–1716* (London, 1963); E. Le Roy Ladurie, *L'Etat royal de Louis XI à Henri IV* (Paris, 1987). For concise review of this literature and the 'new' monarchy debate, see A. Goodman *The New Monarchy* (Oxford, 1988).
4 C. Coleman and D.R. Starkey, eds. *Revolution Reassessed: Revisions in the History of Tudor Government and Administration* (Oxford, 1986); D. Parker, *The Making of French Absolutism* (London, 1983); R. Mettam, *Power and Faction in Louis XIV's France* (Oxford, 1988); N. Henshall, *The Myth of Absolutism* (London, 1992); D.L. Potter, *A History of France 1460–1560 The Emergence of a Nation State* (London, 1995); J. Lynch *Spain 1516–1598* (Oxford, 1991).

1 MONARCHS: PERSONALITIES AND IDEALS OF MONARCHY

1 *The Prince*, by Niccolò Machiavelli translated by George Bull (London, 1961), p. 119.

2 S.B. Chrimes, *Henry VII* (Berkeley and Los Angeles, 1972); R. Hoyle, 'War and Public Finance' in D. MacCulloch, ed., *The Reign of Henry VIII* (London, 1995), pp. 75–99.
3 *Anglica historia*, by Polydore Vergil, edited by D. Hay, Camden Society, 74 (London, 1950); *Vita Henrici VII* and *Annales Henrici VII* by Bernard André in J. Gairdner, *Memorials of King Henry the Seventh* (London, 1858). See A. Fox, *Politics and Literature in the Reigns of Henry VII and Henry VIII* (Oxford, 1989), pp. 17–19.
4 Hall, p. 508.
5 *The Book of the Courtier* by Baldesare Castiglione translated by George Bull (London, 1967), p. 88; BL, Cotton MS Caligula B II, fo. 36 [*LP* I ii, 3342] Norfolk to Wolsey, Montreuil, 7 October 1514.
6 A.-M. Lecoq, *François Ier imaginaire symbolique et politique à l'aube de la Renaissance française* (Paris, 1987), pp. 67–100; see pp. 35–45 for the origins of the salamander myth and its use as a Valois family emblem.
7 R.J. Knecht, *Renaissance Warrior and Patron: The Reign of Francis I* (Cambridge, 1994), pp. 1–14; D.L. Potter, *A History of France 1460–1560 The Emergence of Nation State* (London, 1995) pp. 7–16.
8 K. Brandi, *The Emperor Charles V* trans. C.V. Wedgwood (London, 1965); E.E. Rosenthal, 'The Invention of the Columnar Device of Emperor Charles V at the court of Burgundy in Flanders in 1516', *Journal of the Warburg and Courtauld Institutes* 36, (1973), pp. 198–230; H.G. Koenigsberger, 'The Empire of Charles V in Europe' in G.R. Elton ed., *New Cambridge Modern History* vol. II *The Reformation, 1520–1559* (Cambridge, 1990), pp. 339–76.
9 J. Bérenger, *A History of the Habsburg Empire 1273–1700* trans. C.A. Simpson (London, 1994), esp. pp. 139–90.
10 L.G.W. Legg, *English Coronation Records* (London, 1901); T. Godefroy *Le Cérémonial françois* (2 vols, Paris, 1649), I, pp. 245–55, for the *sacre* of Francis I. English sovereigns were also presented and verbally recognised by the nobility at the outset of the service.
11 T.F. Ruiz, 'Une royauté sans sacre: la monarchie Castillane du bas moyen-age', *Annales* 39 (1984), pp. 429–53; G. Sabatier and S. Edouard, *Les Monarchies de France et d'Espagne (1556–1715)* (Paris, 2001), pp. 23–33. I am grateful to Professor Knecht for drawing my attention to this book.
12 C. Beaune, *La naissance de la nation France* (Paris, 1985) translated by S. Ross Hutton, *The Birth of an Ideology: Myths and Symbols of Nation in Late-Medieval France* (Berkeley, 1991), esp. pp. 70–90. J. Krynen, *L'empire du roi: Idées et croyances politiques en France XIII–XV siècles* (Paris, 1993).
13 M. Bloch, *The Royal Touch: Sacred Monarchy and Scrofula in England and France*, translated by J.E. Anderson (London, 1973).
14 S. Anglo, *Spectacle, Pageantry and Early Tudor Policy* (Oxford, 1969) on English royal entries; T. Ruiz, *Spanish Society 1400–1600* (Harlow,

2001), pp. 143–48; Sabatier and Edouard, pp. 102–8 on Spanish royal entries. For Francis's entry to Lyon see Lecoq, pp. 195–201ff.

15 Q. Skinner, *The Foundations of Modern Political Thought* (2 vols, Cambridge, 1978), vol. I *The Renaissance*, pp. 118–28.

16 *The Education of Christian Prince* by Desiderus Erasmus, translated by N.M. Chesire and M.J. Heath, ed. L. Jardine (Cambridge, 1997), p. 15.

17 J.C. Olin, *Christian Humanism and the Reformation: Desiderius Erasmus, Selected Writings* (New York, 1965) pp. 117–23; An English translation of Erasmus' Letter to Paul Volz; B.E. Mansfield, 'The Three Circles of Erasmus of Rotterdam', *Colloquium: The Australian and New Zealand Theological Review* IV (4) (1972), pp. 4–11.

18 *La Monarchie de France* by Claude de Seyssel, translated and edited by J.H. Hexter and D.R. Kelley (New Haven, 1981), pp. 49–51; 53–4; 82–4.

19 Machiavelli, pp. 90–119; Seyssel, pp. 135–42.

20 M. Keen, *Chivalry* (London, 1984), pp. 8–11; *Le Débat des Hérauts d'Armes de France et d'Angleterre* edited by L. Pannier and P. Meyer (Paris, 1877), pp. 12ff; Ruiz, *Spanish Society*, pp. 171–8; 240–3.

21 *De Regimine Principum* by Stephen Baron, translated and edited by P.J. Mroczkowski, American University Studies Series XVII vol. 5 (New York, 1990), esp. pp. 31–5; 77–81. I am grateful to Dr Maria Dowling for drawing my attention to this source; *The Book Named the Governor* by Sir Thomas Elyot, edited by S.E. Lehmberg (London, 1975).

22 Machiavelli, pp. 125–7.

23 *Utopia*, by Sir Thomas More, edited by J.J. Greene and J.P. Dolan in *Thomas More: Utopia and Other Writings* (New York, 1967), pp. 43–50, 56–7; On the debate in England more generally see A. Fox and J.A. Guy, *Reassessing the Henrician Age: Humanism, Politics and Reform* (Oxford, 1986); J. Guy, 'The Henrician Age' in J.G.A. Pocock, ed., *The Varieties of British Political Thought, 1500–1800* (Cambridge, 1993), pp. 13–46.

24 *The Governance of England*, by Sir John Fortescue edited by C. Plummer (Oxford, 1885), pp. 114–5; H.G. Koenigsberger, '*Dominium Regale* or *Dominium Politicum et Regale,* Monarchies and Parliaments in early-modern Europe' in his *Politicians and Virtuosi: Essays in early-modern History* (London, 1986), pp. 2–4ff.

25 Seyssel, pp. 54–57, 89–104; Skinner, vol. II, *The Age of Reformation*, pp. 260–6; J. Russel-Major, *From Renaissance Monarchy to Absolute Monarchy: French Kings, Nobles and Estates* (Baltimore, 1994).

26 *De L'institution du prince* by Guillaume Budé (Paris, 1547; reprinted Farnborough, 1966).

27 D. Parker, *The Making of French Absolutism* (London, 1983), pp. 1–45; Knecht, pp. 519–40.

28 J. Perez, 'L'idéologie de l'état' in C. Hermann *et al.*, *Le premier âge de l'État en Espagne 1450–1700* (Paris, 1990), pp. 191–216.

29 Fortescue, pp. 118–45.

30 Ibid, p. 123; R. Strong, *Splendour at Court: Renaissance Spectacle and Illusion* (London, 1973); F. Yates, *Astrea: The Imperial Theme in the Sixteenth Century* (London, 1975).
31 A.B. and A. Wyon, *The Great Seals of England* (London, 1887), pp. 67–70.

2 WARRIORS: HONOUR AND MAGNIFICENCE IN WAR AND PEACE

1 K. Brandi, *The Emperor Charles V* trans. C.V. Wedgwood (London, 1965), p. 220.
2 J. Bérenger, *A History of the Habsburg Empire 1273–1700* trans. C.A. Simpson (London, 1994), p. 128.
3 M. Rodriguez-Salgado, *The Changing Face of Empire. Charles V, Philip II and Habsburg Authority* (Cambridge, 1988), p. 30.
4 Keen, *Chivalry* (London, 1984), pp. 219–33; P. Contarmine, *War in the Middle Ages*, translated by M. Jones (Oxford, 1984), esp. pp. 260–96; 355–61.
5 *Commentaires*, by Blaise de Monluc, edited by Ian Roy and published as *The Valois-Habsburg Wars and the French Wars of Religion* (London, 1971), p. 61.
6 Keen, pp. 179–85.
7 P. Begent and H. Chessyre, *The Most Noble Order of the Garter* (London, 1999), esp. pp. 7–18.
8 H. Pauwels ed., *La Toison d'Or: Cinq siècles d'art et d'histoire* (Bruges, 1962), p. 38; Rosenthal, pp. 198–230; M.Tanner, *The last Descendant of Aneas: The Hapsburgs and the Mythic Image of the Emperor* (Yale, 1993).
9 On the exchange of orders between Henry and Francis see D. Starkey, ed., *Henry VIII: A European Court in England* (London, 1991), pp. 94–99.
10 *Historie du gentil seigneur de Bayart composée par le Loyal Serviteur* edited by M.J. Roman (Paris, 1878), pp. 15–75.
11 W.H. Jackson, 'The Tournament and Chivalry in German Tournament Books of the Sixteenth Century and in the Literary Works of Emperor Maximilian' in C. Harper-Bill and R. Harvey, *The Ideals and Practice of Medieval Knighthood: Papers from the first and second Strawberry Hill Conferences* (Woodbridge, 1986), pp. 49–73.
12 Keen, pp. 201–17; S. Anglo, ed., *The Great Tournament Roll of Westminster* (2 vols, Oxford, 1968), I, pp. 54ff; S. Gunn, 'The Early Tudor Tournament' in Starkey, *European Court*, pp. 47–9.
13 H. Soly and J. Van de Wiele, eds, *Carolus: Charles Quint 1500–1558* Catalogue of the *Carolus* exhibition held in Ghent 6 November 1999

to 30 January 2000; Cat. no. 38. Hereafter cited as *Carolus;* C. Blair, 'The Emperor Maximilian's gift of armour to King Henry VIII and the silvered and engraved armour at the Tower of London', *Archaeologia*, 99 (1965), pp. 19–39, esp. pp. 8–14.

14 Brandi, pp. 82–83; R. Tamalio ed., *Ferrante Gonzaga alla corte spagnola di Carlo V (*Mantua, 1991), pp. 178–9. Pandolfo to Isabella d'Este, Burgos, 8 July 1524.

15 BN, MS français 4253, fos.12r/v; P. Hamon, *L'argent du roi: Les finances sous François Ier* (Paris, 1994), p. 5; R.J. Knecht, *Renaissance Warrior and Patron: The Reign of Francis I* (Cambridge, 1994), pp. 109–12.

16 J. Cummins, *The Hound and the Hawk: The Art of Medieval Hunting* (London, 1988), pp. 1–20; Knecht, p. 112 for an account of a similar incident at Amboise in June 1515.

17 Tamalio, *Ferrante Gonzaga*, pp. 82–85, 133–135; W. Bradford, ed., *Correspondence of the Emperor Charles V* (London, 1850), p. 439.

18 Hall, p. 712; *LP* III ii, 1558 Pace to Wolsey, 9 September 1521; S. Thurley, 'The Sports of Kings' in Starkey, *European Court*, pp. 163–6.

19 Hall, p. 535; PRO, E36/217 fos.170–85; Richard Gibson's Revels accounts for the banquet.

20 S. Anglo, *Spectacle, Pageantry and Early Tudor Policy* (Oxford, 1969), pp. 190–208; W. Stirling-Maxwell, *The Entry of the Emperor Charles V into Bologna in 1529* (Florence, 1875); see Chapter 1 for an account of the emperor's emblem.

21 Fo.D.II of the 1513 Pynson edition states that it was 'printed at the commandement of oure soveragne lorde the king henry viii'; Roman, *Le Loyal Seviteur*, pp. i–xvi.

22 E. Arber, ed., *Tudor Tracts 1532–1588: An English Garner* (New York, 1964), pp. 1–8; *Carolus* Cat. no. 227.

23 H. Inalcik, *The Ottoman Empire: The Classical Age 1300–1600* (London, 1973 and 2000), pp. 23–40.

24 D.M. Head, 'Henry VIII's Scottish Policy', *The Scottish Historical Review*, 61 (1982), pp. 1–24; D. Dunlop, 'The Politics of Peace-Keeping: Anglo-Scottish Relations from 1503 to 1511', *Renaissance Studies*, 8 (1994), pp. 138–61.

25 D. Potter, 'The Frontiers of Artois in European Diplomacy, 1482–1560' in *Artois et la diplomatie moderne* (Lille, 1999); H. de Schepper, 'The Burgundian Netherlands' in T.A. Brady, H.A. Oberman and J.D. Tracy, eds., *Handbook of European History 1400–1600* (2 vols., Leiden, 1994), vol 1. pp. 499–533.

26 G. Parker, 'The Political World of Charles V' in H. Soly, ed., *Charles V 1500–1558 and his Time* (Antwerp, 1999), pp. 113–226; R.J. Knecht, *French Renaissance Monarchy: Francis I and Henry II* (London, 1996), pp. 30–46; R. Bonney, *The European Dynastic States 1494–1660* (Oxford, 1991), pp. 79–130.

27 Erasmus, *Education of a Christian Prince*, p. 108; J.G. Russell, *Peacemaking in the Renaissance* (London, 1986), pp. 10–14; R.P. Adams, *The Better Part of Valor: More, Erasmus, Colet and Vives on Humanism, War and Peace, 1496–1535* (Seattle, 1962); J.A. Fernandez, 'Erasmus on the Just War', *Journal of the History of Ideas*, 34 (1973), pp. 209–206; *Utopia* by Sir Thomas More, edited by J.J. Greene and J.P. Dolan, in *Thomas More: Utopia And Other Writings* (New York, 1967), pp. 81–3.
28 For examples of these contrasting approaches to Anglo-French peace see J.J. Scarisbrick, *Henry VIII* (London, 1968), pp. 67–134 and G.R. Elton, *England under the Tudors* (London, 1955) pp. 88–97.
29 BL, Cotton MS Caligula D VI, fo.121r; *LP* I ii, 2956 Henry VIII to Wolsey.
30 C. Weiss, ed., *Papiers d'état du Cardinal Granvelle* (9 vols, Paris, 1841–52), I, pp. 131–3 for the opening statements of the two men at the Calais conference in this account of it addressed to Margaret of Savoy. Hereafter cited as Weiss.
31 *CSPV* IV, 802 Carlo Capello to the Signory, London, 7 September 1532; *Calendar of State Papers, Spanish*, ed., G. Bergenroth, P. de Gayangos (13 vols, London, 1862–1954), IV ii, 993 Chapuys to Charles V, London, 15 September 1532.
32 J.G. Russell, *The Field of Cloth of Gold, Men and Manners in 1520* (London, 1969), esp. pp. 2ff and p. 190; Anglo, pp. 137–60, esp. p. 158.
33 Hall, pp. 610–14; Russell, *Cloth of Gold*, pp. 128–34; Anglo, p. 153.
34 St. P, VI, p. 60 Wingfield to Henry VIII, 18 April 1520; On the detail of this development see G. Richardson, 'The Privy Chamber of Henry VIII and Anglo-French Relations 1515–1520', *The Court Historian* 4 (2) (1999), pp. 119–40.
35 *CSP. Span.* III i, 47 Louis de Praet to Charles V, London 25 March 1525; *LP* XV, 121 Francis I to his ambassador in England, 27 January 1540.
36 G. Mattingly, *Renaissance Diplomacy* (London, 1965), pp. 66–94; J.G. Russell, *Peacemaking in the Renaissance* (London, 1986), pp. 67–89; B. Behrens, 'Treatises on the Ambassador written in the Fifteenth and Early Sixteenth Centuries', *EHR*, 51 (1936), pp. 616–27.

3 WARRIORS: WARFARE AND INTERNATIONAL RELATIONS

1 *Anglica historia*, by Polydore Vergil, edited by D. Hay, Camden Society, 74 (London, 1950), p. 197.

2 S.J. Gunn, 'The French Wars of Henry VIII' in J. Black ed., *The Origins of War in Early Modern Europe* (Edinburgh, 1987), pp. 28–47; *LP* I i, 244 Ordinances establishing the king's spears signed at the top by Henry; K. Watts, 'Henry VIII and the founding of the Greenwich Armouries', in D. Starkey, ed., *Henry VIII: A European Court in England*, (London, 1991), pp. 42–6.
3 P. Contarmine, *War in the Middle Ages* translated by M. Jones (Oxford, 1984), 165–72; A. Jouanna, *La France du XVI siècle 1483–1598* (Paris, 1997), pp. 184–5.
4 F. Lot, *Recherches sur les effectifs des armées françaises des Guerres d'Italie aux Guerres de Religion 1494–1562* (Paris, 1962).
5 J. Lynch, *Spain under the Habsburgs* (2 vols, Oxford, 1981), I, pp. 83–8; R. Quatrefages, 'Le Système militaire des Habsbourg' in C. Hermann *et al.*, *Le Premier âge de l'État en Espagne 1450–1700* (Paris, 1990), pp. 341–79; M.E. Mallett, 'The Art of War' in T.A. Brady, H.A. Oberman and J.D. Tracy, eds., *Handbook of European History 1400–1600* (2 vols, New York, 1994), I, pp. 544–5.
6 *LP* I i, 324, 325. Henry's orders for weapons, placed by his agent in the Netherlands, Thomas Spinelly.
7 BN, MS français 4523, fo.51. P. Contarmine, 'Les industries de guerre dans la France de la Renaissance: l'exemple de l'artillerie', *Revue Historique*, 271 (1984), pp. 249–80; A. Blanchard *et al.*, *Histoire militaire de la France* (4 vols, Paris, 1992), I, pp. 245–8.
8 W. Eisler, 'The Impact of the Emperor Charles V upon the visual arts', Unpublished Pennsylvania State University Ph.D. dissertation, 1983, pp. 98–113.
9 H.M. Colvin, *The History of the King's Works* (6 vols, HMSO, 1963–82), IV, pp. 367–401.
10 D.R. Starkey, ed., *The Inventory of Henry VIII* (London, 1998), I *The Manuscript*, pp.144–6; D. Loades, 'Henry VIII and the Navy' in Starkey, *European Court*, pp. 172–81.
11 C. de La Ronciere, *La marine française* (6 vols, Paris, 1923), III, pp. 409–31; P. Hamon, *L'argent du roi: Les finances sous François Ier* (Paris, 1994), pp. 35–6.
12 Hall, p. 635; F. Braudel, *The Mediterranean and the Mediterranean World in the Age of Philip II* translated by S. Reynolds (2 vols, London, 1972–73), II, pp. 108–115.
13 H.J. Hewitt, *The Organisation of War under Edward III 1338–62* (Manchester, 1966), p. 115.
14 G. Parker, 'The Political World of Charles V' in H. Soly, ed., *Charles V and his Time* (Antwerp, 1999) p. 177 quoting de Beccarie's *Instructions sur la fait de la guerre*, published in Paris in 1548.
15 R. Hoyle, 'War and Public Finance' in D. MacCulloch, ed., *Reign of Henry VIII* (Basingstoke, 1995), pp. 75–99, esp. p. 85; P. Hamon, *L'argent du roi: les finances sous François Ier* (Paris, 1994), pp. 45–7;

Braudel, II, p. 842; R. Ehrenberg, *Capital and Finance in the Age of the Renaissance: A Study of the Fuggers and their Connections*, translated by H.M. Lucas (New York, 1963), pp. 70–113.

16 Hall, pp. 549–51 for a description of the Battle of the Spurs; C. Cruickshank, *Henry VIII and the Invasion of France* (Stroud, 1991), pp. 100–7. The interpretation offered here differs in significant ways from Cruickshank's which is currently the most readily available account. J.J. Scarisbrick, *Henry VIII* (London, 1968), pp. 32–8.

17 T. Rymer, *Foedera, Conventiones, Litterae etc.* (London, 1704–35), XIII, pp. 625–53; Scarisbrick, pp. 68–74ff.

18 G. Richardson, 'Entertainments for the French ambassadors at the court of Henry VIII', *Renaissance Studies* 9 (4) (December 1995), pp. 404–15 for a fuller discussion of these festivities; Russell, *Peacemaking*, Appendix A for a translation of Pace's oration.

19 A.-M. Lecoq, 'Une fête italienne à la Bastille en 1518' in '*Il se rendit en Italie, Etudes offertes à André Chastel*, ed. G. Briganti (Rome, 1987), pp. 149–68.

20 Scarisbrick, pp. 125–34, 439–50; S.J. Gunn, 'The French wars of Henry VIII.'

21 *LP* XX i, 1007 Poynings to Henry VIII, 22 June 1545; A. McKee, 'Henry VIII as Military Commander', *History Today*, (June 199), pp. 22–9.

22 *Ordonnances des rois de France: règne de François Ier* (9 vols, Paris, 1902–92), I, pp. 147–72.

23 R.J. Knecht, *Renaissance Warrior and Patron: The Reign of Francis I* (Cambridge, 1994), pp. 68–77.

24 B.S. Hall, *Weapons and Warfare in Renaissance Europe: Gunpowder, Technology and Tactics* (Baltimore, 1997), pp. 179–83; C. Oman, *A History of the Art of War in the XVIth Century* (New York, 1937).

25 K. Brandi, *The Emperor Charles V* trans. C.V. Wedgwood (London, 1965), pp. 223–36; Knecht, pp. 239–48.

26 Knecht, pp. 330–41.

27 C. Weiss, *Papiers d'état du cardinal de Granvelle* (9 vols, Paris, 1841–52), I, pp. 464–73.

28 J.G. Russell, *Diplomats at Work: Three Renaissance Studies* (Stroud, 1992), pp. 94–152 for the most recent account of these negotiations.

29 Weiss, I. pp. 611–13. Francis's response to proposals made to him on Charles's behalf by the lord of Balancon.

30 Knecht, pp. 330–41.

31 K. Lanz, *Correspondenz des Kaisers Karl V* (3 vols, Leipzig, 1844–46), II, 458 Charles V to Mary of Hungary, Aigues–Mortes, 18 July 1538.

33 Knecht, pp. 385–92 for more detail on this *entente* and Charles's entertainment.

34 Parker, The Political World of Charles V', in Soly, p. 224, quoting the Duke of Sessa to Don Balthasar de Zúñiga, 28 September 1600.

4 GOVERNORS: ROYAL AUTHORITY AND THE ADMINISTRATION OF THE REALM

1 *DNB*, *sub* Sir John Fyneux.
2 See references to this historiography given in the Introduction.
3 G.R. Elton, *The Tudor Constitution: Documents and Commentary* (Cambridge, 1968), pp. 21–30; J. Guy, 'Thomas Wolsey, Thomas Cromwell and the Reform of Henrician Government' in D. MacCulloch, ed., *Reign of Henry VIII*, (Basingstoke, 1995), pp. 35–57.
4 G.R. Elton, *The Tudor Revolution in Government* (Cambridge, 1953), pp. 60–5; 316–69.
5 J. Guy, 'Privy Council: Revolution or Evolution' in C. Coleman and D.R. Starkey, eds., *Revolution Reassessed* (Oxford, 1986), pp. 59–85.
6 D.R. Starkey, 'Court, Council and Nobility in Tudor England' in R.G. Asch and A.M. Birke, eds., *Princes Patronage and the Nobility: The Court at the Beginning of the Modern Age c.1450–1650* (Oxford, 1991), pp. 175–203.
7 S. Gunn, *Early Tudor Government 1485–1558* (London, 1995), pp. 72–108; J.R. Lander, *Government and Community, England 1450–1509* (Harvard, 1980) J. Guy, *Tudor England* (Oxford, 1990), pp. 175–7, 315–17.
8 Guy, *Tudor England* pp. 169–70.
9 R. Reid, The King's Council in the North (London, 1921), esp. pp. 1–165; S. Ellis, 'A crisis of the aristocracy? Frontiers and noble power in the early Tudor State', in J. Guy ed., *The Tudor Monarchy* (London, 1997), pp. 330–40.
10 Guy, *Tudor England*, pp. 173–7; Elton, *The Tudor Constitution*, pp. 147–95, 195– 213; Lander, pp. 35–9.
11 G. Zeller, *Les institutions de la France au XVIe siècle* (Paris, 1948), pp. 112ff.; D. Potter, *A History of France 1460–1560: The Emergence of a Nation State* (London, 1995), pp. 90–105.
12 N.M. Sutherland, *The French Secretaries of State in the age of Catherine de Medici* (London, 1962), esp. pp. 7–17; C.-A. Mayer and D. Bentley-Cranch, *Florimond Robertet (? –1527) Homme d'État Français* (Paris, 1994).
13 R.H. Harding, *Anatomy of a Power Elite: The Provincial Governors of Early Modern France* (Yale, 1978), esp. pp. 1–45; D. Potter, *War and Government in the French provinces: Picardy 1470–1560* (Cambridge, 1993), pp. 64–112, for a detailed account of the governorship of this frontier province, mainly under Charles de Bourbon, Duke of Vendôme.
14 Zeller, pp. 167–75.
15 J.H. Shennan, *The Parlement of Paris* (Stroud, 1998), pp. 128–205; R.J. Knecht, Renaissance Warrior and Patron: The Reign of Francis I (Cambridge, 1994), pp. 90–100, 264–8.

16 J. Dewald, *The Formation of a Provincial Nobility. The Magistrates of the Parlement of Rouen 1499–1610* (Princeton, 1980); R.J. Kalas, 'The Selve family of Limousin: Members of a New Elite in Early Modern France', *The Sixteenth Century Journal*, 18 (2) (1987), pp. 147–72.
17 Zeller, pp. 134–45; J.M.H. Salmon, *Society in Crisis: France in the Sixteenth Century* (London, 1975), pp. 76–9; A. Jouanna, *La France du XVIe siècle 1483–1598* (Paris, 1996), pp. 209–21.
18 H. Rabe and P. Marzhal, '*Comme représentant nostre proper personne*' – 'The Regency Ordinances of Charles V as a Historical Source' in E.I. Kouri and T. Scott eds., *Politics and Society in Reformation Europe* (London, 1987), pp. 78–102.
19 Rabe and Marzhal, pp. 84–6, 92; On Ferdinand's court and council see V. Press, 'The Habsburg Court as Center of the Imperial Government', *Journal of Modern History* 58 Supplement (December 1986), pp. S23–S45.
20 J.M. Headley, *The emperor and his chancellor: A study of the imperial chancellery under Gattinara* (Cambridge, 1983).
21 C. Weiss, ed., *Papiers d'état du Cardinal Granvelle* (9 vols; Paris, 1841–52), II, pp. 549–61; Charles's instructions to Philip, dated Madrid 5 November 1539; K. Brandi, *The Emperor Charles V* translated by C.V. Wedgwood (London, 1965), pp. 485–93.
22 M. Lunenfield, *Keepers of the City. The Corregidores of Isabella I of Castile (1474–1504)* (Cambridge, 1988).
23 H. Kamen, *Spain 1469–1714: A Society of Conflict* (London, 1983), pp. 81–5.
24 P. Rosenfeld, 'The Provincial Governors in the Low Countries,' *Standen and Landen* 17 (1959), pp. 1–47, esp. p. 6. H.H. Rowen, *The Princes of Orange, The Stadholders in the Dutch Republic* (Cambridge, 1988), pp. 1–7.
25 J. Israel, *The Dutch Republic its rise, greatness and fall, 1477–1806* (Oxford, 1995), pp. 21–40.
26 J.J. Scarisbrick, *Henry VIII* (London, 1968), pp. 138–9; Hall, p. 732.
27 *Ordonnances* IX, pp. 550–628, 'Ordonnance general en matière de justice et de police'; Knecht, pp. 352–3.
28 A. Wall, *Power and Protest in England 1525–1640* (London, 2000), esp. pp. 130–80 for a discussion of patterns of resistance in Tudor and Stuart England.
29 S. Haliczer, *The Comuneros of Castile: the forging of a revolution 1475–1521* (Madison, 1981); J. Lynch, *Spain 1516–1598 From Nation State to World Empire* (Oxford, 1991), pp. 51–66.
30 M. Bush and D. Bownes, *The Defeat of the Pilgrimage of Grace* (Hull, 1999); A. Fletcher, *Tudor Rebellions* (London, 1983), pp. 6–39.
31 Knecht, pp. 480–3.

32 H.G. Koenigsberger, 'Prince and States-General: Charles V and the Netherlands (1506–1555)', *Transactions of the Royal Historical Society*, Sixth Series, vol. IV (1994), pp. 127–51.

5 GOVERNORS: REVENUE, REPRESENTATION AND RELIGION

1 Quoted in W. Blockmans, 'The Emperor's Subjects' in H. Soly ed., *Charles V and his Time* (Antwerp, 1999), pp. 227–83, esp. p. 227.
2 H.G. Koenigsberger, 'Dominium Regale or Dominium Politicum et Regale, Monarchies and Parliaments in Early Modern Europe', in his *Politicians and Virtuosi: Essays in Early Modern History* (London, 1986), pp. 1–25; A.R. Myres, *Parliaments and Estates in Europe to 1789* (London, 1975).
3 R. Holinshed, *Chronicles of England, Scotland and Ireland* (6 vols; London, 1807–8), III, p. 826.
4 C.S.L. Davies, 'Tournai and the English Crown 1513–1519', *HJ*, 41 (1) (1998), pp. 1–26. cf. A.K.D. Hawyard, 'The Enfranchisement of Constituencies 1509–1558' *Parliamentary History*, 10 (1) (1991), pp. 1–26.
5 F.C. Dietz, *English Government Finance* (Urbana, 1921), pp. 11–158; J.D. Alsop, 'The Theory and Practice of Tudor taxation', *EHR*, 382 (January 1982), pp. 1–30.
6 Dietz, pp. 159–77; Hoyle, 'War and the Public Finances,' in D. MacCulloch ed., *Reign of Henry VIII*, (Basingstoke, 1995), pp. 83–99; S. Gunn, *Early Tudor Government 1485–1558* (Basingstoke, 1995), pp. 109–62.
7 *The Privy Purse Expences of King Henry the Eighth*, ed., N.H. Nicolas (London, 1827); D.R. Starkey, 'Court and Government' in C. Coleman and D.R. Starkey, eds., *Revolution Reassessed: Revisions in the History of Tudor Government* (Oxford, 1986), pp. 29–58.
8 G.R. Elton, *Tudor Constitution: Documents and Commentary* (Cambridge, 1968), pp. 128–46; J.D. Alsop, 'The Structure of Early Tudor Finance, c.1509–1558' and C. Coleman, 'Artifice or Accident? The Reorganization of the Exchequer of Receipt c.1554–1572' in C. Coleman and D.R. Starkey, pp. 135–62; 163–98.
9 J. Russell-Major, 'Popular Initiative in Renaissance France' in his *The Monarchy, the Estates and the Aristocracy in Renaissance France* (London, 1988), pp. 27–41.
10 J.H. Salmon, *Society in Crisis: France in the Sixteenth Century* (London, 1975), pp. 59–79; D. Parker, *The Making of French Absolutism* (London, 1983), pp. 13–19; Potter, pp. 149–63.
11 P. Hamon, *L'argent du roi: Les finances sous François Ier* (Paris, 1994), pp. 66–96.

12 R.J. Knecht, *French Renaissance Monarchy: Francis I and Henry II* (London, 1996), pp. 20–3; 47.
13 J.D. Tracy, *Holland under Habsburg Rule 1505–1566 the Formation of a Body Politic* (Berkeley and Los Angeles, 1990), pp. 130–46; Israel, p. 40.
14 G. Mutto, 'The Spanish System: Centre and Periphery', in R. Bonney ed., *Economic Systems and State Finance* (Oxford, 1995), pp. 231–59, esp. p. 242.
15 C. Herman and J.-P. Le Flem, 'Les Finances' in Herman *et al.*, *Le premier âge de l'état en Espagne*; pp. 324–39; R. Carande, *Carlos V y sus banqueros* (3 vols; Barcelona, 1977), II, pp. 222–52.
16 Herman and Le Flem, pp. 304–6.; J. Lynch, *Spain 1516–1598 From Nation State to World Empire* (Oxford, 1991), pp. 76–9.
17 J.J. Scarisbrick, *Henry VIII* (London, 1968), pp. 163–97 for what remains the most lucid exposition of the canon law of the divorce available; see also pp. 267–324 for the royal supremacy.
18 D. MacCulloch, 'Henry VIII and the reform of the Church' in his *Reign of Henry VIII*, pp. 159–80; esp. p. 178.
19 D. MacCulloch, *Thomas Cranmer A Life* (Yale, 1996), pp. 185–348; Scarisbrick, pp. 384–423. For the factional manoueuvring at Henry's death, see below.
20 R.J. Knecht, *Renaissance Warrior and Patron: The Reign of Francis I* (Cambridge, 1994) pp. 90–103; Potter, pp. 220–31.
21 R.J. Knecht, 'Francis I, 'Defender of the Faith'?' in E.W. Ives, R.J. Knecht and J.J. Scarisbrick eds., *Wealth and Power in Tudor England: Essays presented to S.T. Bindoff* (London, 1978), pp. 106–27.
22 D. Nicholls, 'Looking for the Origins of the French Reformation' in C.T. Allman ed., *Power, Culture and Religion in France c.1350–1550* (Woodbrige, 1989), pp. 131–44; N.Z. Davis, 'Strikes and Salvation at Lyons' in her *Society and Culture in Early Modern France*, pp. 1–16.
23 M. Greengrass, *The French Reformation* (Oxford, 1987); M. Greengrass, *The Longman Companion to the European Reformation c.1500–1618* (London, 1998), pp. 116–29; Potter, pp. 231–50.
24 H. Schilling, 'Charles V and Religion: The struggle for integrity and unity of Christendom' in Soly, pp. 285–363; M. Hughes, *Early Modern Germany 1477–1806* (London, 1992) pp. 30–60; R.W. Scribner, *The German Reformation* (London, 1986), pp. 35–43; Greengrass, *Companion to the European Reformation*, pp. 43–88.
25 Lynch, pp. 83–94; H. Kamen, *The Spanish Inquisition: A historical revision* (London, 1997), pp. 28–102.
26 *Ibid.*
27 Schilling, pp. 350ff; Greengrass, *Companion to the European Reformation*, pp. 129–41.
28 Knecht, *French Renaissance Monarchy*, pp. 86–96 for a lively, but balanced, presentation of this debate from the 'absolutist' perspective.

6 PATRONS: GOVERNMENT AND THE ROYAL COURT

1 R. Holinshed, *Chronicles of England, Scotland and Ireland* (6 vols, London, 1807–8), III, p. 611.
2 M.J. Heath, 'Erasmus the Courtier' *The Court Historian* 5 (2) (October 2000), pp. 93–104 for an account of Erasmus' experience in and criticism of various European courts.
3 J. Gillingham, *The Wars of the Roses* (London, 1990); M. Hicks, 'Bastard Feudalism, Overmighty Subjects and Idols of the Multitude during the Wars of the Roses', *History* 85 (279) pp. 386–403.
4 Hall, p. 519.
5 H. Miller, *Henry VIII and the English Nobility* (Oxford, 1986), pp. 6–37.
6 G.W. Bernard, 'The Fortunues of the Greys, earls of Kent in the early sixteenth century', *HJ*, 25 (3) (1982), pp. 671–85.
7 S. Gunn, 'Henry Bouchier, earl of Essex (1472–1540)' in G. Bernard, ed., *The Tudor Nobility* (Manchester, 1991), pp. 135–69.
8 Miller, p. 37.
9 S. Gunn, *Early Tudor Government 1485–1558* (Basingstoke, 1995), pp. 23–71.
10 D.R. Starkey ed., *The English Court* (London, 1987).
11 G. Bernard, 'The Rise of Sir William Compton, early Tudor courtier,' *EHR*, 96 (1981), pp. 754–77.
12 G. Richardson, 'The Privy Chamber of Henry VIII and Anglo-French Relations, 1515–1520,' *The Court Historian* 4 (2) (August 1999), pp. 119–40 for a fuller discussion of the adaptation of the French office in England and the role of the privy chamber servants in Henry's relations with Francis I.
13 E.W. Ives, 'Faction at the Court of Henry VIII: The Fall of Anne Boleyn', *History*, 57 (July 1972), pp. 169–88, esp. p. 181. See also his *Faction in Tudor England* (London, 1979).
14 E.W. Ives, *Anne Boleyn* (Oxford, 1986), pp. 349ff.; 'The fall of Anne Boleyn Reconsidered', *EHR* (July, 1992), pp. 651–64; a response to G. Bernard, 'The Fall of Anne Boleyn', *EHR*, 106 (July 1991), pp. 584–610.
15 D.R. Starkey, *The Reign of Henry VIII: Personality and Politics* (London, 1991).
16 A. Jouanna, *La France du XVI siècle 1483–1598* (Paris, 1997), pp. 57–69, notes that the expression 'noblesse de robe' was unknown in the early sixteenth century, emerging only after 1600 when exemption from the *taille* for those holding judicial offices was formalised.
17 S. Carroll, *Noble Power during the French Wars of Religion: The Guise Affinity and the Catholic Cause in Normandy* (Cambridge, 1998),

esp. pp. 14–17. On the structure and development of the Guise affinity under Francis I and Henry II see pp. 53–87.

18 W. Weary, 'La maison de La Trémoille pendant la Renaissance: Une seigneurie aggrandie,' in *La France de la fin du xvème siècle – renouveau et apogée*, ed. B. Chevalier and P. Contarmine (Paris, 1985), pp. 197–214; M. Petitot, ed. *Mémoires de La Trémoille: Mémoires relatifs a l'Histoire de France* vol. 14 (Paris, 1820).

19 Jouanna, pp. 71–83; some of the more relevant and accessible contributions to a vast historiography on patronage include: S. Kettering, 'Patronage in Early Modern France' *French Historical Studies* 19 (4) (1992), pp. 839–62; K.B. Neuschel, *Word of Honor :Interpreting Noble Culture in Sixteenth Century France* (Ithaca, 1989); M. Greengrass, 'Noble Affinities in Early Modern France: The Case of Henry I de Montmorency, Constable of France', *European History Quarterly* 16 (3) (1986), pp. 275–331.

20 R.J. Kalas, 'Marriage, Clientage, Office Holding and the Advancement of the Early Modern French nobility: The Noailles Family of Limousin,' *SCJ*, 27 (2) (1996), pp. 365–83.

21 J. du Tillet, *Receuil des Roys de France* (Paris, 1580), p. 325.

22 M. Chatenet, 'Une demure royale au mileu du xvie siècle: La distribution des espaces au château de Saint-Germain-en-Laye,' *Revue de l'Art* 81 (1988), pp. 20–30.

23 *Mémoires de Martin et Guillaume du Bellay* eds, V.-L. Bourrilly and F. Vindry (4 vols, Paris, 1908–19), I, 63, 98; II 126, 141. see also *CAF*, IX *sub* 'Charles du Solier'.

24 D.L. Potter, *War and Government in the French Provinces: Picardy 1470–1560* (Cambridge, 1993), pp. 113–54.

25 D.L. Potter, *A History of France: The Emergence of a Nation State* (London, 1995) pp. 57–89; R.J. Knecht, *Renaissance Warrior and Patron: The Reign of Francis I* (Cambridge, 1994), pp. 541–54.

26 T. Ruiz, *Spanish Society 1400–1600* (London, 2001), pp. 68–81; G. Sabatier and S. Edouard, *Les monarchies de France et d'Espagne* (Paris, 2001), pp. 137–41.

27 H. Nader, 'Noble Income in Sixteenth-Century Castile: The Case of the Marquises of Mondéjar, 1480–1580', *Economic History Review*, 30 (1977), pp. 411–28; see also H. Nader, *The Mendoza Family in the Spanish Renaissance* (New Jersey, 1979).

28 P. Rosenfeld, 'The Provincial Governors in the Low Countries,' *Standen and Landen* 17 (1959), pp. 1–47; D.R. Doyle, The Sinews of Governance in the Sixteenth Century: Mary of Hungary and Political Patronage,' *SCJ*, 31 (2) (2000), pp. 349–60.

29 G. Redworth and F. Checa, 'The Courts of the Spanish Habsburgs 1500–1700, in J. Adamson, ed., *The Princely Courts of Europe: Ritual, Politics and Culture under the Ancien Régime 1500–1750* (London, 1999); M. Rodriguez-Salgado. 'The Court of Philip II' in R. Asch and

A.M. Birke, *Princes, Patronage and the Nobility, The Court at the Beginning of the Modern Age c.1450–1650* (London, 1991) pp. 205–44.

30 L.P. Gachard, *Collection des voyages des souverains des Pays-Bas* (3 vols, Brussels, 1874), II, pp. 35–6.

31 Redworth and Checa; Sabatier and Edouard, pp. 133–41.

32 M. Cavalli, *Relazione, 1551* in E. Albèri, ed., *Relazione degli ambasciatori veneti al Senato* (Florence, 1839–63) Ist ser., vol. 2, pp. 192–223 esp. p. 206.

33 A.G. Dickens, 'Estate and Household Management in Bedfordshire c. 1540' *Bedford Historical Records Society*, 36 (1956), 38–45 at p. 45.

7 PATRONS: ROYAL ARTISTIC PATRONAGE

1 *St. P.* VIII, p. 482. I have modernised the spelling.

2 R.J. Knecht, *Renaissance Warrior and Patron: The Reign of Francis I* (Cambridge, 1994), pp. 462–77.

3 *Carolus*, Catologue nos. 37 and 40.

4 R. Tamalio, *Federico Gonzaga alla corte di Francesco I di Francia* (Paris, 1994), pp. 292–3. Federico Gonzaga to the Marquis of Mantua, Tours, 12 August 1516; A. Blunt, *Art and Architecture In France 1500–1700* Second Edition (London and New Haven, 1994), pp. 1–83.

5 J.-P. Babelon, *Châteaux de France au siècle de la Renaissance* (Paris, 1989), pp. 110–115.

6 R.J. Knecht, 'Francis I and Fontainebleau', *The Court Historian* 4 (2) August 1999, pp. 93–118.

7 M. Chatenet, *Le Château de Marid au Blois de Boulogne* (Paris, 1987), esp. pp. 49–63, 85–102; Knecht, *Renaissance Warrior*, p. 419.

8 W.L. Eisler, 'The Impact of the Emperor Charles V upon the visual arts', Unpublished Pennsylvania State University Ph.D. 1983, p. 57–74; C. Herrero-Carretero, 'Les tapisseries' in *Charles Quint, Tapisseries et armures des collections royales d'Espagne* (Brussels, 1994), pp. 43–113; *Carolus*, Catalogue no. 55, a view of the royal palace at Brussels by Batholomeus de Momper, dating from the end of the sixteenth century, showing the gallery.

9 E.E. Rosenthal, *The Palace of Charles V in Granada* (Princeton, New Jersey, 1985), esp. pp. 236–64; C. Kubler and M. Soria, eds, *Art and Architecture in Spain and Portugal and the American Dominions 1500 to 1800* (Harmondsworth, 1959).

10 Eisler, pp. 114–119.

11 S. Thurley, *The Royal Palaces of Tudor England: Architecture and Court Life (1460–1547)* (New Haven and London, 1993), pp. 62–5;

H.M. Colvin *The History of the King's Works* (6 vols; HMSO, 1963–82), IV, pp. 192–9.

12 W.G. Thompson, *A History of Tapestry* (London, 1930).

13 Eisler, pp. 85–90.

14 *Carolus*, Catalogue nos. 1, 44 and p. 2 for bronze busts of Charles, Mary of Hungary and Empress Isabella by the Leone and Pompeo Leoni.

15 L.F. Schianchi, *Correggio*, (Florence, 1994), pp. 64–76; C. Hope, 'Federigo II Gonzaga as a patron of painting' in D.S. Chambers and J. Martineau, eds. *The Splendours of the Gonzaga* (London, 1981), pp. 73–5.

16 Eisler, pp. 211–214.

17 *Ibid*, M. Hollingsworth, *Patronage in Sixteenth Century Italy* (London, 1996), pp. 310–312.

18 P. Mellen, *Jean Clouet* (Paris, 1971); Starkey, *Henry VIII: a European Court*, p. 55 for an illustration of the Treaty of Westminster; On the portrait of Francis as king David see Richardson, 'Anglo-French relations', pp. 264–5. The image reproduced there is taken from V. Leroquais, *Les Livres d'Heures de la Bibliothéque Nationale* (4 vols, Paris, 1927), III, Plate CXXIII a.

19 Blunt, pp. 60–83; Babelon, p. 118.

20 S. Schneelbalg-Perelman, 'Richesses du Garde-Meuble Parisien de François Ier: Inventaires inédits de 1542 et 1551' *Gazette des Beaux-Arts*, Series 6, 78 ii (1971), pp. 251–62.

21 Quoted in J. Cox-Rearick, *The Collection of Francis I: Royal Treasures* (New York, 1996), p. 85.

22 B. Cellini, *The Autobiography of Benvento Cellini*, edited and abridged by C. Hope (Oxford, 1983), p. 120.

23 *Ibid*, p. 141.

24 *Ibid*, p. 144.

25 M. Biddle, 'Nicolas Bellin of Modena, An Italian Artificier at the courts of Francis I and Henry VIII', *Journal of the British Archaeological Association*, Third Series, 29 (1966), pp. 106–21.

26 J. Backhouse, 'Illuminated Manuscripts and the Development of the Portrait Miniature' in D.R. Starkey ed., *Henry VIII: a European Court in England* (London, 1991), pp. 88–93; For an argument that it was Francis I himself and not, as is usually believed, his sister Marguerite who sent the Clouet miniatures to England in 1526, see Richardson, 'Anglo-French Relations', pp. 163–6.

27 J. Fritsch; 'Les Arts du Nord' in *Trésors de la Renaissance au château d'Éouen: Dossier de L'Art,* 40 (September 1997), pp. 69–85. T. Campbell, 'Of silk and gold', *Country Life* (October 10, 1991), pp. 92–5.

28 *Chronicle of Santa Cruz*, quoted in K. Brandi, *The Emperor Charles V* translated by C.V. Wedgwood (London, 1965), p. 383.

29 Eisler, pp. 128–43.

30 Fritsch, p. 81; Eisler, pp. 151–4 who suggests the ship may be by Torriano.

31 AN, J947 no. 3, fos. 1–4. Inventory made at Paris on 18 February 1533, countersigned by Breton.
32 *The Privy Purse Expences of King Henry the Eighth* (London, 1827), p. 215; PRO SP1/246 fo. 1 [*LP* Addenda I ii, 1869] Starkey, p. 152. Leseney's astrolable is pictured as plate XI.16.
33 P. Burke, 'Presenting and Re-Presenting Charles V' in H. Soly ed., *Charles V 1500–1558 and his Time* (Antwerp, 1999), pp. 393–476.
34 BN, MS fr.13429 fo. 4b; Knecht, pp. 78–9, 110 reproduces some of the miniatures from this work.
35 BL, Royal MS 2 A XVI; P. Tudor-Craig, 'Henry VIII and King David' in D. Williams ed., *Early Tudor England, Proceedings of the 1987 Harlaxton Symposium* (Woodbridge, 1989), pp. 183–201.

Select bibliography

For background or further reading. Place of publication is London unless otherwise stated.

PRINCIPAL PRIMARY SOURCES

State papers and correspondence

Calendar of State Papers, Spanish, ed. G. Bergenroth, P. de Gayangos (13 vols; 1862–1954).

Calendar of State Papers, Venetian, ed. R. Brown, C. Bentick and H. Brown (9 vols; 1864–98).

Catalogues des actes de François Ier, ed. P. Marichal *et al.* (10 vols; Paris, 1887–1910).

Correspondence of the Emperor Charles V, ed. W. Bradford (1850).

Correspondenz des Kaisers Karl V, ed. K. Lanz (3 vols; Leipzig, 1844–46).

Foedera, Conventiones, Litterae etc., ed. T. Rymer (1704–35).

Four Years at the Court of Henry VIII: Despatches of Sebastian Giustinian, ed. R. Brown (2 vols; 1854).

Letters and Papers, Foreign and Domestic, of the Reign of Henry VIII, eds. J.S. Brewer, J. Gardiner and R.H. Brodie (21 vols; 1862–1932).

Négociations diplomatiques entre la France et l'Autriche, ed. A.J.C. Le Glay (2 vols; Paris,1845).

Ordonnances des rois de France: règne de François Ier, (9 vols; Paris, 1902–75).

Papiers d'état du cardinal de Granvelle ed. C. Weiss, (9 vols; Paris, 1841–52).

State Papers published under the authority of the Record Commission: King Henry VIII, (11 vols; 1830–52).

Ferrante Gonzaga alla corte spagnola di Carlo V, ed. R. Tamalio, (Mantua, 1991).

Federigo Gonzaga alla corte di Francesco I, ed. R. Tamalio (Mantua, 1994).

The Inventory of Henry VIII ed. D.R. Starkey (1998), I, *The Manuscript*.

Commentaries, histories and political tracts

Anglica Historica by Polydore Vergil, edited by D. Hay, Camden Society, 74, (1950).

Commentaires, by Blaise de Montluc, edited by I. Roy and published in English as *The Valois–Habsburg Wars and the French Wars of Religion* (1971).

De Regimine Principum, by Stephen Baron, translated and edited by P.J. Mroczkowski (New York, 1990).

La Monarchie de France by Claude de Seyssel, published in English as *The Monarchy of France*, translated and edited by J.H. Hexter and D.R. Kelly (New Haven, 1981).

Le Cérémonial françois by Theodore de Godefroy, (2 vols: Paris, 1649).

Le Débat des Hérauts d'Armes de France et d'Angleterre edited by L. Pannier and P. Meyer (Paris, 1877), 12ff.

Le Triumphe des Vertuz: Le Triumphe de Prudence by Jean Thenaud, edited by. T.J. Schuurs-Jansen (Geneva, 1996).

Le Triumphe du tres Chrestian roy de France, Loys XII, by Symphorien Champier, edited by G. Trisolini (Rome, 1977).

L'institution du prince by Guillaume Budé (Paris, 1547; reprinted Farnborough, 1966).

The Autobiography of Benvento Cellini written by Himself, edited and abridged by C. Hope (Oxford, 1983).

The Book of the Courtier by Baldesare Castiglione, translated by G. Bull (London, 1967).

The Education of a Christian Prince by Desiderius Erasmus, translated by N.M. Chesire and M.J. Heath, edited by L. Jardine (Cambridge, 1997).

The Governance of England by Sir John Fortescue, edited by C. Plummer (1885).

The Prince by Niccolo Machiavelli, translated by G. Bull (1961).

The Union of the Two Noble and Illustre Famelies of Lancastre and Yorke by Edward Hall, edited by H. Ellis (1809).

Utopia by Sir Thomas More, in J.J. Greene and J.P. Dolan, *Utopia and Other Essential Writings of Thomas More* (New York, 1967).

Vita Henrici VII and *Annales Henrici VII* by Bernard André, in J. Gairdner, *Memorials of King Henry the Seventh* (1858).

INTRODUCTION

General histories of the period

F. Braudel, *The Mediterranean and the Mediterranean World in the Age of Philip II* translated by S. Reynolds (2 vols; 1972–73).
R. Bonney, *The European Dynastic States 1494–1660* (Oxford, 1991).
T.A. Brady, H.A. Oberman, J.D. Tracy, eds., *Handbook of European History 1400–1600* (2 vols; New York, 1994).
C. Coleman and D.R. Starkey, eds., *Revolution Reassessed: Revisions in the History of Tudor Government and Administration* (Oxford, 1986); G.R. Elton, *The Tudor Revolution in Government* (Cambridge, 1953); *England Under the Tudors* (2nd edn, 1974); N. Henshall, *The Myth of Absolutism* (1992); E. Le Roy Ladurie, *L'Etat royal de Louis XI à Henri IV* (Paris, 1987); R. Mettam, *Power and Faction Louis XIV's France* (Oxford, 1988); R. Mousnier, *Les institutions de la France sous la monarchie absolue 1598–1789* (2 vols; Paris, 1974); J. Morrill, 'French Absolutism as Limited Monarchy', *HJ* 21 (4) (1978), pp. 961–72.

1 MONARCHS: PERSONALITIES AND IDEALS OF MONARCHY

Biographies of the monarchs and related sources

K. Brandi, *The Emperor Charles V* translated by C.V. Wedgewood (1965); *Charles–Quint en son temps* ed. Centre Nationale de la Recherche Scientifique (Paris, 1959) A. Fernández-Alvarez, *Charles V* (1975); C. Giry-Deloison, ed., *François Ier et Henri VIII: Deux princes de la Renaissance 1515–1547* (Lille and London, 1995); R.J. Knecht, *Renaissance Warrior and Patron: The Reign of Francis I* (Cambridge, 1994); *French Renaissance Monarchy: Francis I and Henry II* (1996); D. MacCulloch, ed., *The Reign of Henry VIII: Politics, Policy and Piety* (1995); S. McDonald, *Charles V, Ruler and Dynast* (1992); M. Rady, *The Emperor Charles V* (1989); G.J. Richardson, ' "Good friends and brothers"?: Francis I and Henry VIII', *History Today* 44 (9) (1994), pp. 20–26; J.J. Scarisbrick, *Henry VIII* (1968); H. Soly, ed., *Charles V and his Time* (Antwerp, 1999); H. Soly and J. Van de Wiele, *Carolus: Charles Quint 1500–1558* (Brussels, 1999);

D.R. Starkey, *The Reign of Henry VIII: Personalities and Politics* (1991); *Henry VIII: A European Court in England* (1991).

S.B. Chrimes, *Henry VII* (Berkeley and Los Angeles, 1972); E.W. Ives, *Anne Boleyn* (Oxford, 1986); P. Gwynn, *The King's Cardinal: The Rise and Fall of Thomas Wolsey* (1990).

General histories of European kingdoms

J. Bérenger, *A History of the Habsburg Empire 1273–1700* translated by C.A. Simpson (1994); T.N. Bisson, *The Medieval Crown of Aragon* (Oxford, 1986); J. Edwards, *The Monarchies of Ferdinand and Isabella* (1996); J.H. Elliott, *Imperial Spain 1469–1716* (1963); J. Guy, *Tudor England* (Oxford, 1988); J.N. Hillgarth, *The Spanish Kingdoms 1250–1516* (2 vols; Oxford, 1978); M. Hughes, *Early Modern Germany 1477–1806* (1992); H. Kamen, *Spain, 1469–1714* (1983); H.G. Koenigsberger, 'The Empire of Charles V in Europe' in G.R. Elton ed., *New Cambridge Modern History* vol. II *The Reformation, 1520–1559* (Cambridge 1990), pp. 339–76. R. Highfield, *Spain in the Fifteenth Century* (1972); D. Potter, *A History of France: The Emergence of a Nation State* (1995); W. Prevenier, and W. Blockmans, *The Burgundian Netherlands* (Cambridge, 1985); J.D. Tracy, *Holland under Habsburg Rule 1506–1566* (Berkeley, 1990); T.F. Ruíz, *Spanish Society 1400–1600* (2001); G. Sabatier, and S. Edouard, *Les monarchies de France et d'Espagne* (Paris, 2001); G. Woodward, *Spain in the Reigns of Isabella and Ferdinand 1474–1516* (1997).

On European political thought and its development during the Renaissance

A. Brown, *The Renaissance* (1988); A.E. Bakos, ed., *Politics, Ideology and the Law in Early Modern Europe: Essays in honour of J.H.M. Salmon* (Rochester, 1994); J.H. Burns, and M. Goldie, *Cambridge History of Political Thought 1450–1700* (Cambridge, 1991); A. Fernández-Santamaria, *The State, War and Peace: Spanish Political Thought in the Renaissance 1516–1559* (Cambridge, 1977); M. Greengrass, *Conquest and Coalescence: The Shaping of the State in Early Modern Europe* (1991); J.H. Hexter, *The Vision of Politics on the Eve of the Reformation: More, Machiavelli and* Seyssel (1973); G.R. Nauert, *Humanism and the Culture of Renaissance Europe* (Cambridge, 1995); J. Guy, 'The Henrician Age' in J.G.A. Pocock, ed., *The Varieties of British Political Thought, 1500–1800* (Cambridge, 1993); A.J. Rabil, ed., *Renaissance Humanism: Foundations, Forms and Legacy* (3 vols; Philadelphia, 1988), vol. II. *Humanism Beyond Italy*; C.B. Schmitt, Q. Skinner and E. Kessler, *The Cambridge History of Renaissance Philosophy*

(Cambridge, 1988); Q. Skinner, *The Foundations of Modern Political Thought* (2 vols; Cambridge, 1978).

On ideals of monarchy and monarchical institutions

J.M. Bak, ed., *Coronations Medieval and Early Modern Monarchic Ritual* (Berkeley, 1990); D. Canadine and S. Price, eds, *Rituals of Royalty: Power and Ceremonial in Traditional Societies* (Cambridge, 1987); J. Dufournet, A. Fiorato, A. Redondo, *Le pouvoir monarchique et ses supports ideolgiques aux XVIe–XVIIe siècles* (Paris, 1990); H. Duchardt, R.A. Jackson and D. Sturdy, *European Monarchy: Its Evolution and Practice from Roman Antiquity to Modern Times* (Stuttgart, 1992); R. Folz, 'Le Sacre impériale et son évolution Xe–XIIIe siècle' in *Le Sacres des rois: Actes du colloque international d'historie sur les sacres et couronnements royaux* (Paris, 1985); E.H. Kantorowicz, *The King's Two Bodies: A Study in Medieval Political Theory* (New Jersey, 1957); R. Oresko, G.C. Gibbs and H.M. Scott, *Royal and Republican Sovereignty in Early Modern Europe* (Cambridge, 1997); T. Ruiz, 'Une royaté sans sacre: La monarchie Castillane du bas Moyen Age', *Annales* 39 (1984), pp. 429–53; F. Yates, *Astarea: The Imperial Theme in the Sixteenth Century* (1975).

C. Beaune, *La naissance de la nation France* (Paris, 1985), translated by S. Ross Huston as *The Birth of an Ideology: Myths and Symbols of Nation in Late-Medieval France* (Berkeley, 1991); M. Bloch, *Les rois thaumaturges* (Paris, 1961) Published in English as *The Royal Touch: Sacred Monarchy and Scrofula in England and France,* translated by J.E. Anderson (London, 1973); J. Krynen, L'*empire du roi: idées et croyances politiques en France XIII–XV siècles* (Paris, 1993).

J.H. Burns, *The True Law of Kingship: Concepts of Monarchy in Early-modern Scotland* (Oxford, 1996); A. Fox and J. Guy, *Reassessing the Henrician Age: Humanism, Politics and Reform, 1500–50* (Oxford, 1986); J. Guy, ed., *The Tudor Monarchy* (1997); L.G.W. Legg, *English Coronation Records* (1901); A.B. and B. Wyon, *The Great Seals of England* (1887).

2 WARRIORS: HONOUR AND MAGNIFICENCE IN WAR AND PEACE

On chivalry and royal orders

M. Keen, *Chivalry* (Yale, 1984); P. Begent and H. Chesshyre, *The Most Noble Order of the Garter* (1999); H. Pauwels, ed., *La Toison d'Or: Cinq siécles d'art et d'histoire* (1962); C. Van de Bergen-Panten, ed., *L'Ordre de la Toison d'Or de Philippe le Bon à Philippe le Beau* (Brussels, 1996); R. Vilanova, *Capítulo de Toisón de oro celebrado en Barcelona el año 1519* (Barcelona, 1930).

On para-military sports

J. Cummins, *The Hound and the Hawk: The Art of Medieval Hunting* (1988); W.H. Jackson, 'The Tournament and Chivalry in German Tournament Books of the Sixteenth Century and in the Literary Works of Emperor Maximilian' in C. Harper-Bill and R. Harvey, eds., *The Ideals and Practice of Medieval Knighthood: Papers from the First and Second Strawberry Hill Conferences*, (Woodbridge, 1986), pp. 49–73; C. Blair, 'The Emperor Maximilian's gift of armour to King Henry VIII and the silvered and engraved armour at the Tower of London,' *Archaeologia*, 99 (1965), pp. 19–39.

On the ideals of peace and peace-making

R.P. Adams, *The Better Part of Valor: More, Erasmus, Colet and Vives on Humanism, War and Peace, 1496–1535* (Seattle, 1962); J.A. Fernandez, 'Erasmus on the Just War,' *Journal of the History of Ideas*, 34 (1973), pp. 209–16; B.E. Mansfield, 'The Three Circles of Erasmus of Rotterdam', *Colloquium: The Australian and New Zealand Theological Review* IV (4) (1972), pp. 4–11; J.G. Russell, *Peacemaking in the Renaissance* (1986).

3 WARRIORS: WARFARE AND INTERNATIONAL RELATIONS

On medieval warfare and its development in the early-modern period

C.T. Allmand, *The Hundred Years War: England and France at War c.1300–c.1450* (Cambridge, 1989); J. Black, ed., *The Origins of War in Early Modern Europe* (Edinburgh, 1987); P. Contamine, *War in the Middle Ages*, translated by M. Jones (Oxford, 1984); P. Contamine, C. Giry-Deloison and M.H. Keen, eds., *Guerre et societé en France, en Angleterre et en Bourgogne XIVe–Xve siècles* (Lille, 1991); J.R. Hale, *War and Society in Renaissance Europe 1450–1620* (1998); B.S. Hall, *Weapons and Warfare in Renaissance Europe: Gunpowder, Technology and Tactics* (Baltimore and London, 1997); H.J. Hewitt, *The Organization of War under Edward III*

1338–62 (Manchester, 1966); H. Inalcik, *The Ottoman Empire: The Classical Age 1300–1600* (2000); C. de La Ronciere, *La marine française* (6 vols; Paris, 1923); B. Lewis, *The Middle East: 2000 years of history from the rise of Christianity to the present day* (1995); F. Lot, *Recherces sur les effectifs des armies françaises des Guerres d'Italie aux Guerres de Religion, 1494–1562* (Paris, 1962); C. Oman, *The Art of War in the Sixteenth Century* (1979).

On sixteenth-century international relations and diplomacy

S. Doran, *England and Europe in the Sixteenth Century* (1999); J.G. Russell, *The Field of Cloth of Gold, Men and Manners in 1520* (1969); *Diplomats at Work: Three Renaissance Studies* (1992); D.L. Potter, 'The Frontiers of Artois in European Diplomacy, 1482–1560' in *Artois et la diplomatie moderne* (Lille, 1999), pp. 261–75; D. Dunlop, 'The Politics of Peace-Keeping: Anglo-Scottish Relations from 1503 to 1511', *Renaissance Studies* 8 (1994), pp. 138–61; P. Gwynn, 'Wolsey's Foreign Policy: The Conferences at Calais and Bruges Reconsidered', *HJ* 23 (4) (1980), pp. 755–72; D.M. Head, 'Henry VIII's Scottish Policy', *The Scottish Historical Review* 61 (1982), pp. 1–24; G. Mattingly, *Renaissance Diplomacy* (1965); G.J. Richardson, 'Entertainments for the French Ambassadors at the Court of Henry VIII,' *Renaissance Studies* 9 (4), 1995, pp. 404–415; 'Anglo-French Political and Cultural Relations in the reign of Henry VIII', Unpublished University of London Ph.D. dissertation, 1996; 'The Privy Chamber of Henry VIII and Anglo-French relations, 1515–1520', *The Court Historian* 4 (2) (1999), pp. 119–40.

4 GOVERNORS: ROYAL AUTHORITY AND ADMINISTRATION

On the development of royal government in the sixteenth century

P. Chaunu, *L'Espagne de Charles Quint* (2 vols; Paris, 1973); S.J. Gunn, *Early Tudor Government* (1995).
C. Hermann *et al.*, *Le premier âge de l'État en Espagne 1450–1700* (Paris, 1990); R. Evans, *The Making of the Habsburg Monarchy 1500–1700* (Oxford, 1979); A. Jouanna, *La France du XVIe siècle* (Paris, 1996); A.W. Lovett, *Early Habsburg Spain* (Oxford, 1986); J. Lynch, *Spain*

1516–1598: From Nation State to World Empire (Oxford, 1991); D. Parker, *The Making of French Absolutism* (1983); M. Rodriguez-Salgado, *The Changing Face of Empire under Charles V and Philip II* (Cambridge, 1994).

On administrative structures and developments

C. Coleman, and D.R. Starkey, eds., *Revolution Reassessed:Revisions in the History of Tudor Government* (Oxford, 1986); C. Cross, D. Loades and J.J. Scarisbrick, eds., *Law and Government under the Tudors: Essays presented to Sir Geoffrey Elton on his retirement* (Cambridge, 1988); G.R. Elton, *The Tudor Constitution: Documents and Commentary* (Cambridge, 1968); *Studies in Tudor and Stuart Politics and Government* (3 vols; Cambridge, 1974); J.M. Headley, *The Emperor and his Chancellor: A Study of the Imperial Chancellery under Gattinara* (Cambridge, 1983); E.W. Ives, R.J. Knecht and J.J. Scarisbrick, eds., *Wealth and Power in Tudor England: Essays presented to S.T. Bindoff* (1978); J.R. Lander, *Government and Community: England, 1450–1509* (Cambridge, Massachusetts, 1980); J.M.H. Salmon, *Society in Crisis: France in the Sixteenth Century* (1975); J.H. Shenan, *Government and Society in France 1461–1661* (1969); *The Parlement of Paris* (1998); D.R. Starkey, 'Court, Council and Nobility in Tudor England' in R.G. Asch, A.M. Birke, eds., *Princes, Patronage and the Nobility: The Court at the Beginning of the Modern Age 1450–1650* (Oxford, 1991), pp. 175–203; W. Stubbs, *The Constitutional History of England* (3 vols; Oxford, 1874–78); G. Zeller, *Les institutions de la France au XVI eme siècle* (Paris, 1948).

Government in the localities

J. Boucher, *Lyon et la vie Lyonnaise au XVIeme siècle* (Lyon, 1992); J. Dewald, *The Formation of a Provincial Nobility: The Magistrates of the Parlement of Rouen (1499–1610)* (Princeton, NJ, 1980); D.R. Doyle, 'The Sinews of Habsburg Governance in the Sixteenth Century: Mary of Hungary and Political Patronage', *SCJ* 31(2) (2000), pp. 349–60; R.H. Harding, *Anatomy of a Power Elite: The Provincial Governors of Early Modern France* (Yale, 1978); S. Ellis, *Tudor Frontiers and Noble Power: The Making of the British State* (Oxford, 1995); M. Lunenfeld, *Keepers of the City: The Corregidores of Isabella I of Castile 1474–1504* (Cambridge, 1987); D.L. Potter, *War and Government in the French Provinces: Picardy 1470–1560* (Cambridge, 1993); G. Redworth, *Government and Society in Late Medieval Spain* (1993); R. Reid, *The King's Council in the North* (1921).

Attitudes to and resistance to royal authority

M. Bush and D. Bownes, *The Defeat of the Pilgrimage of Grace* (Hull, 1999); N.Z. Davis, *Society and Culture in Early Modern France* (Stanford, 1976); S. Ellis, 'A Border Baron and the Tudor State: The Rise and Fall of Lord Dacre of the North', *HJ* 35 (2) (1992), pp. 253–77; S. Ellis, 'A crisis of the aristocracy? Frontiers and noble power in the early Tudor State', in J. Guy, ed., *The Tudor Monarchy* (1997); A. Fletcher, *Tudor Rebellions* (1983); S. Haliczer, *The Comuneros of Castile: the forging of a revolution 1475–1521* (Madison, 1981); P. Rosenfeld, 'The Provincial Governors from the Minority of Charles V to the Revolt the Low Countries', *Standen and Landen* 17 (1959), pp. 1–63; A. Wall, *Power and Protest in England 1525–1640* (2000).

5 GOVERNORS: REVENUE, REPRESENTATION AND RELIGION

On crown finance and debt

J.D. Alsop, 'The Theory and Practice of Tudor Taxation', *EHR* 382 (1982), pp. 1–30; R. Bonney, ed., *Economic Systems and State Finance* (Oxford, 1995); R. Carande, *Carlos V y sus banqueros* (3 vols; Barcelona, 1977); F.C. Dietz, *English Government Finance 1485–1558* (Urbana, 1921); R. Ehrenberg, *Capital and Finance in the Age of the Renaissance: A Study of the Fuggers and their Connections*, translated by H.M. Lucas (New York, 1963); P. Grierson, *Later Medieval Numismatics* (1979); P. Hamon, *L'argent du roi: Les finances sous François Ier* (Paris, 1994); P. Spufford, *Handbook of Medieval Exchange* (1986).

On the development of representative institutions

F.L. Carsten, *Princes and Parliaments in Germany from the Fifteenth to the Eighteenth Century* (Oxford, 1959); C.S.L. Davies, 'Tournai and the English Crown 1513–1519', *HJ* 41 (1) (1998), pp. 1–26; A.K.D. Hawkyard, 'The Enfranchisement of Constituencies 1509–1558' *Parliamentary History* 10 (1) (1991), pp. 1–26; H.G. Koenigsberger, 'Dominium Regale or Dominium Politicum et Regale, Monarchies and Parliaments in Early Modern Europe', in his *Politicians and Virtuosi: Essays in Early Modern History* (1986), pp. 1–25; 'Prince and States-General: Charles V and the Netherlands (1506–1555)', *Transactions of the Royal Historical Society*, Sixth Series, vol. IV (1994), pp. 127–51; A.R. Myres, *Parliaments and Estates in Europe to 1789* (1975); J. Russell Major, *Representative Institutions in Renaissance*

France 1421–1559 (Madison, 1960); *The Monarchy, the Estates and the Aristocracy in Renaissance France* (1988); *From Renaissance Monarchy to Absolute Monarchy: French Kings, Nobles and Estates* (Baltimore and London, 1994).

On the Reformation and royal reaction

M. Greengrass, ed., *The Longman Companion to the European Reformation c1550–1618* (1998); *The French Reformation* (Oxford, 1987).

R.J. Evans, and T.V. Thomas, *Crown, Church and Estates: Central European Politics in the 16th and 17th Centuries* (1991); H. Kamen, *The Spanish Inquisition A Historical Revision* (1997); D.MacCulloch *Thomas Cranmer, A Life* (Yale, 1996); J.K. McConica, *English Humanists and Reformation Politics under Henry VIII and Edward VI* (Oxford, 1965).

6 PATRONS

On ideas of nobility and the mentality of nobles

J.M. Constant, *La noblesse française aux XVIe et XVIIe siècles* (Paris, 1985); A. Jouanna, *Le devoir de révolte: La noblesse française et la gestation de l'État moderne, 1559–1661* (Paris, 1989); E. Schalk, *From Valor to Pedigree: Ideas of Nobility in France in the Sixteenth and Seventeenth Centuries* (Princeton, 1986); K.B. Neuschel, *Word of Honor: Interpreting noble culture in sixteenth-century France* (Ithaca and London, 1989); G. Bernard, *The Tudor Nobility* (Manchester, 1991); M. James, 'English Politics and the Concept of Honour 1485–1642', *Past and Present* Supplement 3, (1978); H. Miller, *Henry VIII and the English Nobility* (Oxford, 1986).

On royal patronage and affinities

G. Bernard, 'The Rise of Sir William Compton, early Tudor courtier', *EHR* 96 (1981), pp. 754–77; 'The Fortunes of the Greys, earls of Kent, in the early sixteenth century', *HJ* 25 (3) (1982), pp. 671–85; S.J. Gunn, 'Henry Bouchier, Earl of Essex (1472–1540)' in G. Bernard, ed., *The Tudor Nobility* (Manchester 1991), pp. 135–69; M. Hicks, 'Bastard Feudalism, Overmighty Subjects and Idols of the Multitude during the Wars of the Roses', *History* 85 (279) (July 2000), pp. 386–403.

S. Carroll, *Noble Power during the French Wars of Religion: The Guise Affinity and the Catholic Cause in Normandy* (Cambridge, 1998);

M. Greengrass, 'Noble affinities in early modern France: The case of Henri I de Montmorency, Constable of France', *European History Quarterly* 16 (1986), pp. 275–311; R.J. Kalas, 'The Selve family of Limousin: Members of a new elite in Early Modern France', *SCJ* 18 (2) (1987), pp. 147–72; 'Marriage, clientage, office holding and the advancement of the early modern French nobility: The Noailles family of Limousin', *SCJ* 27 (2) (1996), pp. 365–83; S. Kettering, 'Patronage in Early Modern France,' *French Historical Studies* 17 (4) (1992), pp. 839–62; W. Weary, 'La Maison de la Trémoille pendant la Renaissance: une seigneurie aggrandie' in B. Chevalier and P. Contarmine, eds., *La France de la fin du Xve siècle – Renouveau et apogeé* (Paris, 1985); J.B. Wood, *The Nobility of the Election of Bayeux 1463–1666* (Princeton, 1980).

W.S. Maltby, *Alba: A Biography of Fernando de Toldeo, Third Duke of Alba 1507–1582* (Berkeley, 1983); H. Nader, 'Noble Income in Sixteenth-Century Castile: The case of the Marquises of Mondéjar, 1489–1580', *Economic History Review* 30 (1977), pp. 411–28; *The Mendoza family in the Spanish Renaissance* (New Jersey, 1979).

On the structure and functioning of royal courts

R. Asch, and A.M. Birke, *Princes, Patronage and the Nobility, The Court at the Beginning of the Modern Age c.1450–1650* (1991); J. Adamson, ed., *The Princely Courts of Europe: Ritual, Politics and Culture under the* Ancien Régime *1500–1750* (1999); A.G. Dickens, ed., *The Courts of Europe* (1977); M.J. Heath, 'Erasmus the Courtier', *The Court Historian* 5(2) (2000), pp. 93–104; E.W. Ives, *Faction in Tudor England* (1979); V. Press, 'The Habsburg Court as the Center of the Imperial Government', *Journal of Modern History* 58 Supplement (December 1986), pp. S23–S45; J.-F. Solnon, *La Cour de France* (Paris, 1987); D.R. Starkey, 'The King's Privy Chamber 1485–1547', Unpublished University of Cambridge Ph.D. dissertation 1973; 'Representation through intimacy: A study in the symbolism of monarchy and Court office in early-modern England' in I. Lewis, ed., *Symbols and Sentiments: Cross-Cultural Studies in Symbolism* (1977), pp.187–224; *The English Court* (1987).

7 ROYAL ARTISTIC PATRONAGE

Royal propaganda and the image of the monarch

S. Anglo, *Images of Tudor Kingship* (1992); *Spectacle, Pageantry and Early Tudor Policy*, (Oxford, 1969) A.-M. Lecoq, *François Ier imaginaire symbolique et politique à l'aube de la Renaissance française* (Paris, 1987); W.L. Eisler, 'The Impact of the Emperor Charles V upon the visual arts', Unpublished Pennsylvania State University Ph.D. dissertation, 1983; R. Strong, *Art and Power: Renaissance Festivals 1450–1650* (1984); M. Tanner, *The Last Descendant of Aneas: The Hapsburgs and the Mythic Image of the Emperor* (Yale, 1993); H. Trevor-Roper, *Princes and Artists: Patronage and Ideology at Four Habsburg Courts 1517–1633* (1991); P. Tudor-Craig, 'Henry VIII and King David' in D. Williams, ed., *Early Tudor England, Proceedings of the 1987 Harlaxton Symposium* (Woodbridge, 1989), pp. 183–201.

On architecture and sculpture

J.-P. Babelon, *Châteaux de France au siècle de la Renaissance* (Paris, 1989); M. Chatenet, *Le Château de Madrid au Bois de Boulogne* (Paris, 1987); R.J. Knecht 'Francis I and Fontainebleau', *The Court Historian* 4 (2) (1999), pp. 93–118.; C. Kubler and M. Soria, *Art and Architecture in Spain, Portugal and their American dominions 1500 to 1800* (1959); E.E. Rosenthal, *The Palace of Charles V in Granada* (New Jersey, 1985); D.S. Chambers and J. Martineau, eds. *The Splendours of the Gonzaga* (London, 1981); M. Biddle, 'Nicholas Bellin of Modena, An Italian Artificer at the courts of Francis I and Henry VIII', *Journal of the British Archaeological Association*, Third Series, 29 (1966), pp. 106–21.

On paintings and other artistic patronage

M. Hollingsworth, *Patronage in Sixteenth Century Italy* (1996); L.F. Schianchi, *Correggio* (Florence, 1994); S. Schneebalg-Perelman, 'Richesses du garde–meuble parisien de François Ier: inventaires inédits de 1542 et 1551', *Gazette des Beaux-Arts* 78 (1971), pp. 253–304; J. Cox-Rearick, *The Collection of Francis I: Royal Treasures* (New York, 1996); P. Mellen, *Jean Clouet* (Paris, 1971).

Index

Richardson, Glenn.

Renaissance monarchy.

DATE			